THE
WELL·FILLED
TORTILLA
C·O·O·K·B·O·O·K

THE WELL·FILLED TORTILLA

C·O·O·K·B·O·O·K

BY VICTORIA WISE AND SUSANNA HOFFMAN

ILLUSTRATIONS BY LISA HENDERLING

▼

WORKMAN PUBLISHING ▼ NEW YORK

DEDICATION

For each other in collaborative creation
and to the memory of Abe L. Hoffman

Fresh Tomato Salsa, Chive Salsa, Ancho Chili Sauce, and Good and
Plenty Wine-Simmered Vegetables from GOOD AND PLENTY by Vic-
toria Wise and Susanna Hoffman. Copyright © 1988 by Victoria
Wise and Susanna Hoffman. Reprinted by permission of Harper &
Row, Publishers, Inc. Tzatziki Sauce, Salsa Verde, and Carnitas are
previously published adaptations from the same book.

Hominy Tortillas from I HEAR AMERICA COOKING by Betty Fussell.
Copyright © 1986 by Betty Fussell. Reprinted by permission of
Viking Penguin, a division of Penguin Books USA Inc.

Library of Congress Cataloging-in-Publication Data
Wise, Victoria.
    The well-filled torilla cookbook/by Victoria Wise and Susanna
  Hoffman : illustrated by Lisa Henderling.
      p. cm.
    ISBN 0-89480-364-6
    1. Tortillas. I. Hoffman, Susanna. II. Title.
  TX770.T65W57 1990   89-40730
  641.8'2—dc20   CIP

Cover and book design by Lisa Hollander
Cover illustration by Seymour Chwast
Book illustrations by Lisa Henderling

Workman books are available at special discounts when purchased
in bulk for premiums and sales promotions as well as for fund-
raising or educational use. Special editions or book excerpts can
also be created to specification. For details, contact the Special Sales
Director at the address below.

Workman Publishing Company, Inc.
708 Broadway
New York, NY 10003-9555
www.workmanweb.com

Manufactured in the United States of America

First printing June 1990
20 19 18 17 16 15 14 13 12 11

ACKNOWLEDGMENTS

Numerous people in our well-filled lives are due our gratitude for helping us cook and complete this book.

Those who have always been major ingredients are Hank and Ruth Jenanyan, Abe and Florence Hoffman, Arayah and Paul Rude, Deborah and Jerry Budrick, Beverly Jenanyan, Deborah and Levi Bendele, Elaine Fahlstrom, Juanita Godding, Jacqueline and Bill Smalley, Karin and Tim Knowles, Josephine Spoerl, and Joanna Wise.

Dale Ketter and Sienna Nervo and their staff keep the cafe part of our lives cooking and operating. The administration, faculty, staff, and countless students at the California College of Arts and Crafts sample our wares and cheer us on.

Lisa Rich and Robbie Greenberg, Cielo Arango and Claudio Luzarraga, Chad Clausen, May Diaz, Terry Valdez, and Elva Nieves give us the spice for many a taco as well as their lively tales.

Robert Mandel and Bill Chambers, Ray Saunders, Barbara and John Haugeland, Nancy Podbielniak, Marida Hollos, Curt Hardyck, Chooch and Holly Potenziani, Gail Stempler and Stuart Lake, Susan Mitchell, Gale Hayman, Deborah and Dan Kashinsky, Penny Brogden and Tom Nemcik, Tom Sternberg and Violetta Coatta, Patty Unterman, Milton Stern, Craig Brock, David Ramirez, and Howard Sylvester enrich our lives and encourage us in every endeavor.

For their zestful input, we thank our friend and agent Martha Casselman, book designer Lisa Hollander, and our astute and caring editor, Suzanne Rafer.

Finally, Rick, Steve, Jenan, Jesse, and Gabriella enfold us in their love, and we are forever grateful.

CONTENTS

TORTILLAS

SALSAS AND TOPPINGS

THE FILLINGS

SIDE SALADS

TORTILLA DESSERTS

WHY WE DOTE ON WELL-FILLED TORTILLAS

When Europeans discovered the New World, they expected to find gold. Instead they found the tortilla.

Flat pancakes of corn or flour, tortillas can be served warm under an endless variety of fillings and layered with countless salsas and toppings. They can be wrapped around fillings to make well-stuffed packets; used as tasty food scoops; offered up toasted and topped with salad; or served hot and pliable and plain.

Tortillas *are* gold.

Taught to us by Mexican friends and neighbors, and savored at many a cantina meal, well-filled tortillas seduced us years ago. As tacos, enchiladas, burritos, chimichangas, and quesadillas, they enticed us with their freshness, warmed us with their spicy bang, and won us over with their speed and versatility.

Tortilla fillings can encompass all the international flat cake and bread cuisines—the Middle-Eastern pita; the Indian paratha; the French crêpe, and even the fry breads of the Native Americans. And in this book, they do. We present most of the recipes as tacos, with the tortilla simply warmed and softened, or lightly crisped. Among our dishes are all the variations already mentioned, plus flautas, tostadas, quesadillas, and tortilla desserts. With this book we hope already-devoted tortilla-fillers will revel in a multitude of new ideas, and novices will soon become enthusiastic tortilla cooks.

▲▲▲▲▲▲▲▲▲▲▲▲▲▲▲▲▲▲

Our recipes are written for 18 well-filled corn tortillas or 12 well-filled flour tortillas (these are a little larger than the corn), enough to feed four to six. You can gauge your own particular needs and expand or decrease the amounts. Usually grown men can eat from two to five well-filled tortillas, depending on appetite and whether the tortillas are corn or flour. Women usually can devour two to three. Teenagers eat three to four, children one, and guests one of every kind.

▼▼▼▼▼▼▼▼▼▼▼▼▼▼▼▼▼▼

THE LARDER

With a few essentials in the pantry and some fresh produce ready to add to your main ingredient, you have the versatility to create all kinds of well-filled tortillas. We always have on hand:

ACHIOTE PASTE: Made from achiote seeds, also known as *annato* seeds. The paste, which often comes in the form of small "bricks" with the texture of beef bouillon cubes, is sometimes pure achiote and sometimes mixed with other herbs and spices (*achiote condimentado*). The taste is somewhat musky, somewhere between paprika and mild chili powder. Achiote gives a rich earthy zest and pleasing brown-red color to meats, fish, and sauces. Achiote paste is widely available in Latin and Mexican markets and international grocers. Or, you can buy the seeds and pulverize or grind them to use as a seasoning.

ANCHOVIES: We don't use anchovies in our fillings often, but find that occasionally they add that certain punch to both fillings and salsas. Tins of salt-packed anchovies are the best if you can find them. A tin can be easily stored for months. After opening, add a few drops of water to create a brine, cover the tin well, and refrigerate for up to several months. Otherwise, stock several tins of oil-packed anchovy fillets.

BEANS: To make bean fillings or to use as a topping. We prefer, and in this book only use, black beans, which need no presoaking and cook up in 1½ hours. Other beans that are good for tortilla-filling are pinto and red kidney beans. Keep beans in sacks or jars in a dry pantry.

CHEESE: For topping filled tortillas or turning out quesadillas, we always keep three sorts of cheese: a selection of melting cheeses, a fresh crumbling cheese, and a grating cheese.

■ **Melting Cheeses** (*queso asadero*): Cheddar and Jack are the most traditional. We also like Gouda, Edam, Gruyère, Emmentaler, semi-soft sheep's-milk cheeses, sharp Cheddars, such as Cheshire, Wisconsin, or Vermont types, and even Muenster (as long as another more biting cheese is mixed with it to increase its flavor).

■ **Fresh Crumbling Cheeses** (*quesos fresco*): If you can find it in a Mexican market buy *queso fresco*, or substitute Bulgarian or Corsican feta, ricotta, or farmer's cheese with a little feta mixed in to obviate the blandness.

■ **Grating Cheeses** (*queso anejo*): *Cotija, oreado,* or *queso seco* if they are available, or you can use Parmesan, aged Asiago, Romano, Kasseri (softer in texture but similar in taste to Mexican *queso fresco*), or aged Jack.

CHILI PEPPERS: Along with tortillas, chili peppers are the most important ingredient in a well-filled tortilla. There are many varieties of chilies, some small, others large, some mild, others fiery hot. They are available fresh, dried, and canned. Fresh chilies, dried chilies, and canned chilies are somewhat interchangeable but have different flavors and serve for different purposes. We use, and store, all three kinds. Below is a description of those most commonly used.

■ **Fresh Chili Peppers:** In our cooking we use a great many fresh chilies, preferring their fruity flavor and crunchy texture in most of our tortilla fillings. Stored in a plastic bag in the vegetable crisper of the refrigerator, most keep a week to 10 days, with the reds deteriorating somewhat faster than the greens due to their ripeness. Some, such as the large Anaheims or poblanos, keep even longer. We often specify a particular type, but fresh chili peppers can usually be substituted one for the other, although some are distinctly hotter than others. Where we call for serranos, you can use the more commonly available jalapeños, or the milder yellow wax should you care for less heat. Any kind of fresh chili pepper will be more or less hot within its range according to the season. Chilies are mildest in spring, ripening to hotter throughout the summer, and hottest in the fall.

Anaheims: 4 to 5 inches long, tapering to a pointed tip, usually green, but sometimes red. They range from almost bell-pepper-like, to mildly warm.

Fresnos: 2 to 3 inches long, pointed tips, green ripening to red. They look and taste almost like a jalapeño, except they are usually found red, and range from mildly spicy to hot.

Jalapeños: 1½ inches to 3 inches long, rounded tips, green ripening to mottled green and orange. They range from mild to very hot.

Poblanos: 3 to 5 inches long, rounded

rather than elongated shape, dark green ripening to red-brown. Poblanos always have a bit of a bite, ranging to quite hot.

Santa Fe Grandes: 3 to 4 inches long, wider at the stem and curving to a tapered end, pale green ripening through orange to deep red, and hot to very hot.

Serranos: About 1½ inches long and ¼ to ½ inch wide, green ripening to bright red, and mildly hot to fiery.

Yellow Wax (also called *gueros*): 1½ to 2½ inches long, wider at the stem end and tapering to a rounded end, pale yellow ripening to mottled yellow-orange. They can be quite mild to quite hot and have a distinctly bell pepper taste.

■ **Dried Chili Peppers:** Dried chilies are matchless for making rich, pungent sauces and seasoning certain stews. They keep for months or even years in jars or bags in the pantry, in baskets on your counter, or strung on string and hung on walls. We always have on hand a wide supply of dried chilies. The following is a descriptive list of the dried chilies referred to in this book.

Anchos: 3½ to 5 inches long and about 3 inches wide, dark red-brown, and mild to slightly hot. Ancho chilies are a dried version of fresh poblano chilies, and the ones we most often use because they purée beautifully without first having the skins removed.

Cascabels: Round chilies, ¾ to 1½ inches wide, red-brown, fairly hot, but not as fiery as the more common japones.

Chipotles: Tapered, 2 to 3 inches long and about ½ inch wide, definite brown color, quite hot. Chipotles are smoke-dried jalapeños and impart a fiery smoke flavor to sauces and stews.

Guajillos: 2 to 3 inches long and about ¾ inch wide, brown with touches of orange-gold, medium hot, with a pleasing tart fruity flavor.

Japones: About 2 inches long and ¼ inch wide, bright orange-red, and fiery hot.

New Mexicos/Californias/Colorados: 6 to 8 inches long and 1 to 1½ inches wide, bright to dark red, ranging from almost sweet to mildly hot. All are dried forms of fresh Anaheims and their flavor varies slightly depending on where they were grown. These are the large chilies often found strung and called *ristras.*

Pasillas: 5 to 7 inches long and about 1 inch wide, very dark red-brown to almost black, and quite mild to warm. Pasillas, like anchos, are a dried form of fresh poblano chilies. If puréeing them for a sauce, you must scrape the pulp off the skins or accept a slightly "stringy" sauce.

■ **Dried Processed Chili Peppers:** Sold in small tins, jars, or packages, these varieties are easy to store on a cool dry pantry shelf with your other herbs and spices.

Cayenne Pepper: Though usually thought of as a pepper like black pepper, Cayenne is actually a form of powdered chili made from tiny cayenne peppers.

Chili Flakes: Dried chili flakes are made from many kinds of dried chilies, usually hot ones. They are especially good for sprinkling on fried potatoes or seasoning fajitas.

Chili Powder: Also made from many varieties of chilies, including the Cayenne pepper. The best chili powder, and the kind we always call for, is pure ground chili with no cumin or other spices added.

■ **Canned Chili Peppers:** Chili peppers put up well, and several varieties are commonly available in small to gigantic cans. If your market does not carry fresh chilies, Anaheims, jalapeños, and serranos in cans are a good alternative for providing the spice and heat in taco dishes. Canned chilies differ in the amount of heat they contain. Taste each to determine its heat before using it in a recipe. Warning: The oils of canned chilies can be relentlessly hot; to handle them, we wear rubber gloves.

CHOCOLATE: Used extensively as a sauce flavoring, and we also use it for dessert fillings. We keep both a good-quality bitter-sweet chocolate bar for *mole* sauces and a box of cinnamon-and-sugar-flavored Mexican chocolate disks—Ibarra brand, for example—for ice cream sauce.

COCONUT STRIPS: The unsweetened kind found in produce markets and health food stores serves as an intriguing taco topping. If you can't find coconut strips, unsweetened shredded coconut, available in most groceries, can be substituted.

CORNMEAL: To use for a crunchy breading, especially for chili strips and eggplant.

DRIED FRUIT: A delightful addition to many fillings and sauces. We usually use apricots, currants, and golden raisins.

EGGS: With a few eggs in the refrigerator, you can turn out a breakfast, lunch, or dinner taco in no time flat.

FRUIT: For fresh salsas, dessert tacos, and your own pleasure, keep a selection of tropical fruits such as papayas, mangos, and pineapples, and always bananas or plantains and oranges.

HEAVY (WHIPPING) CREAM: To thicken fillings and make sauces. The ultrapasteurized kind, with no gums or stabilizers added, keeps very well in the refrigerator.

HERBS: Those we use include:
- **Bay Leaves:** Fresh or dried.
- **Chives:** Always fresh.
- **Cilantro:** Also called fresh coriander or Chinese parsley. You need plenty of fresh cilantro for our recipes. Coriander seed or ground coriander has a different taste altogether and is not a substitute for fresh cilantro. If you are one of those who does not care for cilantro, you can substitute fresh parsley.
- **Marjoram:** Fresh or dried.
- **Mint:** Preferably fresh.
- **Oregano:** Fresh or dried.
- **Parsley:** Always fresh. Italian flat-leaf is best.
- **Sage:** Fresh or dried.
- **Thyme:** Fresh or dried.

HOMINY: For making the best homemade corn tortillas and pork posole filling. Keep a can of yellow or white "wet" hominy on hand. Canned hominy is precooked and ready to use.

ICE CREAM: A selection, including vanilla, for whipping up tostada sundaes.

MASA HARINA: Used for making tortillas, flour ground from corn, called *masa harina* on the package, can be found in almost any supermarket. It is much finer than corn meal. Store it as you would white flour, according to the climate.

NUTS: Frequently used for a pleasing, crunchy topping for many of our tortillas. Keep on hand almonds, peanuts, pine nuts, and walnuts.

OILS: We prefer to use a healthful oil for all cooking, even where tradition dictates the use of solid vegetable shortening or lard. The most delicious cooking oils are olive oil and peanut oil.

OLIVES: Good-quality Greek black olives and Sicilian green olives can help you through many a last minute flavoring quandry.

PRODUCE: One of the main glories of a well-filled tortilla is salsa, the spicy relish concocted from fresh vegetables and fruit. Fresh vegetables also produce many delicious vegetarian fillings. See the Salsa chapter and the chapter on Potato, Bean, and Vegetable tacos and keep handy: avocados, bell peppers, carrots, corn (when in season, we always have an ear or two to cut kernels from), eggplant, garlic, lemons, lettuce, limes, onions, potatoes, radishes, scallions (green onions), tomatillos, tomatoes (we usually keep plum tomatoes, because they are flavorful most of the year, although in season, any kind of ripe, tasty tomato is fine), and yams or sweet potatoes.

RICE: We don't call for rice in any of the taco fillings in this book, but since it is such a traditional accompaniment, especially to bean tacos, you might want to keep a box of long grain white on hand.

SEEDS: Flavorful and crunchy, seeds are a traditional condiment with filled tortillas. We always keep a jar of shelled pumpkin, shelled sunflower, and sesame seeds.

SOUR CREAM: A must at all times, sour cream is one of the most used filled tortilla toppings. Sealed, it keeps for several weeks. Once opened, a carton lasts a week or so.

SPICES: In addition to chilies, fresh and dried, the spices most used in tacos include: cinnamon, cloves, cumin, curry powder, nutmeg, paprika, and turmeric.

SUGAR: For dessert tacos, have on hand:
■ **Confectioners':** For caramelizing dessert tostadas.
■ **Dark Brown:** For sweetening soft dessert tacos.
■ **Granulated:** For crisping dessert tostadas and sweetening dessert sauces.

TEQUILA: For perking up salsas, fillings, and dessert sauces. We also keep on hand Triple Sec or another orange liqueur, such as Curaçao or Cointreau, to add zip to ice cream sauces.

TOMATOES: In addition to fresh tomatoes:
■ **Canned Tomatoes:** A good, not too salty brand of whole tomatoes and/or tomatoes crushed in purée.
■ **Tomato Paste:** An especially good flavor enricher for many ground or stewed meat fillings. To preserve tomato paste after opening a can but not using it all, transfer the remainder to a glass jar, flatten and smooth it out, then pour about ⅛ inch of oil over the top. The oil acts as a sealer to prevent crusting and keep mold from reaching the tomato paste.

TORTILLAS: We adore homemade tortillas and they are fairly quick to make, but most of the time we use good store-bought tortillas. We keep a plentiful supply of those made without preservatives. What we don't use for tacos, our children use for after-school quesadillas.

■ **Corn:** Nutty and chewy, corn tortillas are best when they are quite fresh. Fresh, they last 3 to 4 days. Freezing dries them out and makes them unpliable.
■ **Flour:** Fresh, they last a week or more, but must be well wrapped as their edges dry out easily. Seal them in a zip-lock bag. Meanwhile, a stash can be kept in the freezer. They thaw in a few minutes in the oven and soften quite nicely when heated for tacos.

VINEGAR: For fillings and dressing side salads:
■ **Cider:** The clear, fruity pungence of cider vinegar is especially suitable, and it is the vinegar we use most often.
■ **Red Wine:** For salad dressings and the occasional sauce, such as Green Tzatziki Sauce, where it works better than cider vinegar.

WHITE FLOUR: We keep white flour, preferably unbleached all-purpose, for making flour tortillas.

WINE: One of our favorite seasonings for any cooking. A splash of red or white wine can add the extra zest and bouquet that lifts a dish out of the ordinary. For most home cooking purposes good-quality jug wines (those that are corked rather than capped and have no additives) do the trick. Have a bottle of red and one of white on hand.

EQUIPMENT

Tortilla cooking requires virtually no special equipment other than the usual battery of pots, pans, knives, mixing bowls, and wooden spoons. The only high-ticket item we could not live without because it allows us to make a salsa in a few quick twists of the wrist is a food processor. One of the smaller, much less expensive "mini" food processors now available is equally helpful. For turning out tacos, we mostly use:

BARBECUE GRILL: Nice for fajitas, but you can also use a griddle or fry pan.

CHEESE GRATER: For cheese toppings and quesadillas.

COMAL: The original tortilla griddle of Mexico. Flat and round, they are made of clay, steel, or best of all, cast iron.

GRIDDLE: An easy way to heat tortillas, but an oven or toaster will work as well.

LARGE FRYING PAN: For frying, simmering, everything. Two large frying pans are even better, especially when cooking for a crowd.

OMELETTE PAN OR OTHER SMALL FRYING PAN: A perfect tool for crisping tortillas.

STEW POT: A large pot such as a stovetop casserole, Dutch oven, or stockpot, preferably heavy and nonstick, for the many stewed meat or vegetable fillings. It is handy, but not necessary, to have.

TORTILLA PRESS: For making your own tortillas (but a rolling pin will do).

TORTILLAS

TORTILLAS:
LITTLE CAKES BECOME
EDIBLE PLATTERS

Tortilla means "little cake." And that is exactly what it is: a thin, flat, unleavened pan "cake" of corn or wheat flour. Tortillas are the plate, the envelope, the folder surrounding a countless array of luscious fillings. The bread of Mexican cooking, originally all tortillas were made from corn that has been ground, the native grain of the New World. Corn tortillas, now largely machine made, are still the most nutritious kind. The preparation that the already nutritious corn goes through to make tortillas turns it into even better nourishment. To remove the waxy hulls and ready it for grinding, corn for tortillas is soaked in lime or ash. This treatment creates a chemical reaction that releases protein and minerals otherwise locked in the kernels.

Corn tortillas are also the more flavorful kind. First the lime-soaked corn is boiled to soften it, then when it is turned into dough and patted into cakes, it is baked or fried. The flavor of corn tortillas, particularly when made from fresh corn dough (*masa*), rather than the now more common commercial dried corn flour (*masa harina*), is unmistakable and unforgettable. It is seedy and nutty, like corn on the cob grilled on a barbecue, or the best of buttery popcorn.

When the Spanish brought wheat to the New World, white flour tortillas came into being. An advantage of flour tortillas is that they can be made very large, so large that just one can hold enough for a meal. They are also flakier

and more delicate. Huge flour tortillas filled with beans and other foods were a handy way for cowpokes to dine around the campfire. Such ranch-style meals in a single package inspired our present rage for burritos.

Recently, tortillas made from whole wheat flour and the blue cornmeal of the Southwest have become available. Whole wheat tortillas make superb substitutes for pita bread or the buckwheat crêpes that usually underpin sour cream and caviar. Blue corn tortillas are delectable as chips for dips or just heated and buttered in place of bread. They have a rich, dense, legume-like corn flavor and a musky aroma.

GOING WITH WHAT WORKS BEST

We prefer wrapping our fillings in the more pedestrian corn or flour tortillas. Occasionally we specify one sort of tortilla or another, but mostly we view them as interchangeable. Their size differs, and our recipes recognize that fact in the number of tortillas called for. Corn tortillas are about 6½ inches in diameter, and three well-filled corn tortillas are usually enough for the avid eater. Flour tortillas are larger, about 8 inches in diameter, and two well-filled ones are a meal for most. Both kinds come packaged and can be found in almost every grocery store these days. They are generally of good quality and flavor. Some have preservatives, however, and some don't. We recommend the preservative-free ones for both taste and health reasons.

If you have a Latin market, Mexicatessen (a Mexican deli), or a tortilla factory—called a *tortilleria*—close by, you can probably buy tortillas very fresh, hot off the press, and extra delicious. In some *tortillerias,* markets, rare Mexican restaurants, and certainly in little villages throughout Central America, you can still purchase hand-patted tortillas

▲▲▲▲▲▲▲▲▲▲▲▲▲▲▲

WELL-FILLED TORTILLAS

BURRITO: Warmed soft tortilla filled and folded like an envelope.

CHIMICHANGA: Tortilla, filled and folded envelope style, then crisped or deep-fried.

ENCHILADA: Tortilla, softened or dipped, filled, rolled into a tube, sauced and cheesed over the top, then baked.

FLAUTA: Tortilla filled, tightly rolled into a flute shape, then fried crisp.

TACO: Soft warm or lightly crisped tortilla filled and folded in half. In North America, the tortilla shell for tacos is often fried hard.

TAPA: In Mexico, a soft tortilla, filled, folded and lightly crisped, much like a chimichanga. In Spain, a snack-size tortilla fried crisp and hard, often in a basket shape, then filled.

TOSTADA: Tortilla fried crisp, either flat or basket shaped, and topped with a salad concoction.

QUESADILLA: Tortilla filled with cheese and crisped until the cheese melts.

▼▼▼▼▼▼▼▼▼▼▼▼▼▼▼

made from *masa harina* or even fresh *masa* ground on *metates.* If you are fortunate enough to happen upon some, buy them immediately, if not to fill, then just to eat.

Packaged flour tortillas last a week or more under refrigeration and freeze well. Packaged corn tortillas tend to get chewy and should be used within 3 to 5 days. They also do not resoften if frozen. Should you buy freshly made tortillas from a Mexicatessen, eat them right away while they are at their freshest.

There is, of course, a way to ensure having the freshest tortillas. Make your own. Homemade tortillas are easy to prepare, especially if you don't mind a few raggedy edges. As with any baking—it takes practice to make perfect pies and cakes—it takes a few tries to make uniform corn or flour "little cakes." But without a doubt, homemade tortillas have the most robust flavor. For those adventuresome souls who would like to make their own tortillas, at least occasionally, we include recipes for corn, flour, and best of all, an almost fresh *masa* pulp tortilla. To approximate the freshly ground wet dough used to make traditional tortillas, we offer a method that combines canned wet hominy kernels and *masa harina* (Hominy Tortillas). Should you want to skip the dough-making step and still press or pat your own tortillas, many Mexicatessens and tortilla factories sell tortilla dough by the pound.

PREPARING TORTILLAS FOR FILLING

TO WARM TORTILLAS

For most tacos and all burritos, the tortillas are simply warmed until they are soft and pliant. To warm tortillas, you can use an oven, steamer, griddle, *comal,* ungreased

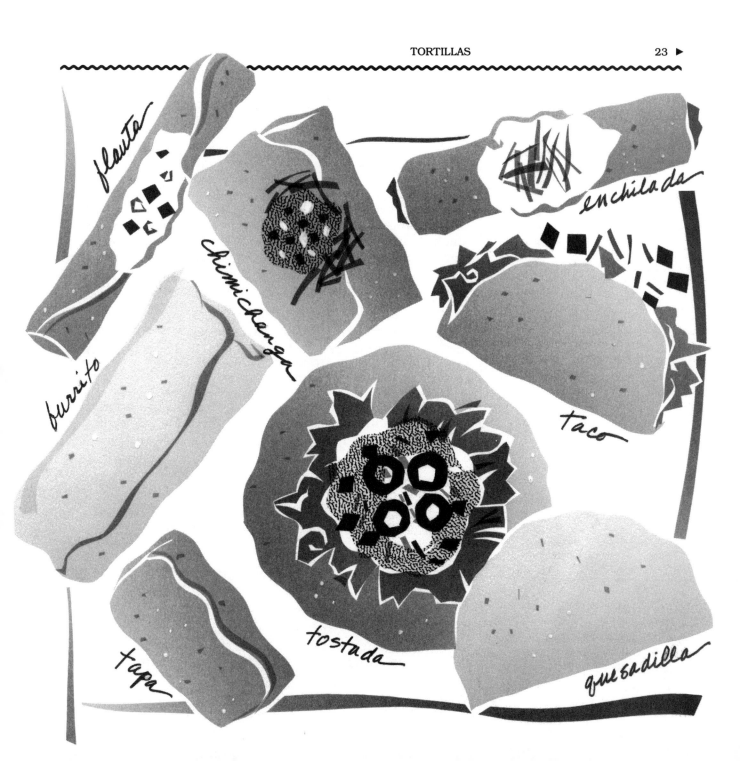

frying pan, or microwave. You can also use a toaster if you are careful to catch the tortilla before it crisps.

In the oven: Heat the oven to 400°F. Place the tortillas on the oven rack and leave for 3 minutes.

In a steamer: Place as many tortillas as you are using in a stack and wrap the stack in a cloth towel or several cloth napkins to enclose completely. Place the wrapped stack in the basket of a vegetable steamer over an inch or so of boiling water. Cover the steamer and leave for 6 to 10 minutes, depending on how many tortillas are in the stack.

On a griddle, comal, or ungreased frying pan: Heat the griddle or pan until hot but not yet smoking. Place a tortilla on the surface and leave for 10 to 15 seconds, until just beginning to puff. Turn and heat briefly on the other side.

In the microwave: Place the tortillas in the microwave without stacking them and microwave for 30 to 45 seconds, until beginning to puff.

In the toaster: Turn the toaster to low, drop in a tortilla, and heat until just beginning to puff.

When serving a crowd, you can soften the tortillas ahead, place them in a cloth-covered bowl or basket, and hold them in a very low oven until ready to serve.

TO CRISP TORTILLAS

When a little crunch is desirable, you can lightly crisp tortillas. To crisp tortillas, fry them in a pan or on a griddle. You can also toast them over a grill, *comal,* or even on a stovetop gas burner, until slightly crunchy but still pliable and not stiff.

In a frying pan or on a griddle: Pour 1 teaspoon oil in

a heavy 9-inch frying pan or onto the griddle. When the oil begins to smoke, add the tortilla and fry for about 1 minute, until beginning to puff. Turn and fry on the other side for 1 minute more. You will need to add a little more oil for each round.

To crisp more than one tortilla at a time, use a larger pan and 2 to 3 teaspoons oil. Fry as many tortillas as will fit, without overlapping, in the pan or on the griddle.

On a grill, comal, or gas burner: Place as many tortillas as will fit without overlapping on a hot grill, *comal,* or over medium heat on a gas burner. Heat until beginning to puff, turn, and heat until crisp but still foldable.

When serving a crowd, you can crisp the tortillas ahead, place them in a cloth-covered bowl or basket, and hold them in a warm oven until ready to serve. They stay warm and fairly crisp, but do soften a little.

TO CRISP A FILLED TORTILLA

To crisp filled tortillas, as for flautas, tapas, and chimichangas, use a frying pan or griddle. Fill the tortilla, then roll or fold it over, roll it up, or tuck in the ends envelope style. Place in a frying pan or on a griddle with a little oil and cook 1 minute. Turn and cook on the other side until golden and crisp, about 1 minute more.

DIPPED TORTILLAS

Dipped tortillas add an extra pleasing tang to many fillings especially those filled with grilled meat or chicken. Particularly good for dipping are Salsa Verde, Fresh Tomato Salsa, Chive Salsa, and Ancho Chili Sauce.

Dip the tortilla in a bowl of whatever salsa or sauce you choose, or spoon the salsa on, spreading it with the back of the spoon. Soften the dipped tortillas in an oven, in an ungreased frying pan, or over a *comal,* or stack and steam

them as described earlier in this section. Dipped tortillas come out especially well when steamed.

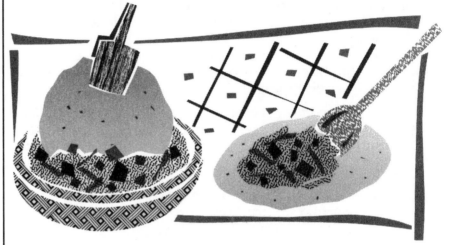

TO FRY TORTILLAS FLAT FOR TOSTADAS

Use a heavy frying pan or griddle. Pour in enough oil to coat the bottom of the pan or griddle. Heat until the oil separates into rivulets but is not yet smoking. Add a tortilla and fry for 1 minute. Turn and fry on the other side until the tortilla is too crisp to fold but not burned, about 1½ minutes more. Remove to paper towels and set aside without stacking until ready to assemble the tostadas.

If you would like tortillas for tostadas without using any oil, heat them in the oven until crisp and no longer pliable. The timing is the same.

TORTILLA TIPS

If surveying longtime tortilla makers, you will probably find that those from central Mexico and points south make corn tortillas, while those from northern Mexico, the Southwest, up through Colorado and California make flour ones. The techniques of making each differ somewhat.

Corn Tortillas: Once the dough is made, you can press, roll, or hand pat it into flat cakes. Forming the tortillas with a press (available at most Mexican grocers for about $10) is easy and fast, but you don't have to have one. You can flatten the dough with a rolling pin as speedily and as well. The shape of the rolling pin matters. It should be evenly cylindrical rather than tapered at the ends. If you don't have this kind, use a dowel or a piece of a broom handle. All nicely serve to flatten the *masa*. Whether you use a tortilla press or rolling pin, there's a trick: plastic wrap. Place an egg-size oval of tortilla dough on a sheet of plastic wrap on the press or work counter. Cover the dough with another sheet of plastic wrap, and then press or roll out. Peel the flattened cake off the wrap and onto the griddle.

To hand pat tortillas, use the method of *tortilleras*, the well-practiced tortilla makers of the Southwest and Latin America. Wet your hands and roll a small ball of dough into the shape and size of a golf ball. With your palms and fingers straight, pat the dough flat until you achieve an even, round cake. The tortillas will be a little thicker than pressed or rolled ones. Unless you are using a press, and especially if using your hands, it takes experience to form perfectly round tortillas. We think tacos are just as good on slightly odd-shaped tortillas. As for ragged edges, you can always trim them off.

Flour Tortillas: You don't use a press or need plastic wrap to make flour tortillas. Roll out a golf-ball-size piece of dough on a lightly floured board or counter as you would pie dough.

▲▲▲▲▲▲▲▲▲▲▲▲▲▲▲

LEFTOVER TORTILLAS

More than just fillable pan cakes, tortillas are the bread that accompanies meals in Mexico and Central America. Whether eaten whole or torn into bite-size pieces, tortillas are used to scoop up vegetables, soak up gravies, mediate between bites, and generally fill the stomach. Like crusts and heels of bread, leftover or broken tortillas need never be wasted. Pieces can be used as crackers for spreads or turned into chips. Tortilla strips can be layered like lasagne noodles in spicy casseroles or crumbled on soups like croutons. Tortillas can also be soaked in milk and turned into pudding. They can be dried out and reground into corn dough for new tortillas. Best of all, when dried like day-old bread, leftover tortilla bits can be lightly fried, then cooked in a sauce of chilies or vegetables, and served like saucy home fries or mixed in with eggs, as in *chilaquiles*.

CORN TORTILLAS

Since *masa*—fresh corn dough—is difficult to find or make, it is *masa harina*—dried and ground corn flour—that is most widely available and widely used to make corn tortillas at home. *Masa harina* is not the same as cornmeal or polenta. These products are simply ground corn. In *masa harina* the corn has been soaked in lime to break down the hulls, then the kernels are ground into a fine flour. Quaker brand *masa harina* is the easiest to find, and it is an excellent product. Occasionally you can find stone-ground *masa harina,* which bears a closer resemblance to fresh *masa* in flavor. When making corn tortillas, it is traditional to use no salt because the lime or ash in the dough replaces it. In our recipe we add a small pinch of salt to bring out the corn flavor, but you can omit it if you choose.

Makes eighteen 6- to 7-inch corn tortillas
Takes 40 minutes to 1 hour, depending on your equipment

4 cups masa harina
½ teaspoon salt
2½ cups hot tap water

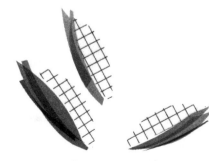

1. Using your hands, mix the *masa harina,* salt, and water together in a bowl until the dough comes together in a soft ball. If using right away, divide the dough into 18 golf-ball-size pieces. Cover with plastic wrap to keep moist while pressing or rolling out the tortillas. If usi..g later, wrap the whole dough ball in plastic wrap. Set aside until ready to press out, or refrigerate, and use within 1 day.

2. To form the tortillas, place a ball of dough between two pieces of plastic wrap. Press with a tortilla press or roll with a rolling pin to make a 6- to 7-inch round between ¹⁄₁₆- and ⅛-inch thick. Set aside in the plastic wrap until ready to cook. The tortillas may be formed in advance and refrigerated overnight.

3. To cook the tortillas, heat a heavy cast-iron frying pan, griddle, or *comal* over medium-high heat. Peel off the plastic wrap and place the tortillas in the pan, one at a time or as many as will fit without overlapping. Cook for 30 seconds, then turn over. Cook for 1 minute, then turn again to the first side. Cook for 30 seconds, until the tortilla puffs slightly but is still pliable. Remove and continue with another round until all of the tortillas are cooked. The tortillas may be cooked in advance, stacked, wrapped in plastic, and refrigerated overnight. Reheat just before serving (page 22).

TIPS

▶ Corn tortilla dough dries out extremely rapidly. It is important to cover the dough with plastic wrap as soon as you make it and keep it covered as you work.

▶ If the tortillas crack around the edges when pressed or rolled, you can smooth them out by pressing on the plastic wrap with your fingers. Or trim the tortillas into even rounds with a knife.

▶ Corn tortilla dough does not suffer from being made in advance and refrigerated overnight as long as it is well wrapped.

FLOUR TORTILLAS

Most traditional recipes for flour tortillas use lard or hard vegetable shortening. We try to avoid them both—lard, because it is cholesterol laden, and shortening, because it contains palm oil, which is good for shelf life but not for blood vessels. We've developed an equally good recipe using vegetable oil or olive oil. Our flour tortillas are very easy to make, particularly for anyone who is accustomed to kneading bread or making pie dough.

Makes twelve 8-inch flour tortillas
Takes about 1½ hours, including 30 minutes resting time for the dough

3 cups unbleached all-purpose flour
⅓ cup vegetable oil, such as corn, safflower, or olive oil
1 teaspoon salt
1 cup warm tap water

1. Place the flour in a mixing bowl. Add the oil and mix together with a fork or your fingers until thoroughly distributed and the flour is crumbly in texture.

2. Mix the salt with the warm tap water and add to the flour. Mix together with your hands until you can gather the dough into a ball. Place the dough on an unfloured board and knead until smooth and elastic, 3 to 5 minutes. Return the dough to the mixing bowl, cover with a towel, place it in a warmish spot, and let rest for up to 2 hours, but no less than 30 minutes. The dough may be wrapped in plastic and stored in the refrigerator. Use within 1 day.

3. To make the tortillas, divide the dough into 12 equal pieces and roll each between your palms to make a ball. Flatten the balls, then place on a very lightly floured board. With a rolling pin, roll each ball into an 8- to 9-inch very thin round. The uncooked flour tortillas may be layered between sheets of plastic wrap and stored in the refrigerator overnight.

4. To cook the tortillas, heat a heavy cast-iron frying pan, griddle, or *comal* over medium-high heat. Place the tortillas, one at a time or as many as will fit without overlapping, in the pan and cook for 30 seconds. If the tortillas puff up, gently press them down with a spatula. Turn and cook on the other side until speckled with brown spots but still pliable and not crisp, about 30 seconds more. Remove and stack as you go, while the tortillas are still warm. Use the cooked tortillas right away or reheat just before serving (page 22).

TIP

▶ As with other tortillas, you can make these in advance and reheat them just before serving.

SOPAIPILLAS

Sopaipillas are a favorite Southwest dessert. To prepare them, sweeten the basic flour tortilla dough with 2 teaspoons of sugar and leaven it with 1 good tablespoon of baking powder. Knead the dough for 3 minutes, then roll it out, and cut it into triangles. As with fritters, drop the triangles into hot oil. Hold them under with a spoon until they puff, then turn until brown all over. Remove the *sopaipillas* and drain. Serve as is, or coat lightly with honey and confectioners' sugar for a quick, easy, and beloved sweet.

HOMINY TORTILLAS

We prefer fresh corn tortillas straight from the pulp beyond all others. But with no grandmother to show us how to soak and grind the corn, and little time or wherewithal, like most modern taco cooks we were stuck with buying fresh tortillas whenever we could find them. Then with great cheers of thanks, Betty Fussell came to our rescue.

Fussell in her spectacular book *I Hear America Cooking* offers a way to have fresh pulpy crunchy tortillas in moments. She adds puréed canned wet hominy to dry *masa harina* and mixes up a dough that is almost a fresh corn pulp duplicate. Her dough is more malleable and easier to roll than dough made with only *masa harina,* and with nutty pieces of white corn kernels dotted throughout the cakes, far more tasty. Using a food processor or food mill to purée the hominy, her technique is no more trouble than mixing plain dry *masa harina* with water. We love her recipe and always use it.

Makes eighteen 6- to 7-inch tortillas
Takes 40 minutes to 1 hour, depending on your equipment

1½ cups canned hominy (most of a 29-ounce can), drained
1½ cups masa harina
¼ teaspoon salt
1 cup hot tap water

1. Purée the hominy in a food processor, blender, or food mill. In a large bowl or the food processor, mix the puréed hominy with the *masa harina,* salt, and water until the dough gathers into a soft ball.

▲▲▲▲▲▲▲▲▲▲▲▲▲▲▲▲▲

White hominy is the corn of grits, and when rolled and toasted, the corn of corn flakes. Mashed it becomes the basis of corn whiskey. From hominy corn and other types of corn we get corn flour for soap and stiffening in dressmaking, corn starch for thickening, corn syrup, and corn oil.

▼▼▼▼▼▼▼▼▼▼▼▼▼▼▼▼▼

2. If using right away, divide the dough into 18 golf-ball-size pieces. Cover with plastic wrap to keep moist while pressing or rolling out the tortillas. If using later, wrap the whole ball of dough in plastic wrap. Set aside until ready to roll out, or refrigerate and use within 1 day.

3. To form the tortillas, proceed as in the Corn Tortilla recipe, step 2, page 28.

TORTILLA CHIPS

Tortilla chips make a crunchy dipper for guacamole or salsa, a cracker substitute for soups or cheese dips, a salad garnish in place of croutons, and a healthful substitute for potato chips. Fry them in a little oil or heat them crisp in the oven to avoid the oil.

Makes 36 tortilla chips
Takes less than 20 minutes

6 corn or flour tortillas, packaged or homemade (if
*   homemade, rolled out and ready to cook)*
Oil (optional)

1. Stack the tortillas and cut through the stack to make 6 triangles out of each.

2. *To fry the tortilla chips,* pour enough oil in the bottom of a heavy frying pan to reach ¼ inch up the sides. Heat until the oil just begins to smoke. Place as many tortilla triangles in the pan as will fit without overlapping. Fry until they puff, about 1 minute. Turn and fry on the other side until crisp, about 1½ minutes more. Drain on paper towels. Continue with another round until all of the triangles are fried.

To crisp the tortilla chips in the oven, heat the oven to 400°F. Lay out the tortilla triangles flat on a baking sheet without overlapping. Bake in the oven for 5 minutes. Turn and bake until crisp, about 5 minutes more.

3. Serve right away or store in an airtight container until ready to use.

▲▲▲▲▲▲▲▲▲▲▲▲▲▲▲▲▲

A long with whole-wheat and blue corn tortillas, many markets now carry rich, crusty bean tortillas made from both black beans and mellow brown pinto beans. They make flavorful snack, and when accompanied by a lively salsa, an appealing hors d'ouevre.

▼▼▼▼▼▼▼▼▼▼▼▼▼▼▼▼▼

SALSAS AND TOPPINGS

STARTING AT THE TOP

If tortillas are the shape of tacos and their like, and fillings are the heart, then salsas are the spirit and toppings the zing. A taco is hardly a taco without them. They add the final touches, lend zest and texture, and make eating tortillas just more fun.

Take a simple roasted chicken filling, add a salsa of dried ancho chili, a swath of guacamole topping, and you have a concoction with soul. Take plain ground beef, drizzle on a purée of tart little green tomatoes, sprinkle cheese over the top, and you get the stuff of food dreams.

Salsas are speedy to make, especially with a food processor or food mill, and with a jar or two in the refrigerator, you're ready when a taco craving hits. No hard rules need hamper your salsa creativity. You can follow the recipes exactly or alter them to suit what's in your kitchen or what pleases your own taste. Play loose with the chili peppers to make the salsa mild, hot, or hotter. Substitute parsley for cilantro. Add radishes or not, scallions or red onions. Mix and match the elements as you choose.

Layered on like a Dagwood sandwich, a taco's customary toppings are chopped tomato, strips of lettuce, spoonsful of sour cream, crumbles of cheese. But why limit yourself? Fried chili strips, toasted nuts and seeds, and dressed cilantro give fillings crunch, spark, and dash. Use one or two salsas. Add on three or four toppings. Variety is the spice of the well-filled tortilla.

▲▲▲▲▲▲▲▲▲▲▲▲▲

SALSA VS SAUCE

When a salsa medley—vegetables, maybe fruits, seeds, or nuts—is uncooked, it's called a *salsa cruda*. When the elements are briefly cooked, the medley is called a sauce. Raw or cooked, what makes salsa or sauce for a well-filled tortilla so refreshing is that it is bound with water, not oil. The pieces are either chunky, cut into about ¼-inch dice, like a chopped salad, relish, or chutney, or else smoothly puréed like a savory jam.

▼▼▼▼▼▼▼▼▼▼▼▼▼

SALSAS

FRESH TOMATO SALSA

The basic *salsa cruda* of Mexican and Southwestern cooking everywhere is Fresh Tomato Salsa. Our special version of Fresh Tomato Salsa, with its six chili peppers, radish, and garlic, is a zippy one. If you would like yours less hot and spicy, reduce the chili quantity. Once chopped and mixed together, its consistency should be like a wet salad with enough liquid to cover the vegetables, but not so much as to drown them. If you can't get the chilies called for, substitute 2 ounces mixed chili peppers—whatever is available.

Makes 2 cups
Takes less than 20 minutes

2 jalapeño chili peppers, stemmed
2 serrano chili peppers, stemmed
2 yellow wax chili peppers, stemmed
3 radishes, trimmed
3 garlic cloves
1 bunch of scallions (green onions), trimmed, or
    ½ medium onion
2 medium tomatoes
1 cup cilantro leaves
¼ teaspoon salt
1 tablespoon tomato paste
½ to 1 cup water

When we opened our Good and Plenty Cafe on the campus of the California College of Arts and Crafts in Oakland, California—student body of 1,200, faculty and staff of 200, and serving most of them, plus plenty of outsiders daily—we decided to feature quesadillas and nachos with our homemade Fresh Tomato Salsa. We thought this spicy accent would appeal to "adventuresome" palates, but we had no idea how their numbers would grow after one taste of the salsa. We timidly began by making 2-cup batches. This quickly increased to double and triple the amount, and as the word spread, our clientele were asking for it on the side with their salads, sandwiches, and soups. Now we're up to gallon batches, tenfold the recipe, everyday.

▲▲▲▲▲▲▲▲▲▲▲▲▲▲▲▲

VEGETABLES IN THE FOOD PROCESSOR

W hen chopping vegetables in a food processor—onions, chili peppers, tomatoes, radishes, or whatever—first halve them or cut them into 1-inch chunks so that they chop up evenly.

▼▼▼▼▼▼▼▼▼▼▼▼▼▼▼▼

1. Coarsely chop the chili peppers, radishes, garlic, scallions, tomatoes, and cilantro in a food processor or with a chef's knife. Transfer to a bowl.

2. Add the salt, tomato paste, and water. Stir to mix well. Use right away or cover and refrigerate for up to 10 days.

TIPS

▶ If you are using a food processor to chop the vegetables, be sure not to overprocess them. The pieces in Fresh Tomato Salsa should be coarse and chunky, not minced.

▶ How much water you add depends on how full and juicy the tomatoes are. If they are soft and ripe, ½ cup water is enough, but if they are very firm, add more, up to 1 cup or so.

TWO RED HOT CHILI-GARLIC SALSAS

E very now and then we crave a truly fiery red sauce. If your constitution can withstand it, a hit of really hot garnish takes your mind off whatever else ails you. Like Chinese hot pepper oil, Moroccan harissa, and Nicaraguan salsa verde, our two hot and sharp Red Hot Chili-Garlic Salsas are especially fine on potatoes, shrimp, meaty fish, and beef. A quarter the usual salsa portion is a plentiful dab on any taco, so we've written the recipes for just one-half cupful. Or use them in conjunction with other salsas when you want a little more heat.

FRESH RED HOT CHILI-GARLIC SALSA

Makes ½ cup
Takes less than 20 minutes

6 garlic cloves
16 to 18 (2 ounces) serrano chili peppers, preferably red,
*   stemmed*
⅛ teaspoon salt
3 tablespoons water

Mince the garlic and chili peppers in a food processor or with a chef's knife. Transfer to a bowl and stir in the salt and water. Serve right away, or cover, refrigerate and use within one day.

DRIED RED HOT CHILI-GARLIC SALSA

Makes about ½ cup
Takes 40 minutes

1½ ounces dried red chili peppers, preferably japones or
*   guajillos, stemmed*
5 garlic cloves
⅓ cup olive oil
¼ teaspoon salt

1. Place the dried chili peppers in a bowl and cover with warm water. Let soak until the chilies are soft, about 30 minutes. Drain.

2. In a food processor, blender, or with a mortar and pestle or chef's knife, mince together the chilies and garlic. Add the olive oil and salt. Use right away or cover and refrigerate.

~~~~~~

TIPS

▶ Since fresh minced garlic becomes stale when refrigerated, but dried chilies do not, to keep this salsa on hand, we make a large batch without the garlic, store it in its oil in the refrigerator, and add the garlic as we serve it.

▶ You can substitute dried Thai chilies (the hottest ever), Szechuan chilies, or in a pinch, dried red chili flakes for the Mexican japones or guajillos in this recipe.

FIESTA SALSA

~~~~~~

From the tortilla wrapping to the salsa topping, corn is a natural complement of tacos. This lively salsa has the corn right in it. One of the tender, sweet, white corn varieties is best; young yellow corn is a second choice. Frozen corn does not work well at all for a fresh salsa; it's better to leave out the corn or wait till next summer.

Makes about 2¼ cups
Takes less than 20 minutes

½ cup fresh corn kernels (1 small ear)
1 medium-size green bell pepper, cored and seeded
½ medium onion
2 red Fresno chili peppers, stemmed
1 large garlic clove
1 cup cilantro leaves
½ tablespoon tomato paste
½ cup water
⅛ teaspoon ground cumin
⅛ teaspoon salt

▲▲▲▲▲▲▲▲▲▲▲▲▲▲▲

As much as the first asparagus or basket of strawberries, the arrival of corn in the market is always a happy event. Corn is at home in salsa, as are most other native American vegetables: chili peppers, bell peppers, and tomatoes.

▼▼▼▼▼▼▼▼▼▼▼▼▼▼▼

1. Bring a small pot of water to boil. When the water boils, drop in the corn, count to five, and drain immediately. Set aside to drip dry.

2. In a food processor or using a chef's knife, coarsely chop the bell pepper, onion, chili peppers, garlic, and cilantro.

3. In a bowl, mix together the tomato paste, ½ cup water, cumin, and salt. Add the chopped ingredients and the corn. Stir to mix. Serve right away, or cover, refrigerate, and use within 1 week.

RED BELL PEPPER-TOMATILLO SALSA

A confetti of colors, a salmagundi of tastes, the sparkle of this salsa is the refreshing, uncooked "little green tomatoes," tomatillos. For a more Southwestern taste, you can use cilantro in place of parsley, but we like the flavor of parsley, especially the robust Italian flat-leaf parsley, in a salsa every now and then.

Makes about 2¼ cups
Takes 20 minutes or less

4 medium tomatillos (about 4 ounces)
1½ large red bell peppers, cored and seeded
1 yellow wax or jalapeño chili pepper, stemmed
½ cup chopped fresh parsley leaves, preferably Italian flat-
*　　leaf*
1½ teaspoons red chili flakes
¼ teaspoon salt
¾ cup water

1. Peel the papery husks off the tomatillos. Rinse the tomatillos and pat them dry.

2. In a food processor or using a chef's knife, coarsely chop the bell pepper, tomatillos, chili pepper, and parsley. Transfer to a bowl and stir in the chili flakes, salt, and water. Serve right away, or cover, refrigerate, and use within 3 days.

TOMATO, PUMPKIN SEED, AND SCALLION SALSA

While water is the moistener in most salsas, every now and then we like to add a little oil. Here, olive or peanut oil enriches the pumpkin seed and basil flavors, making this salsa like a spicy, nutty, chunky pesto. You can emphasize the Adriatic quality of the salsa even more with a touch of chopped anchovy, and as well as on tacos, use it to top pasta!

Makes 2 cups
Takes less than 20 minutes

1 cup shelled pumpkin seeds
4 yellow wax chili peppers, stemmed
Tops from 2 bunches of scallions (green onions)
1 large ripe round or 2 plum tomatoes
¼ cup finely shredded fresh basil leaves
2 teaspoons fresh lemon juice
½ cup olive or peanut oil
1 cup water
¼ teaspoon salt

1. Place the pumpkin seeds in a frying pan and stir over medium heat until toasted, about 5 minutes. Set aside to cool.

2. In a food processor or using a chef's knife, coarsely chop the pumpkin seeds, chili peppers, and scallion tops. Transfer to a bowl.

3. Using a knife, dice the tomatoes into small pieces. Add to the bowl, along with the basil, lemon juice, oil, water, and salt. Stir to mix. Serve right away, or cover, refrigerate, and use within 1 day.

TIPS

▶ To keep the elements discrete and salad-like, we like to hand chop the tomatoes. Use a food processor if you are in a rush, but be sure not to overprocess.

▶ If you are making this salsa when tomatoes are not ripe and juicy, blend 1 tablespoon tomato paste into the water to enhance the tomato flavor.

▲▲▲▲▲▲▲▲▲▲▲▲▲▲▲▲▲

For such a water-laden vegetable, tomatoes love oil. They don't quite absorb it like eggplant, nor bathe in it like garlic. They seem to glaze themselves with it, or treat it like a glistening coating. Oil enriches, actually deepens, tomatoes' flavor. We prefer olive oil as a tomato rinse. It evokes Mediterranean flavors like sun-dried tomatoes and Italian tomato salads. But peanut oil adds a nutty, light film that also appeals.

AVOCADO-PUMPKIN SEED SALSA

In parts of the country where tropical produce is abundant, you can make avocado salsas and guacamoles on the spur of the moment. In other areas, alas, you should plan a few days in advance. A perfect avocado for salsa or mole should be soft all over, but resume its shape after being squeezed, not stay indented. Since most store-bought avocados are rock hard, the softening process often takes a day or two on the windowsill at home.

Makes 2 cups
Takes less than 20 minutes

2 ripe avocados
⅔ cup cilantro leaves
1 serrano chili pepper, stemmed
1⅓ cups fresh parsley leaves, preferably Italian flat-leaf
3 tablespoons shelled pumpkin seeds
1 tablespoon fresh lemon juice
¼ teaspoon salt

1. Cut the avocados in half; remove the pits. Peel the avocado halves and chop the pulp into small chunks. Place in a bowl.

2. In a food processor or using a chef's knife, coarsely chop the cilantro, chili pepper, and parsley. Add to the avocado, along with the pumpkin seeds, lemon juice, and salt. Gently stir with a fork to mix without mashing the avocado. Serve right away.

TIP

▶ If you want to prepare this salsa several hours or even the night before serving, the trick is to retain the avocado pits and tuck them into the salsa. It works like magic to keep the avocado green and fresh.

A ny dish with avocado in it makes people think "guacamole," and head for the bowl, chips in hand, like prospectors locating the treasure of the Sierra Madre. We once made tubs of Avocado-Pumpkin Seed Salsa for a wedding and barely salvaged enough to dress the white fish tacos. We offer two great guacamoles in this book—a basic Guacamole and the Well-Filled Guacamole. But if the hungry hordes insist on treating this salsa as a dip, we suggest you defend yourself by making plenty and getting out the chips.

CHIVE SALSA

Fresh, green, and savory, chive is an inspired salsa seasoning. Together with the aromatic mint and hot chili peppers, it makes a unique and breathtaking taco condiment. If you can't get the chilies called for, substitute about 2½ ounces mixed hot fresh chili peppers, whatever is available.

Makes 2 cups
Takes less than 20 minutes

3 jalapeño chili peppers, stemmed
2 serrano chili peppers, stemmed
3 yellow wax chili peppers, stemmed
2 Fresno or Santa Fe Grande chili peppers, stemmed
4 radishes, trimmed
3 large garlic cloves
2 large or 4 small bunches of chives (about 2 cups when
*   coarsely chopped)*
⅓ cup fresh mint leaves
1 cup cilantro leaves
1 cup water
¾ teaspoon salt

In a food processor or using a chef's knife, coarsely chop the chili peppers, radishes, garlic, chives, and mint. Remove to a bowl. Add the cilantro, water, and salt. Mix well. Serve right away, or cover, refrigerate, and use within 3 days.

TIP

▶ If you're in a pinch for time, go ahead and chop the cilantro along with the rest of the ingredients instead of picking the leaves individually off the stems. The salsa will have a more homogenous texture, less varied and attractive, but still tasty.

Should you care to plant an edible that will give you year-round culinary pleasure, chives are the best candidate. In the garden or in a pot on your kitchen counter, chives thrive. Cut them back and they grow right back up. They are far more hardy than parsley, surviving the winter doldrums—indoors in cold climates or outdoors in mild—whereas parsley falters and fails. Think of chives when you're looking for an oniony taste, for they provide a versatile, clean, and cool alternative to the more familiar bulbous allium.

▲▲▲▲▲▲▲▲▲▲▲▲▲▲▲

Every year the many Spanish-speakers of Northern California hold a Latin American festival in Gilroy. José Feliciano comes to sing, Mexican and Spanish dancers perform, and across a wide grassy field stand booths offering every sort of Latin American food imaginable. The hit of the fair is the Argentine *empanadas*, folded over pie crusts surrounding fillings similar to tortilla fillings. The empanadas are accompanied by a South American salsa made from jalapeños and lots of parsley that is slathered over the outside. We've included our version of the salsa to slather inside North American tacos.

▼▼▼▼▼▼▼▼▼▼▼▼▼▼▼

SOUTH AMERICAN JALAPENO-PARSLEY SALSA

Meat is as central to South American cuisine as it is to North American, and this typical salsa—a *chimichurri*—is a superb meat relish. In Argentina *chimichurri* is served over lean, range-fed, pampas beef steaks. We prefer using green-tasting fresh Italian parsley in this salsa. Should you find only plain canned jalapeños, then do add some vinegar.

Makes about 2 cups
Takes less than 20 minutes

18 canned marinated jalapeño chili peppers
3 tablespoons chopped onion
6 tablespoons fresh parsley leaves, preferably Italian flat-leaf
⅓ cup olive oil

1. Wearing rubber gloves to protect your hands, cut the stems off the jalapeños.

2. In a food processor or using a chef's knife, chop the chili peppers, onion, and parsley into medium-size pieces. Transfer to a bowl. Stir in the oil. Use right away or cover and refrigerate for up to several weeks.

TIP

▶ The special flavor of this salsa depends on using marinated jalapeños. If you cannot find them, use plain canned ones and add ¼ teaspoon dried oregano and 1 teaspoon cider vinegar to the salsa.

GREEN OLIVE-CILANTRO SALSA

Need a switch from tortillas? Or maybe you've run out of them. Green Olive-Cilantro Salsa is excellent in a lettuce leaf taco. Stuff a large curly, romaine, red, or butter leaf with a filling of carnitas, other pork, chicken, duck, fish, beef, or goat, and top with this salsa.

Makes about 2¼ cups
Takes less than 20 minutes

1 pound jumbo green olives (about 2 cups), pitted
2 large garlic cloves
4 serrano chilies, stemmed
1 cup cilantro leaves
1 cup olive oil
1 teaspoon minced lemon zest

In a food processor or using a chef's knife, mince the olives, garlic, chilies, and cilantro. Stir in the olive oil and lemon zest. Serve right away, or cover, refrigerate, and use within 1 week.

TIP

▶ To easily pit olives, tap the olives with a hammer, just hard enough to open the flesh, and pop out the pit.

MENU
▼

OSCAR NIGHT SALSA AND CHIPS PARTY

———

Salsa Verde

———

Green Olive-Cilantro Salsa

———

Fiesta Salsa

———

Avocado-Pumpkin Seed Salsa

———

Mango-Jalapeño Salsa

———

Basic Black Beans

———

A selection of tortilla chips: Corn, flour, blue corn, whole-wheat, and bean, piled high in different baskets.

———

Sopaipillas

LEEK, FETA, AND SOUR CREAM SALSA

Makes about 2 cups
Takes less than 20 minutes

2 small leeks (about 1¾ cups when chopped; see step 1)
¾ cup sour cream
3 tablespoons milk
1 tablespoon fresh lime juice
⅛ teaspoon salt
¼ cup crumbled feta cheese (4 ounces)
*1 small poblano chili pepper (about 2 ounces), stemmed,
    seeded, and minced*

1. Trim the root ends and dark part of the green tops off the leeks. Cut the leeks lengthwise in half. Cut each half into long strips; cut across the strips to finely chop. Wash the leek pieces in plenty of water, drain, and set aside to drip dry.

2. In a bowl, whisk the sour cream until smooth. Whisk in the milk, lime juice, and salt. Add the feta and stir to blend in. Add the leeks and minced chili and mix gently with a fork to blend. Serve right away, or cover, refrigerate, and use within 1 day.

ORANGE-ONION SALSA

Oranges are a solution to staying cool while eating hot. Mingled in a spicy taco, this salsa revives the palate and readies it for the next bite. Make the same salsa with fresh grapefruit, preferably ruby red or Indian River, for a less sweet, more "dry" version. Two small grapefruits are about equal to two large navel oranges.

Makes a bit more than 2 cups
Takes less than 20 minutes

2 large navel or 3 to 4 blood or Valencia oranges
½ cup diced onion
1½ tablespoons chopped Anaheim chili pepper
2 tablespoons cilantro leaves
¼ teaspoon ground cumin

1. Peel the oranges and cut into ¼-inch dice, removing any seeds as you go.

2. In a bowl mix together the oranges, onion, chili pepper, cilantro, and cumin. Serve right away, or cover, refrigerate, and use within 1 day.

Oranges were brought to the New World in the holds of ships commandeered by Spanish *conquistadores.* Their cultivation spread so rapidly that by the time permanent settlers arrived to homestead in Central America, the Caribbean, and Florida, the natives were growing oranges and claiming them as their own. Today oranges are an integral part of New World eating.

Grapefruits are a New World native—some think a hybrid from pomelos and oranges, some think a spontaneous development that appeared in the Caribbean from citrus trees gone wild. Grapefruit, too, has become an integral part of New World fare, from breakfast halves to segments on green salads, and if you use the grapefuit variation, in a citrusy salsa.

PEANUT-GARLIC SALSA

I n Cambodia and Vietnam a peanut-chili dipping sauce is a constant accompaniment to their many taco-like filled pancakes. In Mexico and the Southwest peanuts, though usually not found in a salsa, are often combined with powdered hot chilies and served as a snack. Our Peanut-Garlic Salsa straddles the two cultures. Combined with a hearty portion of garlic, its concentrated flavor is so fiery that a small dab is enough.

Makes 2 cups
Takes less than 20 minutes

8 garlic cloves
2 red Fresno or 3 red serrano chili peppers, stemmed
1⅓ cups peanuts
¾ cup cilantro leaves
¾ cup water
¼ cup fresh lime juice
¼ teaspoon salt (optional, depending on whether peanuts are salted)

1. In a food processor or using a chef's knife, mince the garlic, chili peppers, and peanuts. Add the cilantro and process until coarsely chopped. Or, coarsely chop the cilantro and add to the other ingredients.

2. Transfer to a bowl. Stir in the water, lime juice, and salt. Serve right away, or cover, refrigerate, and use within 1 week.

TIP

▶ If you only have raw peanuts on hand, you can use them if you roast them in an ungreased frying pan over medium heat, stirring until they are browned and toasted all around, about 5 minutes.

M E N U
▼

BACKYARD BARBECUE

———

Grilled Beef, Chicken, and Pork Fajitas with Pan-Grilled Scallions

———

Fresh Tomato Salsa

Sweet and Hot Tomatillo Sauce

Peanut-Garlic Salsa

Well-Filled Guacamole

———

Mexican Bean Salad with Red Chili Vinaigrette

———

Sweet Hominy Chimichangas with Fruit Purées

PEAR-LIME SALSA

Makes 2 cups
Takes less than 20 minutes

2 medium shallots
1 poblano chili pepper, stemmed
2 medium pears
2 tablespoons fresh lime juice
½ teaspoon achiote powder or ⅜ teaspoon chili flakes

1. Mince the shallots and chili pepper in a food processor or with a chef's knife.

2. Halve and core the pears. Cut the pears into small dice.

3. In a bowl, mix together the shallots, chili pepper, pears, lime juice, and achiote powder. Serve right away. Pears are fragile and this salsa will not last overnight.

TIP

▶ Delicate pears should be chopped by hand, not in a food processor.

MANGO-JALAPENO SALSA

Mango, one of the best known fruits of the tropics, makes a pungent and perfect salsa to top many tortilla fillings, both fiery and mild.

▲▲▲▲▲▲▲▲▲▲▲▲▲▲▲▲

We were more than pleased to discover on our last jaunts that among Paris' favorite new restaurants are several devoted to Southwest cuisine. Fresh salsas, the antithesis of the long-cooked, highly concocted French sauces of classical cuisine, are particularly in favor, even to the extent of combining chilies with their beloved fresh pears. Just as we found pear salsas across the United States, we found them in the city of light, and this salsa was inspired by one we ate there. It follows naturally. Paris was the queen city of pears by the time of Louis XI. Every house and manor had them growing in the garden and some 300 varieties were cultivated in the vicinity from the Ile-de-France to Anjou alone. The familiar types we still see today—Anjou, Bosc, William's Bon Christian (named "good Christian" for Louis XI but called "Bartlett" in America), and the Comice—were developed by French pear fanciers. Other types were called such things as "my lady's thigh" they were so fleshy, round, and tender. Any of these, if firm enough, is fine for pear salsa.

▲▲▲▲▲▲▲▲▲▲▲▲▲▲

The China Poblana restaurant on San Pablo Avenue in Berkeley was one of the most charming and unusual restaurants ever. It was owned by a couple, the husband from Goa and the wife from Mexico. He cooked Indian food, she Mexican. They divided their tiny 12-table premise right down the middle, half given over to each cuisine—you had to choose which you would eat as you entered. Still, on either side the food was both hot and cool. For his fiery curries there was mango chutney. For her spicy mole and chili verde, there were fresh mango slices. The restaurant endured like a monument through the 1960s and '70s when we both were students. Then one day we suddenly noticed it had disappeared. We don't know the names of the owners, where they went, or what they are cooking now. But we'd like them to know their joint endeavor still lives in legend. Almost once a week some old Berkeley grad says to us, "Remember the China Poblana on San Pablo Avenue?"

▼▼▼▼▼▼▼▼▼▼▼▼▼▼

Makes 2 cups
Takes less than 20 minutes

2 ripe but firm mangos (2 cups coarsely chopped; see step 1)
½ teaspoon minced jalapeño chili pepper
2 tablespoons coarsely chopped cilantro leaves
1 tablespoon fresh lime juice
¼ teaspoon crushed cardamom or coriander seed

1. Peel the mangos. Using a paring knife, slice through the pulp down to the seed at ¼-inch intervals, first around lengthwise, then horizontally. Cut the pulp from the seed. You will wind up with almond-size chunks.

2. In a bowl, mix together the mangos, chili pepper, cilantro, lime juice, and cardamom. Serve right away.

TIPS

▶ For truly aromatic cardamom or coriander, don't buy the spice ground. It is much better to buy the whole seeds and crush them with a mallet or hammer just before using.

▶ The best mangos for salsa are firm to the touch and still have some green showing through their mottled red, orange, and yellow skins. Softer, riper mangos don't fall into chunks as well and make a mushy salsa.

SALSA VERDE

Set out in cups and there to greet you, Salsa Verde is one of the most familiar salutations to Mexican dining. Based on tomatillos, another of the New World's glorious fruits, Salsa Verde is appealing in its bright green color and fresh, exotic taste. Our recipe is simple, mildly tart, aromatic with cilantro, and very versatile.

Makes 2 cups
Takes less than 20 minutes

12 ounces tomatillos
2 cups cilantro leaves
2 yellow wax or jalapeño chili peppers, stemmed
¼ teaspoon salt

1. Peel the papery husks off the tomatillos. Rinse the tomatillos, place them in a saucepan, and add water to cover. Bring to a boil and simmer until soft to the touch, about 5 minutes. Remove the tomatillos and reserve the water.

2. In a food processor, blender, or food mill, purée the tomatillos along with ½ cup of the reserved cooking liquid, the cilantro, and chilies. Stir in the salt. Cover and chill a little before serving. Keeps for up to 1 week in the refrigerator.

TIPS

▶ To make Salsa Verde by hand, lift the tomatillos out of the cooking water, reserving ½ cup of the water. Finely chop the tomatillos, cilantro, and chili peppers with a chef's knife. Stir in the reserved water and the salt. The sauce will be chunkier than the puréed version, but just as good.

▶ For a more roasted flavor you can bake the tomatillos in the oven or sear them in an ungreased frying pan until barely soft. If you do this, be sure to add ½ cup water to finish the sauce.

Lovers of Mexican food are divided on the issue: Red sauce or green? Emotions run high and opinions are strong when it comes to which basic salsa is the best. (Though lines are often crossed with a subtle, quick dip of the chip into the opposite bowl.) Mexicans are clearly natural diplomats because you usually see a bowl of each on the counters or tables of their cantinas.

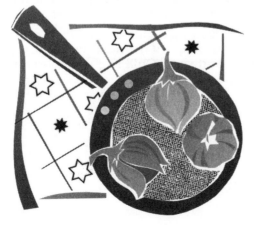

SWEET AND HOT TOMATILLO SAUCE

Onion and sage make a sweet variation of Salsa Verde. When we use them, we like to add extra jalapeños to offset the onion's sweet tang with some extra heat.

Makes about 2¼ cups
Takes less than 20 minutes

8 ounces tomatillos
½ medium-size red onion
1 large garlic clove
3 jalapeño chili peppers, stemmed
½ cup cilantro leaves
¼ teaspoon minced fresh sage leaves or a small pinch of
    rubbed sage

1. Peel the papery husks off the tomatillos. Rinse the tomatillos and place them in a saucepan large enough to hold them in one layer. Add water to cover. Bring to a boil and simmer until they are soft to the touch, about 5 minutes.

2. In a food processor, blender, or food mill, purée the tomatillos, along with ½ cup of the cooking liquid, the onion, garlic, chilies, cilantro, and sage. Chill slightly before using. Keeps for up to 1 week in the refrigerator.

To make a plain baked potato prize-worthy, mix Sweet and Hot Tomatillo Sauce together with cool sour cream. Split open a potato, press it until it is soft and crumbly, and spoon in this spicy combination.

RANCHERO SAUCE

Ranchero sauce is the cowboys' ketchup. On the long rides and cattle drives across the great *estancias* and ranches, it became the sauce of note and necessity in every chuckwagon rolling or resting. Today it still serves to sauce dishes from enchiladas to barbecue. It keeps for weeks, and also is great on (you guessed it) *huevos rancheros*.

Makes 2 cups
Takes less than 20 minutes

1 jalapeño chili pepper, stemmed
1 medium onion
2 garlic cloves
4 medium tomatoes
1½ teaspoons chopped fresh oregano or ½ teaspoon dried
¼ teaspoon pure chili powder
¼ teaspoon salt
½ cup water

1. In a food processor or using a chef's knife, coarsely chop the chili pepper, onion, garlic, and tomatoes. Transfer to a medium-size nonreactive skillet. Add the oregano, chili powder, salt, and water. Cook over medium heat, stirring occasionally, until the tomatoes are soft and the onions are translucent, 12 to 15 minutes.

2. Divide the sauce in half. Purée one half in a food processor, food mill, or mortar. Transfer to a bowl and stir in the remaining sauce. Serve warm, or cover, refrigerate, and use within 10 days.

▲▲▲▲▲▲▲▲▲▲▲▲▲▲

In Phoenix, Arizona, where ranchero sauce is obligatory, it's placed on the tables of every Mexican cafe in large narrow-necked cruets. That way customers can shake it, spill it, or dash it over everything. And they do. The only problem is, the narrow necks are a hindrance for serious salsa consumers, and definitely slow going for salsa and chips. You have to shake the salsa delicately over each chip, a process that requires two hands, one for the chip, one for tipping the cruet, and results in far less salsa than does the scooping method. If you find yourself in Phoenix, there's a solution. Pour the whole bottle out in your appetizer plate, place your plate in the center of the table for your companions to share, and dip away.

▼▼▼▼▼▼▼▼▼▼▼▼▼▼

ROASTED GARLIC, TOMATO, AND ANCHOVY SAUCE

▲▲▲▲▲▲▲▲▲▲▲▲▲

F ew salsas make good canape spreads. They are often too watery or too chunky. Roasted Garlic, Tomato, and Anchovy Sauce—because of its consistency—is a favorite and often-served exception. Combine all the ingredients except for the anchovy. Spread the sauce on wafers or water crackers and top each with a sliver of anchovy fillet.

▼▼▼▼▼▼▼▼▼▼▼▼▼

R oasting turns garlic's biting cloves into a sweet, nutty paste. Combined with roasted tomatoes and anchovy, you get a salsa any Italian would love to spread on bread, dip vegetables into, or drizzle over linguine. We spread it on most meat tacos, but especially love it with goat. Depending on the moistness of the tomatoes, you may have to add water to make the sauce saucy.

Makes 2 cups
Takes 45 minutes

4 whole heads of garlic
4 medium tomatoes
1 serrano chili, stemmed
12 anchovy fillets, preferably salt-packed
½ cup water, if necessary

1. Heat the oven to 500°F.

2. Place the garlic and tomatoes on a baking sheet and roast in the oven until the tomato skins are shriveled, about 15 minutes. Remove the tomatoes and roast the garlic until soft to the touch, 15 to 20 minutes more.

3. When cool enough to handle, peel the tomatoes. Press the pulp out of the garlic cloves using your fingers.

4. In a food processor or using a chef's knife, finely chop the tomatoes, garlic pulp, chili, and anchovies. Transfer to a bowl. If necessary, stir in up to ½ cup water until the salsa is about the consistency of a tomato sauce. Serve right away, or cover, refrigerate, and use within 2 days.

ROASTED RED PEPPER, CHILI, AND PINE NUT SAUCE

One day we ate so much of our Roasted Red Pepper, Chili, and Pine Nut Sauce on chips, we had no room left for the lunch we had prepared. Aha, we thought. Next time we'll substitute ¼ cup good-quality grated Parmesan cheese for the ¼ cup water, and we'll have a wonderful, spicy Italia-Mexicano pasta topping. And we were right! Keep this in mind next time you have a hankering for spaghetti.

Makes 2 cups
Takes 40 to 60 minutes

4 medium-size red bell peppers
6 medium garlic cloves
2 small serrano chilies, preferably red, stemmed
½ cup pine nuts
1 tablespoon cilantro leaves (optional)
¼ teaspoon salt
¼ cup water

1. Heat the oven to 500°F.

2. Place the bell peppers in the oven and roast until charred all around, about 25 minutes. Remove the peppers to a paper bag, twist to seal, and let the peppers steam in the bag for 15 minutes. Peel the peppers with your fingers and a paring knife and remove the seeds.

3. In a food processor or using a chef's knife, mince the bell peppers, garlic, chilies, and pine nuts. Transfer to a bowl. Add the cilantro, salt, and water and stir to mix. Serve right away, or cover, refrigerate, and use within 1 week.

▲▲▲▲▲▲▲▲▲▲▲▲▲▲▲

Near Shreveport, Louisiana, there's an enclave of Spanish among the Cajun people. Their music is the jumpingest and their gumbo the hottest. Their fields are red with every kind of pepper. including sweet red peppers. To top their fresh Gulf oysters, warm their version of tacos—fresh seafood, bits of chicken, frogs' legs ensconced in biscuits—and sauce their crabcakes, they use their favorite spicy elements: garlic, bell pepper, and chilies. We first adapted this Shreveport-style sauce as a topping for our own barbecued oysters. We bought big ones from a Gulf oyster house. In time we craved the sauce on more foods. We added the pine nuts and cilantro and turned it into a taco topping fit for a Cajun king.

▲▲▲▲▲▲▲▲▲▲▲▲▲▲

G raduation at the California College of Arts and Crafts, a huge event that we cater from our on-site cafe, inspired us to make scads of an old favorite recipe, Greek eggplant salad. We concocted the dish the evening before and stashed it in the refrigerator to let the flavors age. Next day we found our manager looking quizzical, dipping tortilla chips into the salad, and asking what this new salsa was. It's not a salsa, we told her, it's eggplant salad. "No way," she said. "This is salsa. Who'd eat something called eggplant salad." And she plastered it on a quesadilla. Taking her cue, we "salsafied" the salad with serrano chilies. Rather than in a pita, it's in a tortilla. Instead of serving it before the lamb and pork, now it's right on top.

▼▼▼▼▼▼▼▼▼▼▼▼▼▼

GREEK SALSA

T hough the eggplant is cooked, making this dish technically a sauce, its fresh flavor and chunky texture make it seem a salsa.

Makes about 2 cups
Takes 1½ hours

1 small eggplant (about ¾ pound)
¼ medium onion
1 to 2 large garlic cloves
½ serrano chili pepper, stemmed
2 tablespoons chopped fresh parsley leaves, preferably
*   Italian flat-leaf*
¼ teaspoon chopped fresh mint leaves or a small pinch of
*   dried mint*
½ teaspoon chopped fresh oregano leaves or ⅛ teaspoon
*   dried*
1½ teaspoons red wine vinegar
1 teaspoon fresh lemon juice
¼ cup olive oil
⅛ teaspoon salt

1. Heat the oven to 450°F.

2. Prick the eggplant once with the point of a knife and place it on a baking sheet in the oven. Roast until soft all the way through to the center, about 50 minutes. Set aside to cool for 10 minutes or so. When cool enough to handle, slit open and scrape out the pulp. Coarsely chop the pulp. Transfer to a bowl.

3. In a food processor or using a chef's knife, coarsely chop the onion, garlic, and chili. Add to the eggplant, along with the parsley, mint, oregano, vinegar, lemon juice, oil, and salt. Stir to blend well. Serve right away, or cover, refrigerate, and use within 1 week.

ANCHO CHILI SAUCE

A long with Salsa Cruda, Salsa Verde, and Ranchero, a dried chili sauce is one of the basics of tortilla cuisine. You can use any of a variety of dried chilies: pasilla, New Mexico, California, or ancho chilies. We prefer anchos for their robust smoky taste and because you don't have to scrape the pulp off the skins before puréeing them. The advantage of a dried chili sauce is its lasting power. It keeps in the refrigerator for many months. If you make a double or triple batch and store it in a jar or plastic container, you are guaranteed to have a sauce on hand for many a spontaneous taco.

Makes 2 cups
Takes 40 minutes

6 ancho chilies (about 4 ounces)
4 large garlic cloves
1½ teaspoons pure chili powder
2½ cups water
½ teaspoon salt

1. Remove the stems and seeds from the chilies. Quarter the garlic cloves.

2. Place the chilies, garlic, chili powder, and water in a saucepan and bring to a boil. Cover, reduce to a simmer, and cook until the chilies are soft, about 15 minutes. Remove from the heat; set aside to cool for 10 minutes.

3. Purée the mixture in a food processor, blender, or food mill. Add the salt and mix well. Serve right away, or cover, refrigerate, and use within 3 months.

ADDITIONAL SALSAS AND TOPPINGS

Throughout this book there appear special salsas and toppings secreted away in the recipes for particular fillings. Many of these salsas and toppings can boost and benefit additional tacos as well.

PASILLA, MINT, AND PICKLED RED ONION SAUCE

We wanted to create a chunky dried chili sauce instead of a smooth one. We also wanted to add a new sort of punch—something like you get from adding vinegar, onions, a touch of sweet, or an aromatic herb—and lift food flavors. The answer was to chop onions coarsely, pickle them in a sweetened vinegar brine infused with mint, and stir them into a rich deep-flavored chili paste. We used pasillas because of their lustrous burnt sienna color and slightly musky taste. Pasilla, Mint, and Pickled Red Onion Sauce makes a luxurious "under" salsa for moistening fillings that are too dry on their own.

Makes 2 cups
Takes 30 minutes

½ cup red wine vinegar
3 tablespoons sugar
3 tablespoons water
1 medium-size red onion, finely diced
10 dried pasilla chilies (4 to 5 ounces), stemmed and seeded
½ cup fresh mint leaves

    1. In a small nonreactive saucepan, bring the vinegar, sugar, and 3 tablespoons water to a boil. Remove immediately.

    2. Place the onion in a bowl. Pour in the vinegar mixture. Set aside for 15 minutes or so while preparing the chilies.

    3. Place the chilies in a saucepan and add water to cover. Bring to a boil. Reduce the heat and simmer until the chilies are quite soft, about 5 minutes. Remove the chilies, reserving the cooking water. When cool enough to handle, scrape the pulp off the chili skins, discarding the skins.

4. In a food processor, blender, or food mill, purée the chili pulp, mint leaves, and ½ cup of the reserved cooking liquid. Transfer to a bowl. Use a slotted spoon to lift the onions from their liquid. Add them, along with 2 tablespoons of their vinegar brine, to the chili mixture. Stir to blend well. Serve right away, or cover, refrigerate, and use within 2 weeks.

▲▲▲▲▲▲▲▲▲▲▲▲▲▲▲▲

Mint is an ever present herb in tortilla cooking. Along with our own summer tomatoes and cluster of chives, we find our need of mint best supplied by growing our own. Growing mint is almost too easy. It loves to take over all available space and wind itself lovingly, but suffocatingly, around the other herbs. Here's a ready solution. Plant the mint in an earthen pot, then embed the pot in the ground. The mint can't spread beyond the boundries of its hidden vessel, yet will grow up amid your other plants, thick, dense, and green.

▼▼▼▼▼▼▼▼▼▼▼▼▼▼▼

YUCATAN SAUCE

We particularly like the mix of ancho and pasilla chilies in this sauce, but you could make it with just one kind or a blend of anchos or pasillas with California, New Mexico, *guajillo*, or *cascabel* dried chilies. Remember, anchos are the only ones you don't have to peel after cooking. Whatever combination of dried chilies you use, the orange and tequila make it fruity, pungent, and festive. Try it with turkey in place of cranberry sauce.

▲▲▲▲▲▲▲▲▲▲▲▲▲▲▲▲

From time to time we hunger for the arid musty aroma that marked the dried chili sauces of our childhood. The sauces we remember when we first had Mexican fare were dense pastes of dried chilies, not the fresh relishes of today. When that lingering sensory memory recurs, we mix up Ancho Chili Sauce, or better yet, Yucatan Sauce with its more intricate flavors. The tequila is an adult addition, just a touch to make the taste and the memory heady.

▼▼▼▼▼▼▼▼▼▼▼▼▼▼▼▼

Makes 2 cups
Takes less than 20 minutes

4 dried ancho chilies (about 2 ounces), stemmed and seeded
4 dried pasilla chilies (about 2 ounces), stemmed and seeded
½ teaspoon pure chili powder
½ teaspoon ground coriander
½ teaspoon ground cumin
1 cup water
¼ medium onion
½ teaspoon chopped orange zest
2 tablespoons fresh orange juice
1 tablespoon tequila, preferably gold

1. Place the chilies, chili powder, coriander, and cumin in a small saucepan. Add the water and bring to a boil. Reduce the heat and simmer until the chilies are soft, about 5 minutes. Remove the chilies, reserving the cooking liquid. When cool enough to handle, separate the ancho from the pasilla chilies. Scrape the pulp off the pasillas, discarding the skins.

2. In a food processor or blender, purée the ancho chilies, pasilla pulp, reserved cooking liquid, onion, and orange zest. Transfer to a bowl. Stir in the orange juice, salt, and tequila. Serve right away, or cover, refrigerate, and use within 3 weeks.

TIPS

▶ For an easy way to separate the ancho from the pasilla chilies, loosely tie together one or the other kind with kitchen string or thread before cooking.

▶ To make this sauce "by hand," purée the chilies with a food mill or mortar and pestle. Mince the onion. Place the chilies and onion along with the reserved liquid in a bowl. Add the remaining ingredients and stir to blend well.

TOPPINGS

THE BASIC SIX TOPPINGS

Shredded lettuce, chopped tomato, shredded cheese, sour cream, chopped avocado, and sliced jalapeño chilies—these are the most common and familiar filled tortilla toppings. They are the ones we envision when we head for a restaurant's taco topping bar and the ones we most rapidly whip up at home.

▲▲▲▲▲▲▲▲▲▲▲▲▲▲▲

We avoid the usual taco complement, iceberg lettuce, which was bred to hold water and has little nutrition. Instead, we prefer stalk lettuces, especially romaine, red leaf, and butter; and "heartless" lettuces—those that grow in patches rather than heads—especially salad bowl and oak leaf, which are substantial types that don't wilt next to hot fillings. Serve lettuce on top of the filling and under the salsa.

▼▼▼▼▼▼▼▼▼▼▼▼▼▼▼

SHREDDED LETTUCE

A winning feature of tacos is that they have their salad right in them. Nothing quite adds vitality like a scattering of fresh crisp lettuce poised right near the first bite.

Makes 4 to 5 cups, enough to top 18 corn or 12 flour tortillas

To prepare: Use 1 large head of romaine, curly leaf, or escarole, or 2 heads of red leaf or butter lettuce. Remove the limp outer leaves. Starting at the top, slice the leaves crosswise into ¼-inch wide strips, stopping at the core. Rinse the shredded lettuce in cool water and spin dry. Serve right away or store in plastic bags in the refrigerator. Use within 5 days.

CHOPPED TOMATO

Juicy and red, ripe and exhilarating, tomatoes infuse life into any taco.

Makes 2 cups, enough to top 18 corn or 12 flour tortillas

To prepare: Use about 1 pound tomatoes (about 2 large, 4 medium, or 6 small), cut into small dice. Serve right away or set aside at room temperature; use within several hours.

To vary: In those seasons when tomatoes are not particularly tasty, a splash of cider or wine vinegar cheers up the flavor. Or, sprinkle on dried basil, oregano, marjoram, thyme, tarragon, or fresh parsley, chives or cilantro.

SHREDDED CHEESE

For many, a taco is not a taco without its cheese topping. Customarily in the United States, this means shredded Jack or Cheddar cheese, but there's no need to limit your choices. Far more varieties of cheese are used in Mexico, and almost any cheese finishes filling a tortilla with aplomb. Use one kind alone or mix two kinds together.

Makes about 3 cups, enough to top 18 corn or 12 flour tortillas

To prepare: Use 12 ounces semisoft yellow or white cheese (such as gouda, Jack, Cheddar, provolone, feta, *queso fresco,* or *queso blanco*); *or* 8 ounces hard grating cheese (such as Parmesan, Romano, aged Asiago, or *cotija*); *or* a mixture. Grate semisoft or hard cheese with a food processor or hand grater.

Break crumbly cheese by hand. Use right away or store in sealed plastic bags in the refrigerator. Most shredded cheese will last up to 2 weeks, but in general does not last as well as cheese in blocks. Watch for mold. In many cases, if it is removed when it first appears, the remainder of the cheese will still be usable. Very hard cheese, once grated, keeps well frozen. Use as much as needed, then return it to a sealed plastic bag and refreeze.

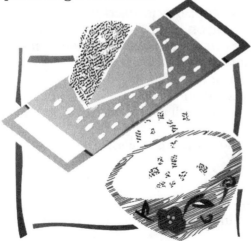

▲▲▲▲▲▲▲▲▲▲▲▲▲▲▲▲

Victoria is an avid gardener, producing crops of lettuce, peppers, squash. Susanna gardens intermittently, with the expectation that whatever she plants must be a stalwart survivor. Neither of us could do without our home-grown tomatoes. Tacos call for fresh ones, good ones, and mostly lots of them. Victoria's many plants give us buckets of frozen Ranchero Sauce. Susanna's at least provide enough to make Fresh Tomato Salsa and Chopped Tomato topping. Store-bought tomatoes sadly have lost their blush and savor. They are grown too sheltered, picked too soon, and shipped too far. But with one or two vines in your kitchen garden, you can have flavorful tomatoes as red as they are ripe. Since good taco eating is better yet with fine tomatoes, we heartily recommend all taco lovers grow their own.

HANDLING CHILI PEPPERS

Although we rarely find the need to protect our hands when slicing fresh chili peppers, canned chili peppers have an insidious effect on bare skin, so we wear rubber gloves when preparing them. And always, when handling any chili pepper, take care not to touch your face or eyes.

SLICED JALAPENO CHILIES

When you don't have any salsa, sliced jalapeño chili peppers bring a taco or other filled tortilla up to temperature. With a salsa, they add extra zip and texture. You can use fresh or canned jalapeños, but keep in mind the canned ones are hotter.

**Makes enough to top 18 corn or
12 flour tortillas**

To prepare: Use 4 ounces fresh jalapeños or one 12-ounce can whole jalapeños. Remove the stems from fresh jalapeños. Stem and seed canned ones. Thinly slice crosswise. Sliced fresh jalapeños keep up to overnight refrigerated in a plastic bag. Canned jalapeños keep indefinitely refrigerated in their juices.

SOUR CREAM

Probably no topping is used in tacos, burritos, chimichangas, or on enchiladas and tostadas as often as sour cream. Sour cream allays dense spices, relieves the heat, and blends with the meat and vegetable juices. We use it with numerous fillings, and suggest that whenever you are at a loss for how to complete a spur-of-the-moment filling, sour cream will almost always do the trick.

**Makes 2 cups, enough to top 18 corn or
12 flour tortillas**

To prepare: Use 2 cups (1 pint container) sour cream. Place the sour cream in a bowl and stir until smooth. Use right away.

To vary: The regular sour cream available in most markets is similar to the sour cream found in northern Mexico. To duplicate the sour cream of central Mexico, stir in 2 tablespoons melted butter. To make a thinner and lighter southern Mexico-style sour cream, stir in ¼ cup light cream.

CHOPPED AVOCADO

Black ones, speckled ones, some so thin-skinned you can chop them peel and all, avocados come in many varieties. The two most commonly available are nubbly, charcoal green Haas and the smooth skinned, bright green Fuerte. Of these, Haas is by far the choice. They are denser and more deeply flavored.

Makes about 2 cups, enough to top 18 corn or 12 flour tortillas

To prepare: Halve 3 medium-size ripe avocados and remove the pits. Scoop out the pulp and chop without mashing. Sprinkle with 1½ tablespoons fresh lime juice and salt to taste. Use right away. Or, to store, tuck the pits back into the avocado mixture, cover with plastic wrap, pressing down to eliminate air pockets, and refrigerate. The mixture will remain brightly colored for 1 day.

To vary: Add about 1 teaspoon black pepper, stir in ¼ cup chopped cilantro leaves, add 2 to 3 minced scallions (green onions), or 1½ teaspoons minced jalapeños.

When the avocado moved north to California and Florida gardens as a lush shade tree, only natives of Mexico and connoisseurs of Mexican botanical treats knew how marvelous the fruit was. For a long while, others ignored the knobby pears, with their buttery, nutty flesh. Now it seems we can hardly get along without avocados. So smooth, they are the perfect companion to spicy Southwest fare, and a natural taco topping. Skinned and chopped, they are sublime, but we like them perked up just a bit with a dash of lime juice and salt.

GUACAMOLE

No sour cream, no cream cheese, no mayonnaise. For guacamole, the famous party treat and favorite taco frosting, unadulterated renditions are the most glorious. Here we offer a traditional, purist's guacamole. The recipe that follows is a special variation.

Makes about 2 cups
Takes 15 minutes

3 medium avocados, preferably Haas
½ medium tomato, finely diced
1½ tablespoons minced onion
1½ teaspoons minced fresh chili pepper
1½ tablespoons fresh lemon juice
½ teapoon salt

Halve the avocados and remove the pits. Use a spoon to scoop out the pulp and place it in a bowl. Add the tomato, onion, chili, lemon juice, and salt. Mash with a fork until the avocado is mostly smooth with a few lumps here and there. Use right away or store as described in Chopped Avocado, page 67.

WELL-FILLED GUACAMOLE

Some of the best recipes for popular dishes are ones that contain an element of surprise. The Well-Filled Guacamole is such a dish. No tomatoes. No onions. Instead tomatillos and lime juice. After one bite you'll join the praising chorus.

Makes about 2 cups
Takes 15 minutes

3 medium avocados
3 medium tomatillos
1½ tablespoons fresh lime juice
¼ teaspoon salt

1. Halve the avocados and remove the pits. Use a spoon to scoop out the pulp and place it in a bowl.

2. Remove the husks from the tomatillos. Rinse the tomatillos; chop them fine. Add to the avocado, along with the lime juice and salt. Mash with a fork until the avocado is mostly smooth with a few lumps here and there. Use right away or store as described in Chopped Avocado, page 67.

TIP

▶ Any of the variations described for Chopped Avocado is equally delicious for this special guacamole.

▲▲▲▲▲▲▲▲▲▲▲▲▲▲▲

FRIED POTATOES

A sprinkling of fried potatoes—everybody's favorite food—brings many a filled tortilla to life. Add them to turkey, chicken, ground meats, and fish fillings. Check the index for the Fried Potatoes recipe and when you use it as a topping, consider preparing the following variations:

ACHIOTE: To add a mild musky flavor and pleasing paprika-red color to the potato topping, sprinkle the potatoes with 1 tablespoon achiote powder while frying.

CHILI FLAKES OR POWDER: To add heat to the potatoes, add ½ tablespoon chili flakes or pure chili powder while frying.

PAN-GRILLED CHILI STRIPS

Strips of fresh chilies roasted in a pan offer a different flourish to a taco. High, dry heat brings out the sugars in the chili strips and produces an almost smoky flavor. Be prepared, though, the smoke given off in pan-grilling can irritate if breathed too deeply.

Makes 1½ cups
Takes 15 minutes

12 ounces fresh poblano or Anaheim chili peppers (6 to 8 peppers), stemmed and seeded
1 tablespoon peanut oil
Salt, to taste

1. Cut the chilies into thin strips.

2. In a large, heavy frying pan, heat the oil over medium-high heat until it begins to smoke. Add the chili strips and fry until wilted but still crunchy, about 5 minutes. Remove to drain on paper towels; salt lightly. Use right away.

TIP

▶ Among heavy skillets, a cast-iron one is the best to use for this and other pan-grilled recipes.

VARIATION

▼

■ Sprinkle the chili strips with 1 tablespoon sesame seeds while frying.

BREADED CHILI STRIPS

L ike tempura or French fried onion rings, breaded chili strips can stand on their own as a snack as well as make a distinctive taco topping. A milk coating before rolling in cornmeal makes the chili strips crunchier; an egg dip makes a richer flavor. Either way, the light cornmeal breading turns out crackly chili strips that fry crisp in very little oil.

Makes 1½ cups
Takes 15 minutes

12 ounces fresh poblano or Anaheim chili peppers (6 to 8
*   peppers), stemmed and seeded*
½ cup milk, or 1 egg mixed with ¼ cup water
¾ cup cornmeal
2 tablespoons olive or peanut oil
Salt, to taste

1. Cut the chili peppers into thin strips. Place the milk or egg/water mixture in a bowl. Place the cornmeal on a plate.

2. In a large frying pan heat the oil over medium-high heat until it begins to smoke. Coat the chili strips first in the milk or egg/water mixture, then in the cornmeal. Add the strips to the oil and cook until the cornmeal is golden and the chilies are limp, 3 to 5 minutes. Remove to drain on paper towels; salt lightly. Use right away.

▲▲▲▲▲▲▲▲▲▲▲▲▲▲▲▲▲

G reen onion, spring onion, scallion, sprinkled on clear soup *à la française*, chopped into hearty beef stir-fries *à la* Hunan, striped across the top of a taco, they are the bulb of a sweet grass. No cuisine in the world lacks them.

▼▼▼▼▼▼▼▼▼▼▼▼▼▼▼▼

PAN-GRILLED SCALLIONS

S callions, quickly singed on a grill or in a pan, are the traditional fajita garnish.

Makes enough for 18 corn or 12 flour tortillas
Takes less than 20 minutes

3 bunches of scallions (green onions), trimmed
Oil
2 tablespoons fresh lime juice
Salt, to taste

1. Cut the scallions into 1-inch lengths.

2. Pour enough oil into a large frying pan to coat the bottom. Wipe out excess oil with a paper towel. Place over high heat until the oil begins to smoke. Add the scallions and stir-fry until the scallions are wilted and blackened in spots, 2 to 3 minutes. Remove to a plate and sprinkle with the lime juice and a little salt. Use right away or cover and refrigerate overnight.

PICKLED ONIONS

R ed, yellow, or white, any onion will do for this mildly sweet and tart pickle. For party fare, you might splurge on shallots or in late spring, use Walla Walla, Texas Sweet 100s, Vidalia, or Maui onions.

Makes about 2 cups
Takes 20 to 30 minutes

2 medium onions, coarsely chopped
½ cup red wine vinegar
1 tablespoon sugar
3 tablespoons water

1. Place the onions in a bowl.

2. In a small nonreactive saucepan, combine the vinegar, sugar, and water. Bring to a boil. Pour over the onions. Set aside to marinate for at least 15 minutes, or cover, refrigerate, and use within 2 weeks.

PICKLED CORN

Unlike many pickled vegetables, pickled corn is too delicate to last. It's best served the day you make it.

Makes about 2¼ cups
Takes less than 20 minutes

3 cups fresh corn kernels (from about 3 medium
*   ears corn)*
⅛ teaspoon Dijon mustard
⅛ teaspoon salt
1 teaspoon sugar
3 tablespoons cider vinegar
½ cup water
1 teaspoon minced jalapeño or serrano
*   chili pepper*

1. Place the corn in a heatproof bowl.

2. Combine the mustard, salt, sugar, vinegar, and water in a small nonreactive saucepan. Bring to a boil, and cook for 1 minute. Pour over the corn; stir in the minced chilies. Set aside to marinate for at least 10 minutes, or up to several hours. Use within 1 day.

Corn is as important to Harry Marx who gardens in the Palisades of New Jersey as it is to any Iowan, Zuni, or Oaxacan. He grows a number of ordinary and fancy varieties, specializing in sweet white corn and the little ears that get jarred whole. We know him as a deli supplier. He never pickled his precious kernels until his recent helpers arrived, Ken, from Korea, and Sergio, from Costa Rica. Together they've developed corn, marinated in vinegar and chili powder as in *kim chee,* jalapeños and onion added *à la costa ricana.* Harry and his men are about to bottle and market the new pickled corn. Even the ladies of Long Island at their salad lunches are asking for the nippy, new condiment, says Harry.

VARIATIONS
▼

■ To turn this topping into an appetizer, simply cut the carrots into thick rounds, cook for a minute or two longer, and keep on the counter to snack from as you turn out the tacos.
■ As a variation add pieces of onion to the carrots. Or, combine the Pickled Carrots, Pickled Corn (page 73), and/or Pickled Onions (page 72).

PICKLED CARROTS

The inspiration for pickled carrots as a topping comes from that bowl of pickled carrots with jalapeños and onion that often serve as a preamble to the meal in Mexican restaurants and *taquerias.*

Makes about 2¼ cups
Takes less than 20 minutes

1 pound carrots
*2 large or 4 small jalapeño chili peppers, stemmed and
    coarsely chopped*
6 large garlic cloves, slivered
1 teaspoon dried oregano
1 cup cider vinegar
2 cups water
⅛ teaspoon salt

1. Peel the carrots. Coarsely chop them in a food processor or with a chef's knife.

2. Place the chili peppers, garlic, oregano, vinegar, water, and salt in a medium-size nonreactive saucepan. Bring to a boil over high heat and cook for 1 minute. Add the carrots and boil for 1 minute.

3. With a slotted spoon or strainer, transfer the carrots to a bowl. Cool the brine in the saucepan. Pour over the carrots. Chill overnight. This will keep for up to several months in the refrigerator.

TIP

▶ After marinating for several days, this topping becomes quite hot. If you like it less or more torrid, add less or more jalapeños as you choose, but remember it takes a while for their full effect to appear.

TOASTED PUMPKIN SEEDS

Bright orange pumpkin is another native of Central America. Its flesh is consumed in late summer and fall, but its seeds serve year round as a snack, a nutty element in *moles,* and a taco topping.

Makes ½ cup
Takes 5 minutes

2 teaspoons vegetable or peanut oil
½ cup shelled pumpkin seeds

Heat the oil in a small frying pan over medium-low heat until it begins to smoke. Add the pumpkin seeds and stir until the seeds are browned and exude a nutty aroma, 1 to 2 minutes. Remove to a bowl and use right away, or store in an airtight jar for up to 1 week.

ROASTING PUMPKIN SEEDS

To roast your own pumpkin seeds, pull the seeds out of the pumpkin. Remove the interconnecting stringy pulp clinging to the seeds. Rinse the seeds and pat them dry. Place on a baking sheet with 1 teaspoon peanut oil; toss to coat all of the seeds. Spread out the seeds and place the baking sheet in a 325°F oven. Roast until golden and crunchy, about 1 hour, stirring and turning from time to time. Serve as is, lightly sprinkled with salt, or shell and then salt lightly. Roasted pumpkin seeds may be stored in an airtight jar for several weeks and toasted as you need them.

DRESSED CILANTRO

Use plain cilantro sprigs to enliven fillings; or chop cilantro leaves with lemon zest to make a south-of-the-border sort of gremolata topping; or try our preferred treatment of dressing the sprigs and laying them lettuce-like across a filling near the nipping edge of the taco. Dressed, cilantro is almost like watercress, dandelion, or spinach salad. It adds moisture, pungency, and crispness, and it blends—as the original taco makers of Mexico knew—with almost any filling.

Makes 2 cups
Takes less than 20 minutes

2 cups cilantro leaves
1 teaspoon cider vinegar or fresh lime juice
1 teaspoon peanut oil
Salt, to taste

Wash and dry the cilantro and place in a bowl. Sprinkle on the vinegar, oil, and salt. Toss to mix well. Serve right away, or cover, refrigerate, and use within 1 day.

TIP

▶ You can make a similar but milder salad-like topping from parsley. Use the grassy Italian flat-leaf parsley, if you can find it, and dress it the same way.

▲▲▲▲▲▲▲▲▲▲▲▲▲▲▲▲

Cilantro seems like everyone's new favorite herb, but it's no Johnny-come-lately. Cilantro is the leafy side of one of the world's longest known spices—coriander. For whatever reason, we have always dealt with members of the carrot family—cilantro, parsley, anise, dill, cumin, caraway, and chervil—in a divided manner. Though all have both aromatic leaves and seeds, we have chosen to enjoy one or the other part, and not both. We nibble the root of carrot, but have the grocer guillotine the leaves. We toss parsley leaves into many a pot and dish, but do nothing with the seeds save plant them. Now thanks to the cooks of China, South America, and many Native American groups, we are no longer so narrow. We use both coriander's seeds and the green leaves, with their marked taste, to make many dishes clearer and more emphatic.

DEVILED PEANUTS AND COCONUT

Indonesians, Polynesians, Southeast Asians, and Indians all know how well peanuts and coconut go together. Usually the two appear as a paste or sauce to complement main dishes of shellfish, pork, or chicken. For the same elements in a taco, we turned the mixture into a topping, deviled with cayenne and sweetened with sugar.

Makes 2 cups
Takes less than 10 minutes

2 tablespoons peanut oil
1 cup roasted, salted peanuts, coarsely chopped
1 cup unsweetened coconut strips or shredded coconut
¼ teaspoon cayenne
1 teaspoon sugar

Heat the oil in a large skillet over medium-high heat until it begins to smoke. Add the peanuts, coconut, cayenne, and sugar. Stir until the peanuts and coconut are lightly browned, 4 to 5 minutes. Transfer to a bowl and use right away, or store in an airtight jar for up to 1 week.

TIP

▶ The small amount of sugar in this topping makes it prone to burn easily. Watch and stir constantly while browning and remove right away.

Halloween brings joy to our gang of children for a reason beyond the usual. To amass candy is entrancing and rule-breaking. To dress in costumes is role-breaking and fun. But to offer one another the pumpkin patch's most crumpled, contorted, and ill-looking examples to carve is a dare and a challenge! Jenan, the youngest, is still let off the hook with a more or less upright specimen, but Gaby and Jesse pick one another true monstrosities. The evening of quibbling and shouting is oiled smooth when the children bring out the first pumpkin pulp and roast the seeds. A little salt, some crunching, some carving, in with the candles, and the jack-o'-lanterns appear. The rest of the seeds are saved for tacos.

THE FILLINGS

THE HEART OF THE MATTER

We come to the heart of the well-filled tortilla—the filling. Central to every taco, burrito, enchilada, chimichanga, flauta, and tapa, is the real matter of the meal: meats, fish, shellfish, vegetables, beans, potatoes, eggs. The range and kinds of tortilla fillings are copious and inspiring. They can be elegant and extravagant. They can spare the pocketbook while still lavishing the desire.

One well-filled tortilla leads to another. Brace yourself for tortilla mania.

BEEF

"Forty thousand youngsters in schools eschew hamburgers," declares our local newspaper. "They only want beef tacos." But parents don't have to read headlines. From coast to coast they have heard the taco call.

Beef came to the ranches of North America and the *estaciones* of South America with the Spanish. The great expanses of plain gave fodder to great herds, and the various breeds, from Angus and Hereford to more heat-resistant types, took to and thrived in the countryside as nowhere before. It follows that tortillas and beef met and married early on, and the combination is still sensational.

WELL-FILLED GROUND BEEF

A basic ground beef tortilla filling—the one you whip up time and again from a pound of simple hamburger meat—doesn't have to be ordinary. With a touch of chili flakes and red wine added to good-quality beef, you have a taco that will please everyone at the family table. We prefer Well-Filled Ground Beef tacos—as we do almost every taco—topped with a salsa. But for younger members at the table, or those who don't care for too much spice, chopped tomatoes, cheese, sour cream, and lettuce are enough to well fill the tortilla.

Serves 4 to 6
Takes less than 20 minutes

2 teaspoons olive or peanut oil
2 medium onions, finely chopped
6 garlic cloves, minced
2½ pounds ground beef chuck or round
1 tablespoon fresh oregano leaves or
*   ¾ teaspoon dried*
¾ teaspoon chili flakes
½ teaspoon salt
1 cup dry red wine
18 corn or 12 flour tortillas, warmed or
*   crisped just before serving*

TOPPINGS
2 cups chopped tomatoes
4 cups shredded lettuce
2 cups shredded cheese
2 cups sour cream
Fresh Tomato Salsa (page 37; optional)

M E N U
▼

FOR THE CHILDREN
———

Well-Filled Ground Beef
Tacos
———

Basic Well-Filled
Quesadilla
———

Coconut Milk Ice Cream
Tostada Sundae

VARIATIONS

▼

FOR THE FILLING
■ Stir ¼ cup of one of the four basic salsas—Fresh Tomato Salsa, Salsa Verde, Ranchero Sauce, or Ancho Chili Sauce (see Index for page numbers)—into the filling along with the wine.
■ Add 1 cup grated zucchini along with the beef and spices.
■ Add 2 tablespoons chopped walnuts or almonds when wilting the onions.
■ Cut 4 thick or 6 thin slices of bacon into ½-inch pieces. Fry until crisp and drain. Add to the filling along with the beef and spices.

FOR THE TOPPINGS
■ The beauty of this basic beef filling is that you can vary the salsa according to whim and what you have on hand. For a classic touch, try the Avocado-Pumpkin Seed Salsa or Fiesta Salsa. For a more exotic combination try Greek Salsa or Peanut-Garlic Salsa (see Index for page numbers).
■ Whole fresh mint or cilantro leaves add an aromatic punch to the beef.
■ Toast pumpkin seeds and sprinkle on top.

1. Heat the oil over medium heat in a large nonreactive frying pan. Add the onions and garlic, and fry until the onions are wilted, about 5 minutes.

2. Add the beef, oregano, chili flakes, and salt and cook, stirring occasionally to break up the chunks of meat, until the meat is browned, about 5 minutes more. Add the wine and continue cooking until most of the liquid evaporates, about 10 minutes more.

3. To assemble, spread about ⅓ cup of the beef filling in the center of a tortilla. Top with tomatoes, lettuce, cheese, sour cream, and Fresh Tomato Salsa, if using it. Fold and serve.

TAMALE-STYLE BEEF

Colorful and heartwarming, Tamale-Style Beef is a company version of our basic beef taco.

Serves 4 to 6
Takes less than 20 minutes

2 teaspoons olive or peanut oil
2 medium onions, finely chopped
6 garlic cloves, minced
1 poblano chili pepper (about 2 ounces), stemmed, seeded,
*   and finely chopped*
2½ pounds ground beef chuck or round
1 medium tomato, finely chopped
2 cups fresh corn kernels (about 2 medium ears)
1 tablespoon fresh oregano leaves or ¾ teaspoon dried
¾ teaspoon chili flakes
½ teaspoon salt
1 cup dry red wine
18 corn tortillas, warmed just before serving

TOPPINGS
4 cups shredded lettuce
2 cups sour cream
Toasted Pumpkin Seeds (page 75)

1. Heat the oil in a large nonreactive frying pan over medium heat. Add the onions, garlic, and chili pepper. Cook until the onions are wilted, about 5 minutes.

2. Add the beef, tomato, corn, oregano, chili flakes, and salt. Cook, stirring occasionally to break up any chunks, until the meat is browned, about 5 minutes. Add the wine and cook until most of the liquid evaporates, about 10 minutes more.

3. To assemble, spread about ⅓ cup of the filling on a tortilla. Top with lettuce, sour cream, and pumpkin seeds. Fold and serve.

▲▲▲▲▲▲▲▲▲▲▲▲▲▲▲

We love tacos, but we miss tamales. We grew up with tamales: Susanna in Denver where tamale vendors used to circle Civic Center with two-wheeled white tamale carts; Victoria all around the world because her New Mexico-raised mother used to have canned tamales shipped to wherever the family was stationed. Making a tamale is an arduous task, even the traditional Mexican families we know make tamales only once a year for the Christmas fiesta. Not willing to do the work, but hungry for the corn flavor, we created Tamale-Style Beef.

▼▼▼▼▼▼▼▼▼▼▼▼▼▼▼

SPANISH-STYLE GROUND BEEF AND PORK

When the people on the plains of Seville and surrounding provinces aren't stuffing green bell peppers with rice, meats, and nuts, they are chopping and adding them to almost every dish. Aside from tomatoes, no other New World vegetable became so much a part of their culinary creativity. In Spain, even the mildest form of that vegetable, the sweet bell pepper, has more bite to it—a sort of warming buzz—than the ones we grow in the United States. To create a more authentic Spanish taste, you might add 1 small yellow wax or poblano chili to this beef and pork filling.

Serves 4 to 6
Takes 30 minutes

2 tablespoons olive or peanut oil
1 medium-size red onion, finely chopped
1 small green bell pepper, cored, seeded,
*   and finely chopped*
⅓ cup pine nuts (about 2 ounces)
1 tablespoon finely chopped orange zest
1 tablespoon fresh thyme leaves or
*   1 teaspoon dried*
1 pound ground beef chuck or round
12 ounces ground pork
½ teaspoon salt
⅜ teaspoon fresh ground black pepper
½ cup dry white wine
18 corn or 12 flour tortillas, warmed or crisped
*   just before serving*

TOPPINGS
4 to 5 scallions (green onions), trimmed and
*   sliced into thin rounds*
1 cup cilantro leaves
2 cups sour cream

1. Heat the oil in a large nonreactive frying pan over medium-high heat. Add the onion, bell pepper, pine nuts, orange zest, and thyme. Cook, stirring occasionally, until the onions are wilted, about 6 minutes. Add the beef and pork. Continue cooking, breaking up the meat chunks with a wooden spoon, until the meat is crumbled and browned through, 6 minutes more.

2. Stir in the wine and simmer until the liquid mostly evaporates and the meat begins to stick to the bottom of the pan, about 6 minutes more.

3. To assemble, spread about ⅓ of the filling in the center of a tortilla. Add the toppings, fold, and serve.

TIP

▶ As for all our ground beef recipes, we recommend using choice-grade ground chuck or ground round. The fat content and blandness of the meat in lesser grade beef makes a less appetizing, less healthful, too greasy filling. Since this recipe also calls for ground pork, which can be quite fatty, you may wish to drain the meat before going on to step 2.

▲▲▲▲▲▲▲▲▲▲▲▲▲▲▲▲

We wanted to pay homage to Spanish cuisine—the fountainhead of many fillings—and how it influenced the taco. But to which Spanish were we to pay tribute? The original Basque people who once occupied the whole Spanish peninsula and their indigenous fare? The Iberian settlers? The seafaring visitors—Phoenicians, Greeks, and Romans—who decided to stay on the fertile plain of Aragon and grow the herbs, oranges, olives, and grapes they brought with them? The marauding northern herders—Visigoths and Franks—who came with their cattle and swine? The Moors with their stark, intense spices? A demographer's maze and food historian's tome proved to be a taco creator's fertile stew. We simply honored them all with a taco, combining the whole pageant—*muy espanole.*

COOKING RICE

Next to beans, rice is the most popular companion dish in Latin American and Caribbean cooking. There's an easy tip for cooking just as much rice as you need for a recipe. Rice doubles in volume when cooked. So, if your recipe calls for ⅔ cup cooked white rice, start with ⅓ cup raw rice and twice as much water (⅔ cup). Place the rice and water in a heavy saucepan small enough so that the water covers the rice by ½ inch. Bring to a boil, reduce the heat to very low, cover, and simmer for 17 minutes. Remove from the heat and set aside until ready to use.

TINY BEEF MEATBALLS

The ubiquitous meatball crops up everywhere. In Sweden they mold meatballs with yesterday's bread. In Italy they place them on a bed of pasta. In Lebanon, they blend them with bulgur and stuff them into pita pockets. In Mexico they bathe them in broth to produce savory soup. But out of the soup and off the pasta, with a splash of red sauce, there's no better place for a meatball than in a tortilla.

Serves 4 to 6; makes about 100 cherry-size meatballs
Takes 20 to 40 minutes

1½ pounds ground beef chuck or round
1 medium onion, finely chopped
⅔ cup cooked white rice
¾ teaspoon ground cumin
¾ teaspoon dried oregano
1½ tablespoons chopped fresh mint leaves or 1½ teaspoons dried
¾ teaspoon salt
Vegetable oil
18 corn or 12 flour tortillas, crisped just before serving

TOPPING
2 cups Ranchero Sauce (page 55)

1. In a medium-size bowl mix together the beef, onion, rice, cumin, oregano, mint, and salt. Roll tablespoonsful of the mixture between your hands to form meatballs, about the size of cherries.

2. Coat the bottom of a large frying pan with oil and set over medium-high heat until the oil begins to smoke. Place as many meatballs as will fit in one uncrowded layer in the pan and sauté, turning one or two times, until browned all around and cooked through, about 6 minutes. Transfer to paper towels to drain. Continue with another round until all of the meatballs are cooked.

3. To assemble, place 6 to 8 meatballs in the center of a tortilla. Spoon some of the sauce over the meatballs. Fold and serve.

TIP

▶ The meatballs can be made up to 2 days in advance and refrigerated. Fry just before serving.

CARNE ASADA

Long before fajitas became popular, taco huts and Mexican hideaways offered Carne Asada. Tender and straightforward, carne asada is steak—thin as a skirt or thick as a sirloin—fried on a griddle or in a pan, shredded or sliced thin, and scooped up with all its juices. In a famous version, *carne asada à la Tampiqueña*, cheese enchiladas, stewed poblano chilies *(rajas)*, beans, and guacamole accompany the broiled and shredded steak, with tortillas on the side. This hearty combination makes a most satisfying meal for hungry appetites. We prefer to pare down the cook's work for family meals with an unfussy taco of seasoned, seared steak, Ranchero Sauce, and a basic guacamole. We add other toppings as time allows or the occasion dictates.

~~~~~~

VARIATIONS

▼

FOR THE TOPPINGS

■ For a more substantial meal, top Carne Asada Tacos with Basic Black Beans.

■ For an American favorite, steak and potatoes, add about 2 tablespoons Basic Fried Potatoes to each taco.

■ Add Fried Poblano Chili Strips for a more torrid taco—you get your vegetables besides.

■ Roast 4 to 6 whole heads of garlic, depending on the size of the heads and your taste, as in the recipe for Roasted Garlic, Tomato, and Anchovy Sauce. Squeeze the garlic pulp over the steak strips before adding the Ranchero Sauce.

■ Sprinkle Toasted Pumpkin Seeds on top of the Ranchero Sauce.

FOR THE SALSA

Carne Asada pairs well with almost any of the salsas in this book with the exception of the fruit-based salsas. Try Sweet and Hot Tomatillo Sauce; Roasted Red Pepper, Chili, and Pine Nut Sauce; or Pasilla, Mint, and Pickled Red Onion Sauce. (See Index for recipe page numbers).

Serves 4 to 6
Takes 40 minutes

2 teaspoons pure chili powder
2 pounds boneless beef steak, cut about ½ inch thick
Salt and freshly ground black pepper, to taste
Oil
2 tablespoons fresh lime juice
18 corn or 12 flour tortillas, warmed just before serving

TOPPINGS
Ranchero Sauce (page 55)
Well-Filled Guacamole (page 69)

1. Rub the chili powder over both sides of the steaks and let them sit at room temperature for at least 30 minutes or overnight in the refrigerator.

2. When ready to cook the steak, sprinkle both sides of the meat with salt and pepper. Rub the bottom of a large nonreactive frying pan with just enough oil to coat. Heat the pan over medium-high heat until the oil begins to smoke. Place as much steak as will fit in one uncrowded layer in the pan. Sprinkle on the lime juice and fry, turning once, until medium rare, about 8 minutes altogether. Remove to a platter and continue with another round until all of the steak is cooked. Set the steaks aside for the juices to settle, 5 to 10 minutes.

3. To assemble, slice the steak across the grain into thin strips. Arrange 4 or 5 slices in the center of a tortilla. Top with Ranchero Sauce and Guacamole. Fold and serve.

TIP

▶ For this dish the steaks should be rapidly seared to seal in juices, leaving the meat pink on the inside. If you have steaks thicker than ½ inch or so, cut them in half through the center to make thinner steaks. Don't worry if your cuts are not neat; they won't show when the meat is sliced for the tacos.

CARNE ASADA GENGHIS KHAN

We particularly enjoy this Far East version of Carne Asada. In order to hold its many toppings, fold the tortilla burrito style.

Serves 4 to 6
Takes 40 minutes

2 teaspoons Dijon mustard
2 tablespoons soy sauce
2 pounds boneless beef steak, cut about ½ inch thick
Vegetable oil
12 scallions (green onions), trimmed and cut into 1-inch
    lengths
6 garlic cloves, cut into thin slivers
1 tablespoon sesame seeds
12 flour tortillas, warmed just before serving

TOPPINGS
Yucatan Sauce (page 61) or Pasilla, Mint, and Pickled Red
    Onion Sauce (page 60)
1¼ cups plain yogurt
Leaves from 12 cilantro sprigs (optional)

1. In a nonreactive pan or dish large enough to hold the meat in 1 or 2 layers, mix together the mustard and soy sauce. Place the steak in the mixture, turn to coat all over, and set aside to marinate at room temperature, between 15 to 30 minutes.

2. Rub a large nonreactive frying pan with enough oil to just coat the bottom. Heat the pan over medium-high heat, and when the oil begins to smoke, place as many steaks as will fit in one uncrowded layer in the pan. Fry, turning once, until medium rare, about 8 minutes. Remove to a platter and continue with another round until all the steaks are cooked. Set the steaks aside for the juices to settle, 5 to 10 minutes.

From the great steppes of central Asia—namely, Mongolia—Genghis Khan rode west. He followed the route called the Gates of History through the Khyber pass (where mustard bloomed along the spice route and long caravans traveled) across the Hindu Kush and Persia. Some say he and his raiding hordes invented yogurt. Used to a native diet of milk with their meals, they carried the frothy white liquid along with them in their saddlebags. Jostled and warmed by their steeds' flanks, the milk fermented into a creamy tart thickness. Genghis Khan never reached Europe, but yogurt did. It even got into tacos—at least into our Mongolian-style tacos.

3. In the same pan, stir-fry the scallions, garlic, and sesame seeds over medium-high heat until the scallions begin to wilt, about 3 minutes. Remove from the heat and set aside until ready to assemble the ingredients.

4. To assemble, cut the steaks across the grain into thin strips. Place 4 or 5 strips in the center of a tortilla. Top with the scallion mixture, whichever chili sauce you are using, and the yogurt. Garnish with cilantro if using. Fold envelope style and serve.

BASIC BEEF FAJITAS IN DIPPED TORTILLAS

A beef fajita is a grilled skirt steak, marinated or not, almost always doused with at least a splash of lime juice before cooking. That's all. Slice it, wrap in a warm corn tortilla, garnish with grilled scallions and a sprinkling of fresh mint, and you turn one of the tenderest, tastiest, and least expensive cuts of beef into a dish for family and nobility alike. If you don't have a grill, you can pan-fry the steak and scallions.

Serves 4 to 6
Takes 20 to 40 minutes

1 medium onion
1 teaspoon pure chili powder
¼ cup fresh lime juice
2½ pounds skirt steak
2 tablespoons olive or peanut oil, if frying the skirt steak
12 scallions (green onions), trimmed
12 corn tortillas
Salsa Verde (page 52)

▲▲▲▲▲▲▲▲▲▲▲▲▲

The reason beef fajitas have risen to fame from Texas barbecues to New York restaurants is they offer us a new version of our favorite home and festive fare—steak. Simple steak, grilled, broiled, or pan-fried, is still the preferred meal from our East coast to our West, our Southern border to our Northern. Fajitas present sliced beef at its most eye-catching and tastebud-stirring—thinly cut, showing its juicy pink core, then enveloped in its own warm tortilla wrapper.

▼▼▼▼▼▼▼▼▼▼▼▼▼

TOPPINGS
⅓ cup thinly shredded fresh mint leaves
2 fresh limes, cut into 12 thin wedges each

1. Grate the onion through the fine holes of a hand grater or mince very fine in a food processor. Place the onion in a non-reactive pan or dish large enough to hold the meat in 1 or 2 layers. Add the chili powder and lime juice and stir to mix. Place the skirt steak in the mixture and turn to coat. Set aside to marinate at room temperature for 30 minutes, turning once, or refrigerate and marinate for up to 2 hours, turning once or twice.

2. *If grilling*, prepare a charcoal fire and allow the coals to burn until they are mostly covered with white ash but a few red spots show through here and there. This will take about 40 minutes. When the fire is ready, remove the skirt steak from the marinade. Place on the grill rack directly over the coals. Grill for 3 to 5 minutes on each side, depending on the thickness of the steak and how well done you like it. Remove the steak to a platter and set aside for the juices to settle, 5 to 10 minutes.

If frying, pour 1 tablespoon of the oil in a large nonreactive frying pan set over medium-high heat until the oil begins to smoke. Place as much of the steak as will fit in one uncrowded layer. Cook for 3 to 5 minutes on each side. Remove, add more oil to the pan, and continue with another round until all the steak is cooked. Set aside to rest for 5 to 10 minutes.

3. While the steak rests, grill or pan-fry the scallions until limp and charred in spots, about 5 minutes. Remove the scallions and cut crosswise into 3 or 4 pieces each.

4. Just before serving, dip the tortillas in the Salsa Verde. Heat in a frying pan or the oven.

5. To assemble, cut the steak across the grain into thin slices. Spread 4 or 5 slices across the middle of a warm dipped tortilla, top with 6 or so pieces of scallion. Sprinkle some mint over the onions. Fold and serve with a lime wedge on the side, to be squeezed on the fajita as it is eaten.

VARIATIONS
▼

FOR THE MARINADE
■ For a more typically Mexican flavor in your marinade, use achiote powder in place of the chili powder in the basic recipe.
■ Marinate the skirt steaks in a mixture of ¼ cup tequila and ½ cup Salsa Verde (see Index).
■ For an Asian flavor, marinate the skirt steaks in a mixture of ⅓ cup soy sauce, ⅓ cup fresh lemon juice, and 2 teaspoons minced fresh chili pepper.

FOR THE TOPPINGS
■ Add a dollop or two of sour cream on top of the mint.
■ Add a tablespoon or so of chopped tomatoes on top.
■ For a little more spark, add a touch of Salsa Verde or Chive Salsa along with or in place of the grilled scallions. For a more substantial taco, top your fajita with Greek Salsa or Avocado-Pumpkin Seed Salsa (see Index for page numbers).

FOR THE TORTILLAS
If you want to skip the step of dipping the tortillas, heat them in a 400°F oven for 3 minutes and brush with melted butter before filling.

ORIENTAL STIR-FRY BEEF

When we discovered our neighborhood Chinese restaurant was wrapping its mu shu pork in tortillas instead of making its own pancakes, we had an explosion of ideas for Chinese-style tacos. We went on a binge creating various stir-fries wrapped in tortillas—chicken chow mein, Mongolian beef, kung pao pork, egg fu yung. All of them are wonderful, speedy, and eliminate the wait for the rice. Below is one of our stars, a colorful medley of stir-fried beef and vegetables, topped with Peanut-Garlic Salsa, and ready for folding. No chopsticks necessary.

Serves 4 to 6
Takes 20 minutes or less

2 tablespoons peanut oil
1 pound beef steak, preferably top round, cut into thin strips
½ pound eggplant (3 oriental or ½ regular), cut into
    small cubes
½ small red bell pepper, cored, seeded, and cut into
    very thin strips
1 yellow wax chili pepper, minced (about 2 tablespoons)
6 scallions (green onions), trimmed and cut into thin rounds
2 garlic cloves, pressed or minced
1 teaspoon grated fresh ginger
1 cup bean sprouts (about 4 ounces)
2 tablespoons Oloroso ⸏ erry or other sweet sherry
2 tablespoons soy sauce
¼ teaspoon salt
18 corn or 12 flour tortillas, warmed just before serving

TOPPINGS
4 cups shredded lettuce
Peanut-Garlic Salsa (page 50)

1. Heat the oil in a large nonreactive frying pan or wok over high heat until the oil begins to smoke. Add the beef strips and stir-fry until lightly browned, about 1½ minutes. Transfer the meat to a bowl and set aside.

2. Add the eggplant, bell pepper, chili pepper, scallions, garlic, and ginger to the pan and stir-fry over medium-high heat until the eggplant is soft, 4 or 5 minutes. Add the bean sprouts, sherry, soy sauce, and salt. Stir-fry for 1 minute more.

3. To assemble, place about ⅓ cup of the filling in the center of a tortilla. Top with shredded lettuce and Peanut-Garlic Salsa. Fold and serve.

TIP

▶ You can make this dish like a spring roll instead of a mu shu pork by filling the tortilla like a fat flauta and then recrisping it (page 25).

VARIATION

▼

■ For an Oriental Stir-Fry taco that is: more like Mu Shu Pork—substitute strips of pork for the beef; more like Kung Pao Chicken—substitute lightly battered strips of chicken breast for the beef; more like Princess Prawns—substitute medium-size deveined fresh shrimp for the beef.

▲▲▲▲▲▲▲▲▲▲▲▲▲▲

Passing the Sangre de Cristo mountains, that turn blood red in the sunset, then rolling down Raton Pass from southern Colorado to New Mexico, eventually you arrive in Taos. In the center of town lies Kit Carson's house and a plaza lined with old adobes. In days gone by, the only places to eat were the hotel dining room at the old stagecoach station or truckstops. The town has changed now. There are fancy new Southwest-cuisine restaurants and opera. Still the hills are sage blue in the afternoon. The pace is easy, and since Chili Colorado is sure to be on the menu, Susanna always makes a side trip when visiting home. This is our version of the famous Tex-Mex dish wrapped in, instead of served with, tortillas.

▼▼▼▼▼▼▼▼▼▼▼▼▼▼

CHILI COLORADO

Although Chili Colorado is considered the flagship dish of Tex-Mex cuisine, no one agrees on exactly what all goes into it. Cook-offs take place every year for the best home version. Beaneries and elegant Southwest grills present their own offerings. The twist in our rendition is the toppings of thickened cream and fresh cilantro.

Serves 4 to 6
Takes 1½ hours

1½ pounds boneless beef chuck roast
8 ounces boneless pork butt
2 tablespoons peanut or olive oil
½ large onion, coarsely chopped
1 large garlic clove, pressed or minced
2½ teaspoons pure chili powder
¼ teaspoon ground cumin
1 small bay leaf
½ teaspoon salt
1⅓ cups canned tomatoes in purée
1 cup water
*18 corn or 12 flour tortillas, warmed or crisped just before
    serving*

TOPPINGS
*2 cups heavy (whipping) cream, whipped until slightly
    thickened*
Dressed Cilantro (page 76)

1. Cut the chuck roast and pork into strips about ⅛ inch thick by ½ inch wide, trimming away any excess fat as you go.

2. Heat the oil in a large nonreactive stew pot set over medium-high heat. Add as much meat as will fit in one uncrowded layer and cook until browned, 4 minutes. Transfer to a bowl and continue with another round until all of the meat is browned.

3. Return all of the meat to the pot and add the onion, garlic, chili powder, cumin, bay leaf, salt, tomatoes, and water. Bring to a boil. Partially cover and cook over medium heat for 1¼ hours. (This stew also can be cooked, covered, in a preheated 400°F oven for 1¼ hours.)

4. To assemble, place about ⅓ cup of the filling in the center of a tortilla. Pour 1 tablespoon or so of the thickened cream over the filling and top with the Dressed Cilantro. Fold and serve.

SPICY OVEN-STEWED BEEF

Serves 4 to 6
Takes 1½ hours

2½ pounds boneless beef chuck roast
2 tablespoons olive or peanut oil
¼ teaspoon ground coriander seed
3 whole allspice berries
¼ teaspoon whole peppercorns
1 pound tomatoes, preferably plum, coarsely chopped
2 medium onions, coarsely chopped
2 large garlic cloves, coarsely chopped
1½ teaspoons chopped fresh oregano or ½ teaspoon dried
1 tablespoon achiote paste or 2 teaspoons pure chili powder
    plus ½ teaspoon cayenne
½ teaspoon salt
1 cup dry red wine
2 cups water
18 corn or 12 flour tortillas, warmed or crisped just before
    serving

TOPPINGS
1 large onion, finely chopped
¼ cup chopped fresh oregano leaves or 1 tablespoon dried
2 limes cut into 6 to 9 wedges each

No longer able to take an occasional weekend escape as we used to in childless days, one weekend we decided to try a getaway bringing our children along. We packed them up in Victoria's station wagon and headed for the snow-covered hills of Lake Tahoe. Cross-country skiing at Sugar Pine Park was the target; the end of the intermediate trail was the goal. After Susanna took the last hill on her *derrière*, and Victoria lugged her skis for a quarter mile while the kids rolled in the snow laughing at us, we knew we needed a taco. Preferably a stewy, beefy, winey, winter one. The ski rental hut had a small grocery complete with a good-looking chuck roast for sale. Red wine was in abundance; the rental cabin was well stocked with spices. Ever taco-minded we had brought the tortillas. Two hours later, feet up, fire crackling, we had Spicy Oven-Stewed Beef tacos, with marshmallows on sticks to follow.

▲▲▲▲▲▲▲▲▲▲▲▲▲▲▲

We love rabbit and make good rabbit tacos using exactly the same ingredients we do in Spicy Oven-Stewed Beef tacos, substituting rabbit for the beef. If you too enjoy a lean rabbit dish, two cut-up fresh rabbits equal the amount of beef in this recipe. Shred the meat from the bones after stewing, as you would for a chicken filling.

▼▼▼▼▼▼▼▼▼▼▼▼▼▼

1. Heat the oven to 400°F.

2. Cut the chuck roast into pieces, about ¾ inch thick by ½ inch long, trimming away any excess fat as you go.

3. Heat the oil in a large nonreactive stew pot over medium-high heat. Add as much meat as will fit in one uncrowded layer and cook until browned, about 4 minutes. Transfer to a bowl. Continue with another round until all of the meat is browned.

4. While the meat browns, place the coriander, allspice, and peppercorns on a paper towel. Fold the towel over the spices and crush them with a mallet or hammer.

5. Return all the meat to the pot and add the crushed spices, tomatoes, chopped onions, garlic, oregano, achiote paste, salt, wine, and water. Bring to a boil. Cover and place in the oven. Cook until the meat is tender, 1¼ hours. (This stew can also be cooked on top of the stove, covered, over medium heat. The timing is the same.)

6. To assemble, place about ⅓ cup of the stew filling in the center of a tortilla. Top with some finely chopped onion and a sprinkle of oregano. Squeeze a lime wedge over all. Fold and serve.

BEEF BEER STEW

Don't just drink good beer with tacos; stew the taco filling *in* the beer. In this rich, remarkably flavorful filling we call for amber beer. Amber beer with its longer roasted, malty taste adds a husky character and special sweetness to the beef and onions. We especially like to use one of the good amber beers of Mexico, such as Dos Equis, the Filipino San Miguel, or San Francisco's Anchor Steam.

Serves 4 to 6
Takes 1½ hours

1¾ pounds boneless beef chuck roast
2 tablespoons peanut or olive oil
3 medium onions, coarsely chopped
2 large garlic cloves, pressed or minced
2 cups amber beer
1½ tablespoons red wine vinegar
1 small bay leaf
1½ teaspoons fresh thyme leaves or
    ½ teaspoon dried
¾ teaspoon salt
½ teaspoon freshly ground black pepper
2 cups fresh corn kernels (about 2 medium ears), or
    1½ cups frozen corn kernels, thawed
18 corn or 12 flour tortillas, warmed or crisped
    just before serving

TOPPINGS
Roasted Red Pepper, Chili, and
    Pine Nut Sauce (page 57)
½ cup chopped fresh jalapeños
3 teaspoons minced lemon zest

1. Cut the chuck roast into strips, about ⅛ inch thick by ½ inch long, trimming away any excess fat as you go.

2. Heat the oil in a large nonreactive stew pot over medium-high heat. Add as much meat as will fit in one uncrowded layer and brown for about 4 minutes. Transfer to a bowl. Continue with another round until all of the meat is browned.

3. Return all of the meat to the pot and add the onions, garlic, beer, vinegar, bay leaf, thyme, salt, and pepper. Bring to a boil. Cover and simmer over low heat for 1 hour. Stir in the corn. Continue cooking until the meat is tender, about 15 minutes more. (This stew also can be cooked in a preheated 400°F oven. The timing is the same.)

4. To assemble, place about ⅓ cup of the filling in the center of a tortilla. Top with a few dollops of Roasted Red Pepper Sauce and the toppings. Fold and serve.

▲▲▲▲▲▲▲▲▲▲▲▲▲▲▲▲

This filling is a good one to make in advance and reheat. It becomes even better as the various elements blend in the pot. Since corn easily overcooks, though, don't add it until you reheat the dish.

▼▼▼▼▼▼▼▼▼▼▼▼▼▼▼▼

MOROCCAN-STYLE BEEF

In Morocco you might find the filling for this gaily colored beef taco plumped out with chick-peas and raisins and pocketed in a crisp-fried pita bread. You might also find the same dish made with lamb, chicken, rabbit, goat, or squab in place of beef.

Serves 4 to 6
Takes 1½ hours

1½ pounds boneless beef chuck roast
2 tablespoons peanut or olive oil
1 medium red- or white-skinned potato, cut into small cubes
3 medium carrots, peeled and diced
1 medium turnip, peeled and diced
1 large garlic clove, pressed or minced
1 teaspoon ground cumin
½ teaspoon saffron threads or ¼ teaspoon saffron powder
½ teaspoon ground turmeric
½ teaspoon salt
½ teaspoon freshly ground black pepper
½ tablespoon tomato paste
3 cups water
18 corn or 12 flour tortillas, warmed just before serving

TOPPINGS
2 cups plain yogurt
Orange-Onion Salsa (page 49)
1 cup crumbled feta cheese (optional)
1 cup thinly shredded fresh mint leaves (optional)

1. Cut the chuck roast into strips about ⅛ inch thick by ½ inch wide, trimming away any excess fat as you go.

2. Heat the oil in a large nonreactive stew pot set over medium-high heat. Add as much meat as will fit in one uncrowded layer and cook until evenly browned, about 4 minutes. Transfer to a bowl and continue with another round until all of the meat is browned.

3. Return all of the meat to the pot. Add the potatoes, carrots, turnips, garlic, cumin, saffron, turmeric, salt, pepper, tomato paste, and water. Bring to a boil. Partially cover and simmer for 1¼ hours. (This stew also can be cooked, covered, in a preheated 400°F oven. The timing is the same.)

4. To assemble, place about ¼ cup of the filling in the center of a tortilla or pita bread. Top with some yogurt, salsa, crumbled feta, and mint leaves. Fold and serve.

TIPS

▶ We list the feta and mint leaves as optional toppings for festive occasions. For quick family meals, the yogurt and salsa complete the flavors in a simple and satisfying way. If you are making the dish for a special event, you could also add toasted slivered almonds to the toppings.

▶ Rather than wrapping Moroccan-Style Beef as a taco, you can mound the filling in the center of a platter, surround it with rice, barley, grits, or real semolina, and serve the tortilla or pita and various toppings on the side like a couscous dish. Then, of course, you need a dab of fiery sauce, such as one of the Two Red Hot Chili-Garlic Salsas (see Index).

It was in Morocco that Victoria discovered spice bazaars, *bisteeya* (pigeon pie with its powdered sugar-dusted crust), couscous, and *khboz mikla* (flat round breads cooked on a griddle). The bread was used to scoop up the spicy meat and vegetable stews, chick-peas, and torrid *harissa* sauce. Victoria's head was quite dizzy with recipe ideas when she came home armed with small packets of turmeric and cumin, bottles of cardamom pods and saffron threads. This is our version of a Moroccan couscous stew with flat bread and fiery sauce, the whole North African theme turned into a taco.

PORK

The Americas sent the tomato, potato, pepper, and pumpkin to the rest of the world, but the world sent the pig to us. Pigless—except for the peccary—until de Soto brought 13 hogs into Florida, there are now some 60 million in the United States alone, with countless more throughout Canada and Central and South America. Today our wild pigs, with their matted coats, curled horns, and skittery temperaments stem from some that gave up the thin veneer of domesticity, fled the pigpen, and returned to feral living.

Currently, pork is the second-favorite meat in North America, but throughout much of the rest of the world it is the primary and most beloved meat. Pigs, along with chickens, are the easiest meat animal to keep. They were also one of the first animals domesticated. As soon as there were villages, there were pigs in sties and on spits. As for pigs and pancakes, the match was made long ago—mu shu pork, *carnitas* with fresh hot tortillas, pigs in a blanket, ham sandwiches.

Pork is perfect for tortilla fillings. The bits of meat are tender. The flavor of pork melds with fruits, peppers, vegetables, spices, cheese, creams, and almost any kind of sauce.

If you're going to make a pig of yourself, do it with a pork taco.

QUICK AND EASY GROUND PORK

We endure a major and continuous disagreement on the best way to build ground pork tacos. Victoria prefers the lettuce next to the meat filling, the sour cream over, and the salsa well separated from the layers by dolloping it on top. Susanna likes the salsa with all its vegetable elements spread right on top of the pork filling, then the sour cream to cool, and the crunchy lettuce on top. We agree on one thing: any way you build it, pork makes a scrumptious use-any-salsa, use-any-topping taco.

Serves 4 to 6
Takes 20 minutes or less

2½ pounds finely ground pork
1 large onion, finely chopped
4 large garlic cloves, minced
2 yellow wax chili peppers, stemmed and finely chopped
2 teaspoons dried oregano
½ teaspoon salt
½ cup dry red wine
18 corn or 12 flour tortillas, warmed or crisped just before
   serving

TOPPINGS
2 cups chopped tomatoes
2 cups chopped avocado
Dressed Cilantro (page 76)
½ cup chopped fresh jalapeño chili peppers (optional)
2 cups sour cream (optional)

   1. Place the pork, onion, garlic, chili peppers, oregano, and salt in a large heavy ungreased frying pan. Cook over medium-high heat, stirring occasionally to break up the chunks of meat,

---

VARIATIONS
▼

FOR THE FILLING:
■ Stir ½ teaspoon or so pure chili powder into the filling along with the other seasonings.
■ Add ½ teaspoon cumin along with the other seasonings.
■ Sage, marjoram, and thyme are all good substitutes for the oregano in the basic recipe. Use the same amount.
■ For a sublimely rich Mexican accent, add 3 tablespoons grated bittersweet chocolate and ⅛ teaspoon cinnamon along with the other seasonings. See also Tequila Sausages with Chocolate Mole Sauce (see Index) for another ground pork and chocolate combination.

FOR THE SALSA
■ Chive Salsa—especially good with the chocolate and cinnamon variation in the filling.
■ Peanut-Garlic Salsa—also especially good with the chocolate and cinnamon variation.
■ Salsa Verde (See the Index for recipe page numbers.)

▲▲▲▲▲▲▲▲▲▲▲▲▲▲▲▲

We got a call one morning from Wynch-Meyer Ranch in Boonville, California—where food and words are loved so much, the townspeople made up their own language, the main phrase of which is "bal gorms," meaning "good chow." They had one pig left to sell from a canceled order. Were we interested? Were we! The pig had been fed only corn and figs and ours dressed out at a plump 240. What this meant to us, besides some hams, some chops, and some ribs, was having enough ground pork to well-fill tortillas throughout the winter. As a thank-you to the Wynch-Meyers, we visited in the spring and made a triple batch of our Quick and Easy Ground Pork filling for them to enjoy. Now they give out copies of the recipe with every pig sale.

▼▼▼▼▼▼▼▼▼▼▼▼▼▼▼▼

until the pork is browned, about 5 minutes. Add the wine and simmer until most of the liquid evaporates, about 5 minutes more.

2. To assemble, spread about ⅓ cup of the pork filling in the center of a tortilla. Top with chopped tomatoes, chopped avocado, Dressed Cilantro, and chopped jalapeños and sour cream if using it. Fold and serve.

TIP

▶ The pork for this filling should be medium or finely ground. Too large a grind and the meat will be tough.

PORK AND CORN MEATBALLS

Serves 4 to 6; makes about 150 cherry-size meatballs
Takes 20 minutes or less

2½ pounds ground pork
2 medium onions, finely chopped
3 serrano or 2 jalapeño chili peppers, stemmed and finely chopped
5 garlic cloves, pressed or minced
1½ cups fresh corn kernels (1½ to 2 medium ears)
2 large eggs
1½ teaspoons salt
3 cups cornmeal
1 tablespoon peanut or olive oil
18 corn or 12 flour tortillas, warmed just before serving

TOPPINGS
Ranchero Sauce (page 55)
3 cups shredded Jack cheese
4 cups shredded lettuce

1. Place the pork, onions, chili peppers, garlic, corn, eggs, and salt in a large bowl. Using your hands, mix together to blend well.

2. Spread the cornmeal on a plate or countertop. Shape tablespoonfuls of the pork mixture into cherry-size meatballs. Roll the meatballs in the cornmeal to coat all around.

3. In a large frying pan, heat the oil over medium heat until it begins to smoke. Add as many meatballs as will fit in one uncrowded layer. Fry, turning to brown all around until cooked through, about 10 minutes. Remove to a platter and continue with another round until all of the meatballs are cooked.

4. To assemble, place 10 or so meatballs in the center of a tortilla. Top with Ranchero Sauce, shredded cheese and lettuce. Fold and serve.

TIP

▶ You can make the meatball mixture up to 3 days in advance, rolled or unrolled. Do not coat with cornmeal until you are ready to cook them.

M aria Jones, in her cafe El Sombrero 30 miles outside Davenport, makes a taco that is positively Iowan and that inspired our Pork and Corn Meatball filling. While visiting relatives in close-by Moline, Illinois, Susanna heard about Maria's food, and borrowed a car in order to chase down the restaurant.

Maria is a tenth generation Spanish-American and has been a Davenport dweller for the past five decades. The pigs Maria uses for pork in the cafe she runs with her husband, Ed, come right from their own or neighbors' farms and are as big as a set of Mack truck wheels. The corn comes from their fields, and she freezes ears to have all winter. She creams the corn for her tacos and adds it as a topping, while we stir the corn right into the meatball mixture. She also keeps the chili peppers out, to be layered on top.

The coconut palm is a gracious gift of nature. Almost every element of it produces something to use or to eat. The long fronds provide the thatch that shingles the rooftops of huts, cabanas, dance halls, and churches in tropical climates worldwide. The sugary sap when distilled becomes an alcoholic drink known as arrack. The bark becomes baskets and household vessels. Then there is the coconut. The white meat of the nut is both eaten and used in products ranging from soap to margarine. The oil of the nut is used for cooking and in skin care, and there still remains the milk. Coconut milk is the basic cooking liquid of perhaps one-third of the world's population. The coconut milk used in Cambodian, Burmese, Philippine, Ceylonese, and African cooking, as well as canned coconut milk, though, is not what we drank as kids when we broke open a coconut and found the milky liquid there. That is yet another gift of the coconut palm, a delicious, refreshing drink. Coconut milk for cooking is the liquid squeezed from the grated coconut pulp. Rich and buttery, it acts both like butter and stock to thicken and flavor fish, fowl, vegetable, and pork soups and stews.

CAMBODIAN-STYLE GROUND PORK

The inspiration for this filling comes from a Cambodian restaurant, the Sayonn, in Berkeley. They serve a variation of the dish surrounded by vegetables.

Serves 4 to 6
Takes 20 minutes or less

2½ pounds ground pork
8 anchovy fillets, finely chopped
2¼ teaspoons paprika, preferably Hungarian sweet
¾ teaspoon pure chili powder
¼ teaspoon cayenne
1¼ cups coconut milk
1 medium jicama, peeled and coarsely grated
1 tablespoon fresh lime juice
18 corn or 12 flour tortillas, warmed or crisped just before serving

TOPPINGS
1 small eggplant, cut into very thin, 1½-inch-long strips
½ small green cabbage, finely shredded
5 pickling cucumbers, peeled and coarsely grated
½ cup fresh mint leaves

1. Place the pork, anchovies, paprika, chili powder, and cayenne in a large ungreased frying pan. Cook over medium-high heat, stirring occasionally to break up the chunks of meat, until the pork is browned, about 5 minutes. Add the coconut milk and cook until almost all of the liquid evaporates, about 10 minutes.

2. Mix the jicama with the lime juice.

3. To assemble, spread about ⅓ cup of the pork filling in the center of a tortilla. Top with the jicama, eggplant, cabbage, cucumbers, and mint leaves. Fold and serve.

TEQUILA SAUSAGE WITH CHOCOLATE MOLE SAUCE

T equila, the most famous and widely exported liquor of Mexico, can not only add dash to Margaritas and the sunrise after many a Sunrise, it gives unique flair to ground pork sausage. Made from the *agave* cactus that flourishes over the dry terrains throughout Mexico, tequila has a spiky, pungent flavor, different from the smoothness of brandy or the fruitiness of wine. In the filling below, we top off tequila sausage with a *mole* of chocolate.

Serves 4 to 6
Takes 30 minutes

TEQUILA SAUSAGE
2½ pounds ground pork
7 garlic cloves, pressed or minced
2 teaspoons chopped fresh sage leaves or ¾ teaspoon rubbed sage
1¼ teaspoons fennel seeds
¼ teaspoon cayenne
1¼ teaspoons salt
⅔ cup tequila, preferably gold
18 corn or 12 flour tortillas, warmed or crisped just before serving

TOPPINGS
Chocolate Mole Sauce (recipe follows)
Pan-Grilled Scallions (page 72)
Dressed Cilantro (page 76)
2 cups chopped tomatoes
2 limes, cut into 6 to 9 wedges each

▲▲▲▲▲▲▲▲▲▲▲▲▲▲▲

Behind the glass case you see hot sausage, sweet sausage, frankfurters, andouille, breakfast links, pork patties, salami, chorizo, linguiça, in bulk, stuffed in chain links, wrapped in caul, or patted into cakes. Sausage making seems a mysterious craft, but sausage is really ground meat mixed with a selection of herbs and spices. It's easy to make your own fresh, additive-free sausage at home. Purchase some ground pork and add the elements you choose: garlic, onion, chilies, herbs, nuts, wine, and even other meats. A basic guideline is, 1 pound of ground meat will take about ¾ teaspoon of salt, plus the other flavorings. Fry up loose or shape into patties or meatballs. First, though, we suggest this tip: Fry a small piece to test whether the seasonings please you before cooking the whole batch.

▼▼▼▼▼▼▼▼▼▼▼▼▼▼▼

1. To make the Tequila Sausage, place the pork in a large bowl. Add the garlic, sage, fennel seeds, cayenne, salt, and tequila. Mix together with your hands to blend well. Use right away, or cover and refrigerate for up to 2 days.

2. Crumble the sausage into a large frying pan. Cook over high heat, stirring occasionally to break up any chunks, until thoroughly browned, about 10 minutes.

3. To assemble, spread about ⅓ cup of the sausage in the center of a warm or crisp tortilla. Top with Chocolate Mole Sauce, Pan-Grilled Scallions, Dressed Cilantro, and chopped tomatoes. Fold and serve with a thin wedge of lime on the side.

CHOCOLATE MOLE SAUCE

Makes about 2 cups
Takes 20 minutes

2½ cups chicken stock or broth
5 garlic cloves, pressed or minced
2½ ounces bittersweet chocolate
⅓ cup pure chili powder
⅛ teaspoon grated nutmeg

1. Place all of the ingredients in a medium saucepan and bring to a boil over medium heat. Reduce the heat and simmer, stirring occasionally, until the chocolate melts and the sauce thickens, about 15 minutes.

2. Serve right away, or cover, refrigerate, and use within 2 weeks. Freeze for longer storage.

TEQUILA SAUSAGE IN RED AND GREEN MOLE SAUCE

When served in its homeland, tequila is usually followed by a chaser of *sangrita,* a spicy red condiment. Here we offer tequila sausage topped with just such a condiment, red and green chili mole.

Serves 4 to 6
Takes 30 minutes

2½ pounds Tequila Sausage (page 105)
18 corn or 12 flour tortillas, warmed or crisped just before
  serving

TOPPINGS
Red and Green Mole Sauce (recipe follows)
4 cups shredded lettuce
2 cups chopped avocado

  1. Crumble the sausage in a large frying pan. Cook over high heat, stirring to break up any chunks, until thoroughly browned, about 10 minutes.

  2. To assemble, spread about ⅓ cup of the sausage meat in the center of a tortilla. Top with the Red and Green Mole Sauce, shredded lettuce, and chopped avocado. Fold and serve.

RED AND GREEN MOLE SAUCE

Makes about 2¼ cups
Takes less than 20 minutes

▲▲▲▲▲▲▲▲▲▲▲▲▲▲▲▲▲

Though tequila is the special ingredient in this sausage, if you don't have a bottle of it on hand, there are three possible substitutes: Gin with its juniper berry taste and aroma, and *rakia* or *grappa,* both distilled from grape pulp and still redolent of its flavor.

▼▼▼▼▼▼▼▼▼▼▼▼▼▼▼▼

1 pound tomatillos
4 radishes, trimmed
2 jalapeño chili peppers, stemmed
½ cup parsley leaves, preferably Italian flat-leaf
2 tablespoons pure chili powder
¼ teaspoon salt

1. Peel the papery husks off the tomatillos. Rinse the tomatillos. Place in a saucepan, and add water to cover. Bring to a boil and simmer until soft to the touch, about 5 minutes.

2. In a food processor, blender, or food mill, purée the tomatillos along with the radishes, chili peppers, parsley, chili powder, and salt. Serve right away, or cover, refrigerate, and use within 5 days.

VARIATIONS
▼

It was actually breakfast rather than dinner, that led us to our Chorizo taco variations, but we have subsequently devoured both for many a supper. Still, to add zany innovation and spice to that most unvarying and often uninspiring morning meal, have one or all of these spectacular tacos.
■ Chorizo and Breaded Chili Strips with shredded Jack cheese and Grapefruit-Onion Salsa.
■ Chorizo and Breaded Chili Strips with chopped tomato and Leek, Feta, and Sour Cream Salsa (see Index for recipe page numbers).

WELL-FILLED CHORIZO

Chorizo, that wonderful peppery Mexican sausage, has changed considerably from its original Spanish link. In Mexico, chorizo starts with fresh pork and is infused with chili powders, garlic, spices from both Spain and Mexico—cinnamon bark, clove, *epazote,* coriander seed—and a dousing of cider vinegar. The chorizo from each district of Mexico differs, with that from Toluca reputed to be the best. If you must find a substitute, use linguiça or andouille. The combination of chorizo and corn tortillas is rightfully traditional, and we always choose corn over flour tortillas for this taco. By the way, don't be fooled by liquid chorizo. It is a flavoring, not a sausage.

Serves 4 to 6
Takes less than 20 minutes

2 pounds chorizo sausage
18 corn tortillas, warmed or crisped just before serving

TOPPINGS
Breaded Chili Strips (page 71)
3 cups shredded Cheddar cheese
2 cups chopped tomatoes
2 cups sour cream

1. Slice the chorizo into ¼-inch-thick half rounds. Preheat a large frying pan over medium-high heat. Add the chorizo, and cook until browned, about 3 minutes.

2. To assemble, spread about ⅓ cup chorizo in the middle of a tortilla. Top with Breaded Chili Strips, shredded cheese, chopped tomato, and sour cream. Fold and serve.

TIP

▶ How you fry your chorizo is actually a matter of personal style. For tacos, we like to slice the links in half rounds first because they cook so quickly, but you can also toss  the links whole into a pan, fry them that way, and cut them up after, remembering to cook them a little longer.

▲▲▲▲▲▲▲▲▲▲▲▲▲▲▲▲

Pig-by-the-Tail, Victoria's French delicatessen, was famous for its *crudités,* its pâtés—the duck liver or the chicken with sorrel perhaps the all-time winners— and its sausages. There were Champagne sausages in links small enough to stuff a chicken breast, country sausages, *crêpinettes,* turkey sausages, Pittsburgh Italian sausages, and then an award-winning chorizo. On chorizo-making day, a haze of chili powder hung like a red cloud above the cutting tables. The giant Hobart mixer chomped away at the cinnamon, nutmeg, and *epazote* to balance the chili powders. The sausage spicings were like a *mole* rolled into the pork rather than separate elements. The person at the casing filler had to be quick at the twist to fill them just right, tie them off at either end, and bundle the links in fours. Eager customers watched from the kitchen door, vying to buy the sausage as it came off the stuffer. But a truly fine chorizo must age at least overnight, so chef Chooch smiled and took orders as he hung the links to dry. By the end of the day, chili-dusted and chili-dry, we toasted the chili spirits with a beer.

▼▼▼▼▼▼▼▼▼▼▼▼▼▼▼▼

QUICK PAN-FRIED PORK FAJITAS

Pork fajita is not common, but there's no reason why it shouldn't be. The tenderloin, the tender and tasty, boneless long strip from under the rib section, grills or fries quickly and slices easily into thin ribbons perfect for a tortilla filling. All sorts of sauces—dried chili, plain tomato *cruda*, every fruit salsa—and any topping can don a pork fajita. You can also crust the tenderloin in a nut coating for a crunchy fajita. Here, in a quick but full-meal version, we simply fry thin rounds of pork tenderloin and layer the meat in a tortilla together with potatoes, red peppers, sour cream, and torrid South American Jalapeño-Parsley Salsa. Depending on the size of the pig, the tenderloin can vary from ½ pound in a suckling pig to 1½ pounds or more from a real porker.

Serves 4 to 6
Takes 20 minutes or less

3 pounds pork tenderloin
Salt and freshly ground pepper,
*　　to taste*
Oil to coat the pans
18 corn or 12 flour tortillas, warmed or
*　　crisped just before serving*

TOPPINGS
3 large red bell peppers, cored, seeded,
*　　and cut into thin, 1½-inch-long strips*
Basic Fried Potatoes (page 210)
South American Jalapeño-Parsley Salsa
*　　(page 46)*
2 cups sour cream

1. Cut the pork tenderloins crosswise into ¼-inch-thick rounds. Lightly salt and pepper each piece.

2. Coat 2 large frying pans with oil and set over medium-high heat until the oil begins to smoke. Add as much pork as will fit in one uncrowded layer and fry for 1½ minutes. Turn and continue cooking until the juices are no longer pink but the meat is still moist, about 1½ minutes more. Remove to a platter and continue with another round if necessary.

3. To assemble, place about ⅓ cup of the meat in the center of a tortilla. Top with red pepper strips, Fried Potatoes, South American Jalapeño-Parsley Salsa, and sour cream. Fold and serve.

TIP

▶ You can also grill the pork for fajitas. See the cutting and grilling directions on page 112.

See the cutting and grilling directions on page 112.

VARIATIONS

▼

FOR THE TOPPINGS
■ Sauté the red pepper strips in a little olive or peanut oil, along with some garlic slivers.
■ Make a ½ batch of Potato and Roquefort Cheese Melt and use as a topping for the pork fajitas, along with Pear-Lime Salsa (see Index for recipe page numbers).

FOR THE SALSA
Most salsas go well with pork fajitas.

PORK FAJITAS AND YAMS IN A DIPPED TORTILLA

The same quality that makes pork adaptable to smoking, curing, and salting—all of which subtly or sharply alter the flavor of the meat—also makes it particularly suitable for marinating in the home kitchen. Along with fish and fowl, pork quickly takes on flavors from an immersion in oil, wines, or savories. Plain, unmarinated pork fajitas are unquestionably good, but marinated, the thin slices develop a taste that is quite unforgettable. The longer the meat sits in the marinade, the better.

Serves 4 to 6
**Takes 20 minutes or less, plus several hours of
      marinating time**

3 pounds pork tenderloin
¼ cup peanut oil
1½ teaspoons chili flakes
*2 tablespoons chopped fresh mint leaves or
      2 teaspoons dried*
6 garlic cloves, pressed or minced
Salt, to taste
*3 medium or 1½ large yams, peeled and
      cut into ½-inch dice*
18 corn or 12 flour tortillas
*Pasilla, Mint, and Pickled Red Onion Sauce
      (page 60)*

TOPPING
4 cups shredded lettuce

1. Cut the tenderloins crosswise in half to make 1 thicker piece and 1 thinner piece. Cut each thicker piece lengthwise in half to make 2 thinner pieces. The pieces should be approximately equal thickness. (See the illustration, facing page, for how to cut a tenderloin.)

2. In a large dish, mix together the peanut oil, chili flakes, mint, and garlic. Add the pork and turn to coat on all sides. Salt lightly. Refrigerate to marinate for several hours, preferably overnight, turning once or twice. Remove the tenderloins when ready to cook; reserve the marinade.

3. *If grilling,* prepare a charcoal fire and allow the coals to burn until they are mostly covered with white ash but a few red spots show through here and there. This will take about 40 minutes. When the fire is ready, place the pork on the grill rack directly above the coals. Grill for 5 minutes. Turn and grill for 5 to 7 minutes more, depending on the thickness, until the juices are no longer pink but the meat is still moist. Remove to a platter and set aside to allow the juices to settle, 5 to 10 minutes.

If frying, set 2 large frying pans over medium-high heat until quite hot. Add as much meat as will fit in one uncrowded layer. Fry for 6 minutes. Turn and continue cooking for 5 to 7 minutes more, depending on the thickness, until the juices are no longer pink but the meat is still moist. Remove to a platter; continue cooking another round if necessary.

4. While the juices settle, cook the yams. Using one of the same pans used for frying or a clean one if you are grilling, heat the reserved marinade over medium-high heat. Add the yams and fry, stirring occasionally, until cooked through, about 5 minutes. Drain on paper towels; salt lightly.

5. Just before serving, dip the tortillas in 1 cup of the Pasilla, Mint, and Pickled Red Onion Sauce. Heat in a frying pan or the oven (page 25).

6. To assemble, slice the tenderloins crosswise into thin rounds. Place about ⅓ cup of the meat in the center of a tortilla. Top with fried yams, shredded lettuce, and the remaining 1 cup of Pasilla, Mint, and Pickled Red Onion Sauce. Fold and serve.

▲▲▲▲▲▲▲▲▲▲▲▲▲▲▲▲▲

Yam and ham. Yam and bacon. Yam and pork. Yam and pig is one of the world's most common food duos. It's the African, Polynesian, Melanesian, Indonesian version of meat and potatoes. Yams were among the first farmed crops. As pigs were among the first tamed animals, pairing the two was a natural. Still a renowned and delicious coupling, it's the main feature of luaus, carnivals, and festivals under many a tropical sky.

▼▼▼▼▼▼▼▼▼▼▼▼▼▼▼▼▼

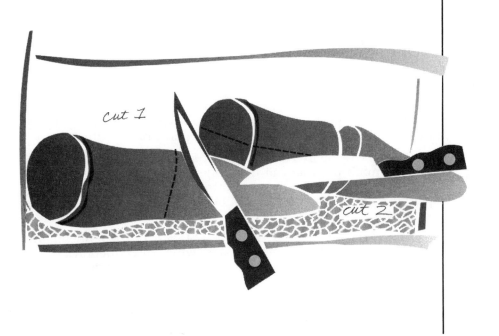

cut 1

cut 2

Our friend Chad spent part of his youth in the Peace Corps in Brazil. He served in a village where pigs foraged about town, settling together in one great muddy wallow exactly in the center of the main road. Chad decided to show the villagers a more prosperous way to raise pigs. He got a lovely white piglet he named Lady Bird, built her a proper pen and put her on a proper pig diet. Unfortunately, just as Lady Bird reached her prime, she contracted a sort of jungle fever peculiar to pigs and met her soul's departing. The only saving grace of Lady Bird's passing, from Chad's point of view, was that at least she didn't end up in a *feijoada*, the traditional dish of Brazil. In *feijoada* black beans and mixed dried meats are stewed together with pork loins and numerous pork parts, including pigs' ears, pigs' feet, and pigs' snouts. Upon returning to the United States, Chad instituted a memorial to Lady Bird he calls the annual "pignic." He buys plenty of beer and roasts a whole pig. (We wonder what Lady Bird would think of this tribute.) In some ways our pork and fennel filling is not unlike *feijoada*, without the miscellaneous pig parts. *Feijoada* is served over rice and accompanied by manioc, kale, and oranges. We place our pork stew in a tortilla instead, use aromatic fennel in place of kale, and top it all with Orange-Onion Salsa.

PORK, FENNEL, AND PARSNIPS

Serves 4 to 6
Takes 1½ hours

3 pounds boneless pork butt or 4½ pounds bone-in
1 tablespoon peanut or olive oil
1 fennel bulb, trimmed, quartered, then cut into ⅛-inch slices (2¼ cups)
2 ounces parsnips, peeled and cut into ¼-inch slices
1 medium onion, coarsely chopped
3 large garlic cloves, pressed or minced
1½ teaspoons pure chili powder
¾ teaspoon salt
1½ cups dry white wine
18 corn or 12 flour tortillas, warmed or crisped just before serving

TOPPINGS
Orange-Onion Salsa (page 49)
4 cups shredded lettuce

1. Cut the pork into ½-inch cubes or strips, trimming off any excess fat as you go. If using bone-in pork, reserve the bone.

2. Heat the oil in a large stew pot set over medium-high heat. Add as much pork as will fit in one uncrowded layer and cook until lightly browned, about 5 minutes. Remove the meat to a platter, and continue cooking another round until all of the pork is browned.

3. Return all of the pork to the pot. Stir in the fennel, parsnips, onion, garlic, chili powder, salt, wine, and pork bone. Bring to a boil. Reduce the heat and simmer until the pork is tender, about 1 hour.

4. To assemble, spread about ⅓ cup of the pork stew in the middle of a tortilla. Top with the Orange-Onion Salsa and shredded lettuce. Fold and serve.

CHILI VERDE

hili Verde is a classic Southwestern stew of pork and green chili peppers. The dish calls for Anaheim chilies, mildly spicy and smoky when roasted. The widespread modern version of Chili Verde, and our basic recipe here, utilizes canned Anaheim chilies, labeled "whole green chilies," that can be found in almost any grocery store. For a special treat, though, take the trouble to roast and peel fresh Anaheim chilies. Use 1½ pounds and follow the procedure for roasting red peppers (page 57, step 2).

Serves 4 to 6
Takes 3½ hours

3 pounds boneless pork butt or 4½ pounds bone-in
1 tablespoon peanut oil
1 large onion, cut into ¼-inch dice
6 garlic cloves, coarsely chopped
2 jalapeño chili peppers, stemmed and coarsely chopped
1 tablespoon fresh oregano leaves or 1 teaspoon dried
Salt and freshly ground black pepper
2 cans (4 ounces each) peeled whole green chilies, drained
1½ cups light beef or pork stock
18 corn or 12 flour tortillas, warmed or crisped just before
*   serving*

TOPPINGS
Dressed Cilantro (page 76)
2 cups chopped tomatoes

1. Cut the pork into ½-inch cubes or strips, trimming off any excess fat as you go. If using bone-in pork, reserve the bone.

2. Heat the oil in a large frying pan set over medium heat. Add the onion, garlic, chili peppers, oregano, and ¾ teaspoon salt. Cook until the onion is wilted, about 5 minutes. Remove the mixture to a large stew pot.

3. In the same pan, add as much pork as will fit in one layer. Sprinkle lightly with salt and pepper and cook over medium-high heat until lightly browned, about 5 minutes. Remove the pork and add it to the pot. Continue with another round until all of the pork is browned.

4. While the pork is browning, cut the canned chilies into ¼-inch-wide strips. Add the chilies to the pot, along with the stock, reserved pork bone if you have one, and 1½ quarts water. Bring to a boil. Reduce the heat to the barest simmer, and partially cover the pot. Cook, stirring occasionally, for 2½ hours, or until the pork shreds easily when pressed with a wooden spoon.

5. To assemble, spread about ⅓ cup of the chili verde in the center of a tortilla. Top with Dressed Cilantro and chopped tomatoes. Fold and serve.

TIP

▶ As a sinful addition to this taco, you can turn the pork fat you trim off the meat into a crackling topping. Mince the fat, place on a baking sheet, and bake in a 350°F oven for 2 hours while the chili stews. Pour off the rendered fat. Sprinkle the cracklings over the top of the taco.

▲▲▲▲▲▲▲▲▲▲▲▲▲▲

Diminutive Lisa, who is not at all diminutive when organizing and directing the movements of a film crew, is the "queen" of chili verde in our circle. How she has time to ferret out dishes while working the nonstop schedules the movies demand, we don't know. But, when shooting a film in Japan, she became expert at Japanese cooking. After visiting China, her meals from a wok became a wonderment. This time she'd been on location in Chama, New Mexico, for many months when we arrived at her house. The stories she tells after a cinema excursion are always worth a long afternoon. She regaled us for several hours with tales of action and reconnoitering on the set, then disappeared into the kitchen. She returned bearing a steaming pot and a basket of hot tortillas, "But the best story I have," she said, "is this," and proceeded to serve us New Mexico Chili Verde. It was perfection and we offer her recipe here.

CARNITAS

E very Saturday throughout Mexico, people wait in line for the long-cooked pork "little meats" to appear in stores and stands. These hungry shoppers buy *carnitas* wrapped in a tortilla, spice them with a salsa, and off they go to finish the marketing. Along with ground beef, pork *carnitas* is the quintessential tortilla filling and favorite snack throughout Mexico. There's no escaping that the dish takes a long time to cook—worth every minute of the wait. But there is an escape from the traditional method of stewing the pork in lard. In a bow to modern guidelines for lower cholesterol, we simmer the pork in wine and water. The results don't lack an iota of flavor. In fact, we think the dish is better this way.

Serves 4 to 6
Takes 3½ hours

3 pounds boneless pork butt or 4½ pounds bone-in
4 garlic cloves
2 teaspoons fresh oregano leaves or ½ teaspoon dried
1 bay leaf
⅓ cup dry white wine
1 teaspoon freshly ground black pepper
¾ teaspoon salt
18 corn or 12 flour tortillas, warmed or crisped just before
*   serving*

TOPPINGS
Well-Filled Guacamole (page 69)
2 cups chopped tomatoes
2 cups sour cream

   1. Cut the pork butt into ½-inch cubes or strips. If using bone-in pork, reserve the bone. Place the meat and bone, if you have it, in a large heavy pot, along with the garlic, oregano, bay leaf, wine, pepper, and salt. Bring to a boil over medium heat. Stir to mix the ingredients. Partially cover and cook at a bare simmer for 2 hours.

2. Remove the cover and add ½ cup water. Increase the heat to medium-high and continue cooking, stirring every 10 minutes or so, until the pork is very soft and shreds easily when prodded, about 1 hour. (If the pork begins to stick to the bottom of the pan during the last part of cooking, reduce the heat to prevent burning.)

3. Remove and discard the bay leaf. Stir gently with a fork to break up and shred the meat.

4. To assemble, spread about ⅓ cup carnitas in the center of a tortilla. Top with Well-Filled Guacamole, chopped tomatoes, and sour cream. Fold and serve.

TIP

▶ Cubing boneless pork is easier than carving one's way around a bone-in pork butt, but adding the bone to the pot lends a definite depth of flavor to any stew. We recommend using bone-in cuts, dropping the bone into the stew pot, and fishing it out when the dish is done.

PORK AND HOMINY

Hominy is a big husky corn of the flint or dent variety. There are five types of corn, all of which were established crops in America long before Europeans arrived. "Pop" and "flint" have hard outer shells. "Dent" is most hard, with a soft waxy depression in the middle. "Flour" corn is what native Americans mainly used, while "sweet" corn—of many hues and sizes—is the corn we generally eat today, on or off the cob. Hominy is the corn used for

---

MENU

▼

HOMAGE TO CORN

Fiesta Salsa with Hominy Tortillas

Pork and Hominy Tacos with Pickled Corn Topping

Brazilian-Style Fish Tacos

Mock Tamale Tacos

Sweet Hominy Chimichangas with Two Fruit Purées

grits, and along with other flint and dent corns is what is ground for cornmeal, *masa,* and polenta. The taste of hominy, slaky and mineral-like, differs from that of sweet corn. It's a treat to eat hominy soft and whole, and the way to taste it at its best is by eating *posole,* pork and hominy stew. When serving this stew as a taco, corn tortillas are a must.

Serves 4 to 6
Takes 3 hours

3 pounds boneless pork butt or 4½ pounds bone-in
2 teaspoons peanut oil
1 pig's foot, quartered (optional)
1 medium onion, coarsely chopped
3 large garlic cloves, chopped
1½ cups canned Italian plum tomatoes, chopped, with juices
    reserved
1 tablespoon chopped fresh oregano leaves or 1 teaspoon
    dried
½ teaspoon salt
1 can (29 ounces) hominy, drained
18 corn tortillas, warmed or crisped just before serving

TOPPINGS
Ancho Chili Sauce (page 59)
2 cups chopped avocados
¼ cup chopped fresh oregano leaves or 2 tablespoons dried
2 limes, cut into 10 wedges each

   1. Cut the pork butt into ½-inch cubes or strips, trimming off any excess fat as you go. If using bone-in pork, reserve the bone.

   2. Heat the oil in a large stew pot set over medium-high heat. Add as many pieces of pork as will fit in one uncrowded layer and cook until browned on all sides, about 5 minutes. Remove and continue cooking another round until all the pork is browned.

   3. Return the pork to the pot, along with the pig's foot, onion, garlic, tomatoes and their juices, oregano, salt, pork bone, and

I n El Paso, Texas, summer is the season when the toads come out. They cover roadways, tile walkways, make barge brigades across swimming pools, crawl into air conditioners, hop over thresholds, and by and large make navigation around homes and shops impossible. It doesn't matter. It gives everyone a good excuse to throw up their hands, relax and eat *posole.* You can get *posole* and pork in soups or stews. Sometimes chicken is added, sometimes pumpkin seeds. One cafe uses tomatillos, another sprinkles the dish with bacon. A squirt of lime is always added. The same dish, thicker, makes a great taco filling— a lot better than eating hominy as corn nuts. We've transported the famous El Paso dish for a tortilla filling, but not the famous El Paso toads!

3 quarts water. Bring to a boil. Reduce the heat and simmer until the pork shreds easily with a spoon, about 2 hours.

4. Stir in the hominy and simmer for 15 minutes more. Remove the pig's foot and any bones. Cut the pig's foot into ½-inch wide strips, discarding the bones. Return the meat to the pot.

5. To assemble, spread about ⅓ cup of the pork and hominy stew in the middle of a tortilla. Top with Ancho Chili Sauce, chopped avocado, oregano, and a squeeze of lime. Fold and serve.

TIP

▶ A pig's foot adds immeasurably to the depth of flavor in this dish, and we recommend searching one out.

To make a Sunday dinner of Pink Ham and Red Banana tacos an unusual and standout affair, we suggest adding squash blossoms to the filled tortilla, if the season is right. Available throughout most of the summer in specialty markets, the blossoms are, suprisingly, both delicate and crunchy. Sauté them lightly, then sprinkle them with a pinch of salt. Better still, bread the blossoms as we do with our Breaded Chili Strips (see Index), and fry them very quickly in hot oil.

PINK HAM AND RED BANANAS

Sunday dinner used to feature a huge ham studded with cloves, circled with pineapple, dotted with maraschino cherries, and as if that didn't make it sweet enough, it was glazed with brown sugar or honey. Along with it, to soften and absorb, were biscuits. Families are smaller now, so a whole ham seems a mighty big project. When we crave the taste of ham, the answer is a ham steak. Ham steak is quick to cook and goes well with fruit. One we prefer is red banana. Not as cloying as pineapple, red bananas take the salty edge off the ham. If you can't find red bananas, use plantains or unripe yellow bananas.

Serves 4 to 6
Takes 20 minutes or less

Vegetable oil
2 pounds ham steak or slices, cut ¼- to ½-inch-thick
2 tablespoons balsamic or red wine vinegar
6 red bananas, peeled, and cut into ¼-inch dice
18 corn or 12 flour tortillas, warmed or crisped just before
*   serving*

TOPPINGS
Salsa Verde (page 52)
Dressed Cilantro (page 76)
2 cups sour cream (optional)

1. Coat a heavy frying pan with the oil and set over medium-high heat until the oil begins to smoke. Add as many ham steaks as will fit in one uncrowded layer. Fry, turning once, until browned on both sides and warmed through, 5 to 10 minutes, depending on the thickness.

2. Just before the ham steaks are done, add the vinegar. Turn to coat both sides of the meat. Cook until the liquid evaporates, about 1 minute. Remove to a platter.

3. When cool enough to handle, cut the ham into thin ½-inch-long strips.

4. To assemble, spread about ⅓ cup of ham in the middle of a tortilla. Arrange about ⅓ cup of the bananas over the ham. Top with Salsa Verde, Dressed Cilantro, and sour cream. Fold and serve.

VARIATIONS

▼

FOR THE TOPPINGS
Plump out the taco with cheese, especially Jack or white Cheddar. Add Breaded Chili Strips or substitute Basic Fried Potatoes for the bananas (see Index for recipe page numbers).

FOR THE SALSA
Instead of Salsa Verde use: Tomato, Pumpkin Seed, and Scallion Salsa, or double the fruit flavors with Orange-Onion Salsa, Mango-Jalapeño Salsa, or Pasilla, Mint, and Pickled Red Onion Sauce (see Index for page numbers).

LAMB AND GOAT

Sheep and goats are the flocks of mountain and desert herders ranging from Asia to Africa, to the western areas of North America, and down the *cordillera* of South America.

Domestic sheep appear early in human history, showing up well before settled villages emerged in Mesopotamia between the Tigris and Euphrates rivers. Interestingly, the bones found indicate that the majority of animals eaten were lambs, not sheep. It seems our forefathers had already taken a fancy to the young milk-fed meat over the more gamy older animals.

Another common meat throughout much of the globe is tender goat. Indeed, goat is often preferred. In *birria*, a traditional dish throughout Central and South America, goat is stewed with spices, and the sweetest of young goats are the Easter meals of numerous nations.

The many people who husband lambs and goats tend to roam far from home minding their animals. Much as our contemporary families, they eat at different times, grab a bit from a pot and something to wrap the food in. In woven satchels, leather pouches, and brown bags, they carry a piece of juicy meat wrapped in a slice of bread, a flat cracker, a tortilla. Here we follow their example and offer fillings of succulent lamb and goat.

ZESTY GROUND LAMB

What ground beef is to America and ground pork is to the French and Italians, ground lamb is to the Lebanese, Armenians, Iraqis, Persians, on into India and beyond. In these exotic nations, ground lamb is molded and woven into countless taco-esque sorts of compositions. People spread it on cracker bread, stuff it in dough, pack it in cabbage leaves, and use it to make kebabs. In a tortilla, rich ground lamb satisfies and gratifies.

Serves 4 to 6
Takes 20 to 40 minutes

2 tablespoons olive or peanut oil
2 medium onions, finely chopped
4 medium garlic cloves, pressed or minced
2 pounds ground lamb
2 large russet potatoes, cut into ¼-inch dice
2 medium tomatoes, coarsely chopped
¾ teaspoon ground allspice
⅛ to ¼ teaspoon cayenne, depending on taste
¾ teaspoon chopped fresh rosemary leaves or ¼ teaspoon
    dried
¾ teaspoon salt
1½ cups dry red wine
18 corn or 12 flour tortillas, warmed or crisped just before
    serving

TOPPINGS
Fresh Tomato Salsa (page 37)
2 cups sour cream

1. Heat the oil in a large heavy frying pan over medium heat. Add the onions and garlic and cook until the onions are wilted,

"Let's get out of town," said Victoria, on a particularly green and sunny March day. "We need a rest. Let's drive to Hearst's Castle." And so we set off in Susanna's sports car. The grass on the treeless fields by the sea at San Simeon had sprouted fresh and verdant. Baby lambs roamed with their moms over the rolling turf. We went on every tour the castle offered: the main rooms, outer houses, upstairs, new wing, all rococo and della Robbia-ed, tiled, gilded, and burnished. We found charming rooms at a small seaside motel, but eating was a problem, with only massive tourist highway stops, it seemed. Dauntless, we sought out a hidden village and in it found a little inn run by longtime California natives named Ortega. They served us ground lamb tacos, strangely accompanied not by cool Margaritas, but a local semisweet Semillon. We still serve ground lamb tacos with a crisp, not too dry, California white wine.

VARIATIONS
▼

As with all our basic ground meat tacos, you can glorify basic ground lamb tacos with myriad elements:

FOR THE TOPPINGS
Breaded Chili Strips, Dressed Cilantro, shredded cheese, shredded lettuce, Toasted Pumpkin Seeds. Or, top off Zesty Ground Lamb with toasted walnuts, browned as in the Toasted Pumpkin Seed recipe. Walnuts are one of lamb's most eloquent accompaniments. The variation of ground lamb tacos that follows calls for walnuts as part of the filling.

FOR THE SALSA
Chive Salsa, Tomato, Pumpkin Seed, and Scallion Salsa, Two Red Hot Chili-Garlic Salsas (either the fresh or the dried version (see Index for recipe page numbers).

about 5 minutes. Add the lamb, potatoes, tomatoes, allspice, cayenne, rosemary, and salt. Cook, stirring occasionally to break up any chunks, until the meat is browned, about 10 minutes. Add the wine and cook until the liquid evaporates, about 10 minutes.

2. To assemble, spread about ⅓ cup of the lamb filling in the center of a tortilla. Top with the Fresh Tomato Salsa and sour cream. Fold and serve.

TIP

▶ Ground lamb tends to be rather oily and to produce quite a quantity of rendered fat while frying. You can cut down on this problem by using very lean lamb, preferably from a butcher. Otherwise, sauté the lamb separately, drain off the fat, and add it to the other ingredients right before adding the wine.

GROUND LAMB, EGGPLANT, AND WALNUTS

Southern Europeans have always known exactly what to do with eggplant. They mix it with lamb, tomato, oil, wine. Northern Europeans have never been so assured in their eggplant dealings. One of the best of their efforts is to serve it with a walnut sauce. The recipe below blends the two worlds into a convivial middle European taco.

Serves 4 to 6
Takes 30 minutes

2 tablespoons olive or peanut oil
1 eggplant (about ¾ pound), cut into ¼-inch dice
½ cup walnuts, coarsely chopped
1 medium onion, finely chopped
2 garlic cloves, pressed or minced
2 fresh chili peppers, stemmed and finely chopped
2 pounds ground lamb
1 tablespoon tomato paste
1 cup dry red wine
¾ teaspoon salt
18 corn or 12 flour tortillas, warmed or crisped just before
    serving

TOPPINGS
Red Bell Pepper-Tomatillo Salsa (page 41)
4 cups shredded lettuce
2 cups crumbled feta cheese

1. Heat the oil in a large, heavy frying pan set over medium heat. Add the eggplant, walnuts, onion, garlic, and chili peppers. Cook until the eggplant and onion are wilted, about 5 minutes. Add the lamb. Cook, stirring occasionally to break up any chunks, until the meat is browned, about 10 minutes. Stir in the tomato paste, wine, and salt; blend well. Continue cooking until most of the liquid evaporates, about 10 minutes more.

2. To assemble, spread about ⅓ cup of the lamb filling in the center of a tortilla. Top with Red Bell Pepper-Tomatillo Sauce, shredded lettuce, and crumbled feta cheese. Fold and serve.

MENU
▼

*SUBLIME SUPPER FOR
SIX FOOD LOVERS*

———

*Pasilla, Mint, and Pickled
Red Onion Sauce*

*Roasted Garlic, Tomato,
and Anchovy Sauce*

Hominy Tortillas

———

*Mini Shrimp Tostadas
with Sweet Potatoes*

*Ground Lamb, Eggplant,
and Walnut Tacos*

———

*Fried Pineapple and
Orange Tacos with Grated
Chocolate*

———

*Coffee with grated
Mexican chocolate*

GROUND LAMB AND DRIED APRICOTS

▲▲▲▲▲▲▲▲▲▲▲▲▲

The Hunza people, who live just beyond the Hindu Kush in the Karakoram mountain range above Jammu and Kashmir, are reputed to live to the ripest old ages in the human race. One hundred and twenty years is not an uncommon life span, and many souls reach 130 or more. Why? No one knows for sure, but their unique diet may be the reason. They eat apricots daily, fresh and dried, skin to kernel, from birth to demise. Since they are a mountain dwelling people whose terrain favors the occupation of herding over farming, what little meat they eat is usually lamb. Apricot most surely makes a fine companion to lamb and we, the less long-lived, recommend the duo. In the Hunza tradition, this filling is fine for a lettuce leaf in place of the tortilla. We also suggest this same recipe for goat.

▼▼▼▼▼▼▼▼▼▼▼▼▼

We like to serve these well-filled tortillas chimichanga style. The final crisping softens the cabbage and provides a desirable crunch.

Serves 4 to 6
Takes 20 to 40 minutes

2 tablespoons olive or peanut oil
1 medium onion, finely chopped
4 garlic cloves, pressed or minced
1⅓ cups dried apricots, finely chopped
2 pounds ground lamb
¼ teaspoon cardamom seeds
½ teaspoon ground cumin
¾ teaspoon salt
1 cup dry white wine
12 flour tortillas

TOPPINGS
Avocado-Pumpkin Seed Salsa (page 44)
2 cups sour cream
4 cups shredded Napa cabbage, sprouts, or lettuce
   (preferably romaine)

Vegetable oil

1. Heat the olive oil in a large, heavy frying pan over medium heat. Add the onion, garlic, and apricots. Cook over medium heat until the onion is wilted, about 5 minutes. Add the lamb, cardamom, cumin, and salt. Brown, stirring occasionally to break up any chunks of meat, about 10 minutes. Stir in the wine and cook until most of the liquid evaporates, 10 minutes more.

2. To assemble, spread about ⅓ cup of the lamb filling in the center of a flour tortilla. Top with Avocado-Pumpkin Seed Salsa, sour cream, and cabbage, sprouts, or lettuce. Fold chimichanga style and continue until all of the chimichangas are assembled.

3. Pour enough vegetable oil into a large frying pan to coat the bottom. Set over high heat. A few at a time, place the folded tortillas in the pan and fry until browned, about 30 seconds per side. Serve hot.

LAMB SHANKS WITH TOMATOES, CORN, AND ANCHOVIES

Serves 4 to 6
Takes 2 hours

1 tablespoon olive or peanut oil
4 lamb shanks (9 to 10 pounds)
Salt and freshly ground black pepper, to taste
8 medium tomatoes, coarsely chopped
2 whole heads of garlic, cloves separated and peeled
6 anchovy fillets, coarsely chopped
1 tablespoon fresh thyme leaves or 1 teaspoon dried
3 cups dry white wine
2 cups fresh corn kernels (about 2 medium ears)
18 corn or 12 flour tortillas, crisped just before serving

TOPPINGS
1 cup chopped fresh jalapeño chili peppers
4 cups shredded lettuce
2 cups sour cream

▲▲▲▲▲▲▲▲▲▲▲▲▲▲▲

Every now and then amid the hills and alkaline flats of Nevada you spot a cone-shaped hut or tent, a spitted campfire, and often a shaggy tethered pony. These are the campsites of Basque sheep herders. Natives of the European continent long before invasions of Celts came roaring down from the far-off steppes of western Russia, the Basques took to the hills of the Pyrenees in the face of incursion. To this day Basques speak a non-Indo-European language related to no other. In the great mountains between Spain and France they keep their own culture, customs, dances, and lingo. And they herd sheep. At the turn of this century, Basque shepherds were encouraged to immigrate in order to tend the flocks of the similarly mountainous western United States.

In San Francisco numerous Basque restaurants still survive, where a series of hearty courses centering around a single entrée of the day are passed down the long "family-style" tables. Of all the fare, lamb shanks and bread is the best. Sometimes the lamb is stewed with peppers, sometimes with tomato or anchovies. The Basques scoop the savory meat onto sourdough bread and chow down. We suggest the same with crisp tortillas.

1. Divide the oil between 2 large nonreactive stew pots and set over medium-high heat until the oil begins to smoke. (Or see *Tip* below.) Place the lamb shanks in the pots and brown on all sides, sprinkling with salt and pepper as you go. Add the tomatoes, garlic cloves, anchovies, thyme, and wine. Bring to a boil. Reduce the heat to a simmer, cover the pots, and cook until the meat is falling away from the bones, about 1½ hours. Stir in the corn and remove the stew from the heat immediately.

2. Using a slotted spoon, lift the lamb, tomatoes, garlic, and corn out of the stewing liquid, or drain off the liquid into a bowl.

3. When cool enough to handle, pull the lamb meat from the bones and shred the meat. Combine the shredded meat with the tomatoes, garlic, and corn. Skim the fat off the stewing liquid.

4. To assemble, spread about ⅓ cup of the lamb and vegetables in the center of a tortilla. Moisten with a little of the skimmed broth. Top with chopped jalapeños, shredded lettuce, and sour cream. Fold and serve.

TIPS

▶ Since the lamb shanks are bulky, and they need to stew a long time, you need two pots to cook a whole recipe's worth. If 2 large stew pots are not part of your kitchen battery, you can brown the meat on the stovetop and transfer it to a large baking dish to cook, covered, in a 350°F oven. The timing is the same. Because of the tomato and wine, any pot or baking dish you use should be nonreactive to avoid a bitter, metallic taste.

▶ You can stew the lamb shanks up to 2 days in advance. Refrigerate the dish without removing the meat from the bones. Gently reheat, then proceed with the recipe. The corn is best if added when you reheat.

GARLIC-ROASTED LAMB SHANKS

We usually think of stewing a lamb shank, as in *osso buco*. But you can also treat the shank like a mini leg of lamb. It roasts to perfection and produces the same kind of full-flavored morsels that dark meat lovers insist on. As with any roast, plenty of garlic is never out of order.

Serves 4 to 6
Takes 2½ hours

4 lamb shanks (9 to 10 pounds)
24 garlic cloves, cut into slivers
Salt and freshly ground black pepper, to taste
2 large red bell peppers
2 cups cooked chick-peas
1½ tablespoons fresh lime juice
1½ tablespoons olive oil
¼ teaspoon salt
18 corn or 12 flour tortillas, warmed or crisped just before
    serving

TOPPINGS
South American Jalapeño-Parsley Salsa (page 46)
2 cups sour cream

1. Heat the oven to 475°F.

2. With your fingers, push the garlic slivers into the natural openings in the lamb shanks and sprinkle liberally with salt and pepper. Arrange the lamb shanks and bell peppers in a single layer in 1 or 2 roasting pans. Roast for 10 minutes. Reduce the oven heat to 350°F and roast until the peppers are soft and the skins are wrinkled, about 1 hour more. Remove the peppers and continue roasting the shanks until the meat is well browned and pulling away from the bones, about 50 minutes more. Remove

MENU
▼

IN HONOR OF
THE CRESCENT
MOON—
A NEAR EAST
TACO FESTIVAL

———

Greek Salsa and Tortilla
Chips

———

Sesame Chicken Fajitas
with Orange-Onion Salsa

Garlic-Roasted Lamb
Shanks in a Taco with
Dried Red Hot Chili-Garlic
Salsa

Sweet Ricotta and
Candied Fruit Flautas

VARIATION
▼

■ You can sauté the red peppers instead of roasting them. Remove the stems and seeds and cut the peppers into ½-inch-wide strips. Sauté the pepper strips in ⅛ inch of olive oil or peanut oil until quite wilted and cooked through, 15 to 20 minutes.

and let cool enough to handle.

3. When the peppers are cool, use your fingers and a paring knife to peel off the skins. Remove the stems and seeds; cut the peppers into thin strips. Set aside.

4. When the lamb shanks are cool enough to handle, remove the bones and shred the meat.

5. In a bowl, toss the chick-peas with the lime juice, oil, and ¼ teaspoon salt.

6. To assemble, spread about ⅓ cup of the lamb in the center of a tortilla. Top with bell pepper strips, chick-peas, South American Jalapeño-Parsley Salsa, and sour cream. Fold and serve.

LEG OF LAMB AND LIMA BEANS WITH MINT AND LIME

Sweet sliced roast lamb is a longtime, worldwide favorite. Great medieval feasts featured joints of mutton carried out on silver platters. Easter festivals star legs of lamb sizzlingly presented with bowls of shimmering mint jelly. Irish wakes soothe grieving relatives with whiskey and lamb. Yugoslavs make celebrations joyful with a hindquarter of lamb, brandy, and figs. The same sweet slices of roast lamb tuck readily into a tortilla. In a nod to the English tradition, we like our roast lamb tacos perked up with fresh mint leaves.

Serves 4 to 6
Takes 1½ to 2 hours

1 leg of lamb (3½ pounds), at room temperature
3 garlic cloves, cut into slivers
Salt and freshly ground black pepper, to taste
½ cup water
1 package (10 ounces) frozen baby lima beans
1 tablespoon fresh lime juice
1 cup shredded fresh mint leaves
18 corn or 12 flour tortillas, warmed or crisped just before
    serving

TOPPINGS
Fresh Red Hot Chili-Garlic Salsa (page 39)
2 cups sour cream

1. Heat the oven to 475°F.

2. Trim any excess fat off the outside of the lamb leg. Push the garlic slivers into the natural openings in the meat and sprinkle the top and sides with salt and pepper. Set the leg in a roasting pan. Roast for 15 minutes. Reduce the oven heat to 350°F and roast until a meat thermometer registers 140°F in the center, about 1 hour more. Remove the lamb from the oven and set it aside to settle the juices, at least 15 minutes.

3. While the lamb rests, bring the water to a boil in a small saucepan. Add the lima beans and cook until warmed through, about 2 minutes. Drain the limas in a colander. Set aside to cool and drip dry, about 10 minutes. When cool, place in a bowl and toss with the lime juice and ¼ cup of the mint leaves.

4. Carve the lamb into thin strips. Skim the fat off the juices in the roasting pan. Moisten the lamb with the skimmed juices.

5. To assemble, place about ⅓ cup of the lamb in the center of a tortilla. Top with lima beans, some of the remaining shredded mint, Fresh Red Hot Chili-Garlic Salsa, and sour cream. Fold and serve.

TIP

▶ Leg of lamb meat is especially tasty at room temperature, when the juices have settled back into the meat, making it tender and succulent. You can cook the leg up to several hours in advance and carve it just before serving.

▲▲▲▲▲▲▲▲▲▲▲▲▲▲▲▲

Victoria's sister, Deborah, and her husband, Jerry, moved from the city to California's gold country in order to bottle the fabulous spring water there, which they fittingly call Aquad'or. Since their holding extends over several acres and many vintners and fine barbecuers reside nearby, they decided to purchase and raise a few goats and sheep. By early spring they also had a little lamb. No example of the tender and vulnerable, this "poor little lamb" was a hellion. He took enormous delight in trampling the water lines and splashing in the Aquad'or. He broke into the house and rampaged through the children's bedroom. He chased the Springer spaniel until the sorry dog broke down and trembled. We dreamed of him ground into taco filling, sliced into fajitas, roasted to shred. But did we make tacos of this lamb? Of course not. We couldn't go through with the deed. Instead, on slaughtering day, we bought a leg of lamb at the grocery store and made the roast lamb and lima bean recipe featured here while we toasted his existence. The lamb lives on like the pig in Charlotte's web, chewing hay and poison oak, greeting schoolchildren, sometimes with a chase and sometimes like a docile kitten bleeting for a pat, growing ever more rotund. He has been appropriately renamed Rambo.

BASIC LAMB FAJITAS

Almost everyone loves a good lamb chop, maybe marinated, pan-fried or grilled, sauced with a jelly, chutney, or salsa. A good chop gives the satisfying flavor of
lamb when roasting a whole leg seems too arduous or
produces too much meat. Chops cut from the leg and
boned lend themselves to slicing and turn out tender morsels perfect for a lamb fajita. They are quick-frying, juicy,
and nicely acquiescent to a soak in beer marinade.

Serves 4 to 6
Takes less than 20 minutes plus several hours or
    overnight for marinating

MARINADE
1 small chili pepper, stemmed and minced
2 garlic cloves, pressed or minced
¼ cup cilantro leaves, coarsely chopped
2 teaspoons achiote paste
Small pinch of ground cloves or cinnamon
½ cup amber beer

2½ pounds boneless lamb steaks, cut ¼- to ½-inch thick and
    trimmed of fat
Salt to taste, if grilling, or 1 teaspoon rock salt or gros sel, if
    frying the fajitas
18 corn or 12 flour tortillas, warmed or crisped just before
    serving

TOPPINGS
Roasted Red Pepper, Chili, and Pine Nut Sauce (page 57)
Dressed Cilantro (page 76)
2 limes, cut into 6 to 9 wedges each

1. In a large nonreactive dish, mix together the chili pepper,
garlic, cilantro, achiote, cloves, and beer. Place the lamb in the
marinade and turn each piece to coat all sides. Cover and refrig-

erate for several hours, or overnight, turning once or twice.

2. *If grilling,* prepare a charcoal fire and allow the coals to burn until they are mostly covered with white ash but a few red spots show through here and there. This will take about 40 minutes. When the fire is ready, remove the lamb from the marinade. Salt the meat on both sides. Place on the grill rack directly over the coals. Grill for 3 to 5 minutes per side, depending on the thickness of the lamb and how well done you want the meat. Remove to a platter and set aside for the juices to settle, 5 to 10 minutes.

If frying, spread the rock salt over the bottom of a large heavy frying pan and set over medium-high heat until the skillet begins to smoke. Add as much lamb as will fit in one uncrowded layer. Cook for 3 to 5 minutes per side. Remove and continue with another round until all the lamb is cooked.

3. Cut the lamb fajitas crosswise into thin strips.

4. To assemble, spread about ⅓ cup of meat in the center of a tortilla. Top with Roasted Red Pepper, Chili, and Pine Nut Sauce, Dressed Cilantro, and lime juice. Fold and serve.

GREEK-STYLE LAMB FAJITAS WITH TZATZIKI SAUCE

A traditional Greek yogurt and garlic sauce, called *tzatziki*, makes for a special variation of lamb fajitas.

Serves 4 to 6
Takes 20 to 40 minutes plus several hours or overnight
   for marinating

▲▲▲▲▲▲▲▲▲▲▲▲▲▲▲

As a tourist, fresh and confused, you enter the hustle and bustle of Athens. Sooner or later you walk down Hermou Street past the two sunken Byzantine churches, or along Athiniou by the cheap clothing shops, tool booths, and worry-bead vendors, or down the hill from the Plaka past Pandrosos Street's jumble of tourist goods, toward the odors of Monesteraki Square. The smells draw you to round the corner, and there they are, the *souvlaki* stands. One after another vertical spits packed with ground lamb, maybe some other meats, spices, and herbs, rotate in their upright grills. Each plier of the *souvlaki*, also called *gyros* in America, forms his meat according to his own secret recipe. Each also has his own version of tzatziki, some with more cucumber, others less, some salty, some peppery, some runny, some thick. Some of the vendors heat their pita breads, others fry them. They all slice down the outer cooked edge of the meat, letting it fall into a special scoop. They dab on the sauce, throw on the toppings, swaddle the ingredients in the bread, and twist the whole shebang in transparent paper. Plato's school and the site where Socrates drank his last tea lie but steps away. You wander through the street into the ancient agora wondering if the same compelling aromas wafted through the streets in bygone days. Our Greek-Style Lamb Fajitas with its Tzatziki Sauce evokes the spinning *souvlaki* and the reverie.

▼▼▼▼▼▼▼▼▼▼▼▼▼▼▼

2½ *pounds boneless lamb steaks, cut ¼- to ½-inch thick and trimmed of fat*
Marinade from Basic Lamb Fajitas, page 132
18 *corn or 12 flour tortillas, crisped just before serving*

TOPPINGS
Tzatziki Sauce (recipe follows)
2 *bunches spinach, well washed, stems removed, leaves thinly shredded (5 cups)*
1 *large red onion, finely chopped*
2 *cups chopped tomatoes*

1. Follow the recipe for the Basic Lamb Fajitas through step 2.

2. Cut the cooked lamb fajitas crosswise into thin strips.

3. To assemble, spread about ⅓ cup of the meat in the middle of a tortilla. Top with Tzatziki Sauce, shredded spinach, chopped onion, and chopped tomato. Fold and serve.

TZATZIKI SAUCE

Makes 2 cups
Takes 10 minutes

1 *small cucumber*
1½ *cups plain yogurt*
2 *garlic cloves, pressed or minced*
1½ *tablespoons red wine vinegar*
½ *teaspoon salt*
¼ *teaspoon freshly ground black pepper*

1. Peel the cucumber. Shred through the large holes of a hand grater.

2. In a bowl, whisk the yogurt until smooth. Add the cucumber, garlic, vinegar, salt, and pepper. Stir to blend. Serve right away, or cover, refrigerate, and use within 1 day.

LAMB FAJITAS WITH LIME, TEQUILA, AND SOUR CREAM SAUCE

An unusually hot April day and the first grilling of the year prompted us to create a cooling sauce for spring lamb fajitas. The fajitas were devoured by the end of the day, but we found our families utilizing the tangy sauce on this and that throughout the week. We've added it to our list of sauces to have on hand.

Serves 4 to 6
Takes 20 to 40 minutes plus several hours or
overnight for marinating

2½ pounds boneless lamb steaks, cut ¼- to ½-inch thick and
trimmed of fat
Marinade from Basic Lamb Fajitas, page 132
18 corn or 12 flour tortillas, warmed or crisped just before
serving

TOPPINGS
2 bunches watercress, large stems removed
½ cup toasted slivered almonds (see Box)
1½ cups black pitted olives, preferably Calamata, pitted and
coarsely chopped
Lime, Tequila, and Sour Cream Sauce (recipe follows)

1. Follow the recipe for Basic Lamb Fajitas through step 2.

2. Cut the lamb fajitas crosswise into thin strips.

3. To assemble, spread about ⅓ cup of the meat in the center of a tortilla. Top with the watercress, almonds, a light sprinkling of black olives, and the Lime, Tequila, and Sour Cream Sauce. Fold and serve.

TOASTING ALMONDS OR PINE NUTS

To toast ½ cup of slivered almonds or whole pine nuts, place 1 tablespoon vegetable oil in a frying pan over medium heat. Add the nuts and stir until lightly browned, 2 to 3 minutes.

LIME, TEQUILA, AND SOUR CREAM SAUCE

Makes 2 cups
Takes about 5 minutes

2 cups sour cream
1 tablespoon tequila, preferably gold
2 tablespoons fresh lime juice

Combine the sour cream, tequila, and lime juice in a small non-reactive saucepan. Set over medium heat and whisk until just boiling. Simmer for 1 minute to burn off the alcohol and thicken the sauce. Remove and use right away, or cover and refrigerate for up to 3 days. Reheat over low heat before serving.

MENU

▼

EVENING ELEGANCE

Quesadillas with Goat Cheese and Deviled Walnuts

Lamb Fajitas with Lime, Tequila, and Sour Cream Sauce
or
Brazilian-Style Fish Tacos with Salsa Verde, Corn, and Black Olive Sauce

Avocado and Grapefruit Salad with Lime Jalapeño Vinaigrette

La Bamba Flautas

GOAT WITH LEEK, FETA, AND SOUR CREAM SALSA

O n spits, in pits, in pans, goat is roasted in court-yards, town squares, and by roadside taverns from nation to island. Here we suggest goat roasted Italian style with rosemary and lemon. We add a touch of spice to complement the taco filling for which the goat is intended. One hour in the marinade suffices to lend the goat meat its flavor, but all-day marinating imparts even more savor.

Serves 4 to 6
Takes 2½ hours

2 tablespoons fresh lemon juice
1 tablespoon pure chili powder
⅓ cup olive oil
1½ teaspoons fresh rosemary leaves or ½ teaspoon dried
1½ teaspoons salt
1 hindquarter (leg and loin section) from a young goat (about 4 pounds)
18 corn or 12 flour tortillas, warmed or crisped just before serving

TOPPINGS
Leek, Feta, and Sour Cream Salsa (page 48)
Toasted Pumpkin Seeds (page 75)
4 cups shredded lettuce

1. In a nonreactive roasting pan large enough to hold the goat hindquarter, mix together the lemon juice, oil, chili powder, rosemary, and salt. Place the goat in the mixture and turn to coat all around. Let marinate at room temperature for at least 1 hour or up to all day.

I t's easier to get kid goat than you think. Around Easter time you can find it under the name *cabrito* at Latin American butchers, *capretto* at Italian butchers, and *katsikia* at Greek butchers, and many butchers freeze a good supply for people who crave the delicious meat at other times of the year. Our favorite suppliers are R. Izacopi in San Francisco's Italian North Beach section or butchers in the Spanish Mission district. The young goat offers delectable meat— sweet, tender, and not at all gamy. The adult, though stronger in flavor than the kid, is still less pungent than mutton. We recommend using the hindquarter for creating an abundant tortilla filling. If you like goat as much as we do, you can substitute goat for the lamb in any of the lamb filling recipes, and vice versa.

2. Heat the oven to 475°F.

3. Place the goat and marinade in the oven and roast for 15 minutes. Reduce the heat to 350°F and roast until an instant reading thermometer registers 135° to 140°F in the thick part of the leg, 45 to 55 minutes more. Remove the roast and set it aside to settle the juices, at least 15 minutes.

4. Carve the goat meat off the bones and cut the meat into shreds. Moisten the meat with the juices from the roasting pan.

5. To assemble, place about ⅓ cup of the meat in the center of a tortilla. Top with Leek, Feta, and Sour Cream Salsa, Toasted Pumpkin Seeds, and shredded lettuce. Fold and serve.

MENU

▼

*CINCO DE MAYO
PARTY*

———

*Goat Steeped in
Cider Vinegar
and White Wine Tacos*

*Tacos de Carnitas with
Basic Black Bean
Topping*

*Fried Tomatillo, Onion,
and Cream Tacos*

———

*Gala Nachos with Mango-
Tequila Sauce*

GOAT STEEPED IN CIDER VINEGAR AND WHITE WINE

Whether roasting, stewing, or braising constitutes the best culinary treatment for goat is a matter of monumental discussion. For an undeniably successful stovetop goat, we offer here a spicy, braised rendition, reminiscent of long-stewed Central American goat dishes, that will fill your house with pungently luring aromas. Mind you, roasting and braising goat are interchangeable enough that the goat in this recipe can be marinated in the stewing liquid together with the same spices, then roasted.

Serves 4 to 6
Takes 1½ hours

1 hindquarter (leg and loin section) from a
    young goat (about 4 pounds)
2 tablespoons achiote paste
½ teaspoon ground cinnamon
½ cup olive oil
¾ cup cider vinegar
2¼ cups dry white wine
12 garlic cloves, pressed or minced
2 tablespoons fresh oregano leaves or
    2 teaspoons dried
1 teaspoon salt
18 corn or 12 flour tortillas, warmed
    just before serving

TOPPINGS
South American Jalapeño-Parsley
    Salsa (page 46)
2 cups sour cream

1. Cut the goat hindquarter in half at the joint between the top of the leg and bottom of the loin section so the pieces will fit in a large roasting pan. Rub the goat meat all over with the achiote paste and cinnamon.

2. Heat the oven to 400°F, if you are roasting the goat.

3. Heat the oil in a large nonreactive roasting pan set over medium-high heat. Add the goat pieces and brown on both sides, about 10 minutes. Remove the goat and set aside. Add the vinegar and white wine to the pan and bring to a boil, stirring to loosen any bits that are stuck to the bottom. Return the goat to the pan and add the garlic, oregano, and salt. Cover and simmer on top of the stove or in the oven until the meat easily shreds, 45 to 55 minutes. Remove from the heat and set aside until cool enough to handle.

4. Carve the goat meat off the bones and cut the meat into shreds. Moisten the meat with the stewing juices.

5. To assemble, spread about ⅓ cup of the meat in the center of a tortilla. Top with South American Jalapeño-Parsley Salsa and sour cream. Fold and serve.

S usanna lived for four years in a Greek village while she did anthropology field work. There goats numbered as many as people, and she grew to dislike the beasts for: eating her flowers; dropping their droppings on her roof which she had to keep swept because it was a runoff for her cistern; and their milk, which she couldn't stand to drink and couldn't stand to waste. Then again, she grew to love the goats for: their milk which she turned into the most sublime caramel custard; their perching on pinnacles in the most comical manner; and their flesh provided the most ambrosial of Easter morning dinners. With no wood for ovens in the village, the goat meat was stewed such as we stew it in this taco, and Easter goat dinner was in the morning because everyone spent the entire night from Holy Saturday to Resurrection Sunday in church. The villagers came home at dawn with a blest candle to mark a cross above the household doorway, rekindle all their lamps anew, and eat goat heartily.

CHICKEN

Nearly as soon as they were tamed—strangely late and well after tortillas were waiting for them—chickens were banned from many a city for rousing the populace with their urge to greet the dawn. But it didn't take long for people to realize their culinary worth was worth the wake up.

The reasons are legion. Unlike bigger beasts, chickens take no year or two to reach meal readiness. They hatch by the dozen and are ready to stew in weeks. They are inexpensive to raise, and meanwhile they produce eggs to pay for their meager keep. They aren't limited to season; they can be the bird at Easter or Christmas.

Mostly, though, what's made chickens the world's most prevalent poultry is their fleshy succulence. Chicken meat is soft, tender, moist, and quick cooking. It takes to every ethnic rendering and adapts to any good spicing or saucing. As a filling chicken produces tacos that have no match in versatility, satisfaction, and edibility.

BASIC CHICKEN FAJITAS IN A DIPPED TORTILLA

From the quick-stop counters to elegant lunchrooms, chicken fajitas are popping up everywhere. Serve them basic and unadorned. Better yet, season them, sauce them, bean them, top them.

Serves 4 to 6
Takes less than 20 minutes

2½ pounds skinless, boneless chicken breasts
2 teaspoons pure chili powder
Salt, to taste
2 tablespoons olive oil, if frying
18 corn or 12 flour tortillas, dipped and heated just before
    serving

TOPPINGS
Fresh Tomato Salsa (page 37), Salsa Verde (page 52), Sweet
    and Hot Tomatillo Salsa (page 54), or Red Bell Pepper-
    Tomatillo Salsa (page 41)
4 cups shredded lettuce

1. Place a piece of waxed paper or plastic wrap on a countertop or cutting board. Place one chicken breast on top and cover with another piece of waxed paper or plastic wrap. With a mallet, hammer, or other pounding device, pound the chicken breast ⅛ inch thick. Continue in the same way until all the breasts are flattened. Set aside until ready to cook, or cover and refrigerate for up to 2 days.

2. When ready to cook the fajitas, remove the waxed paper or plastic wrap from the flattened breasts. Sprinkle both sides

FOR THE SEASONINGS
In place of the chili powder, use achiote, oregano, marjoram, sage, or a mixture of paprika and cayenne pepper.

FOR THE TOPPINGS
■ A special way to do chicken fajitas is to sprinkle grated cheese on the chicken breast as it cooks on the second side. This way the cheese melts and coats the meat. Or, you can sprinkle grated cheese over the chicken strips just before serving.
■ Add a few spoonsful of sour cream on top just before serving.

FOR THE SALSAS
■ In addition to the four salsas listed in the recipe, chicken fajitas go well with many of the salsas in this book. In particular, we like: Ancho Chili Sauce; Yucatan Sauce; Avocado-Pumpkin Seed Salsa; Greek Salsa; Leek, Feta, and Sour Cream Salsa; Mango-Jalapeño Salsa; Peanut-Garlic Salsa; Pasilla, Mint, and Pickled Red Onion Sauce; and Tomato, Pumpkin Seed, and Scallion Salsa (see Index for recipe page numbers).

of each breast with the chili powder and salt. Set aside while preparing the grill or frying pan.

3. *If grilling*, prepare a charcoal fire and allow the coals to burn until they are mostly covered with white ash and a few red spots show through here and there. This will take about 40 minutes. When the fire is ready, place the chicken breasts on the grill rack directly above the coals. Cook until no longer pink but still moist in the center, about 1½ minutes on each side.

If frying, divide the oil between 2 large frying pans and set over medium-high heat until the oil begins to smoke. (You can use 1 frying pan to save on dishes and cook the fajitas in several rounds.) Add as many chicken breasts as will fit in one uncrowded layer. Cook until no longer pink but still moist in the center, about 1½ minutes on each side. Remove, and drain off any liquid from the pan. Continue cooking another round until all of the breasts are cooked.

4. Just before serving, dip the tortillas in whatever salsa you are using. Heat in a frying pan or in the oven.

5. Cut the chicken into thin strips.

6. To assemble, place about ⅓ cup of chicken in the middle of a tortilla. Top with salsa and some shredded lettuce. Fold and serve.

TIPS

▶ When you pound the chicken breasts, small pieces are likely to fall away. Just stick them back on or fry them separately. It doesn't matter for a taco since the chicken is cut into small pieces anyway.

▶ When frying the chicken fajitas, it is important to heat the oil until you can see smoke. Hot searing and rapid cooking is what turns the pounded breast into a chicken fajita.

▶ If you are grilling, remember the cooking time given for the recipe does not include preparing the fire.

▲▲▲▲▲▲▲▲▲▲▲▲▲▲▲

Turn Chicken Fajitas into party fare by accompanying them with a festive beverage. For lunch or midweek dinners, serve them with a Mexican-style fruit or flower water—fresh iced water flavored with lime, tamarind, watermelon, almond, or *jaimaica* (hibiscus).

For hibiscus, almonds, and tamarind, first steep the blossoms, nuts, or pods in boiling water, then strain the water, add sugar to taste, and chill.

For watermelon, lime, orange, strawberry, and other fruits, crush the fruit, retaining all the pulp and juices. Add cold plain or sparkling water and sugar to taste. Chill.

For evening, serve a crisp white, fruity wine, such as a dry Semillon or Sauvignon Blanc, or Champagne flavored with a touch of grenadine or cassis.

▼▼▼▼▼▼▼▼▼▼▼▼▼▼▼

PUERTO RICAN CHICKEN FAJITAS

The combination of chicken and bananas, especially the not-so-sweet, slightly tart sibling of bananas, plantains, appeals to us so much we call for it in two dishes, this one and the Roast Chicken and Plantains.

Serves 4 to 6
Takes less than 20 minutes

2½ pounds skinless, boneless chicken breasts
⅔ cup pine nuts, finely chopped
Salt, to taste
2 to 4 tablespoons olive oil, if frying
3 plaintains (about 2 pounds), or 4 large green bananas,
  peeled and cut into ¼-inch-thick rounds
18 corn or 12 flour tortillas, warmed or crisped just before
  serving

TOPPINGS
2 cups sour cream
Orange-Onion Salsa (page 49)
4 cups shredded lettuce (optional)

1. Place a piece of waxed paper or plastic wrap on a countertop or cutting board. Place one chicken breast on top and cover with another piece of waxed paper or plastic wrap. With a mallet, hammer, or other pounding device, pound the chicken breast ⅛ inch thick. Continue in the same way until all the breasts are flattened. Set aside until ready to cook, or cover and refrigerate for up to 2 days.

2. When ready to cook the fajitas, remove the waxed paper or plastic wrap. Coat both sides of each chicken breast with the pine nuts and salt lightly. Set aside while preparing the grill or frying pan.

Plantains, along with rice and beans, are the great staple and daily fare of the Caribbean and lower Gulf of Mexico. In the Mexican state of Tabasco, plantains are served sliced to garnish rice, cut up for a soup vegetable, mashed to use as a thickening agent, and most interestingly of all, mixed with tortilla dough to make banana tortillas. Our forays to the Cuba Cafe in San Francisco, where plantains accompany every meal and the succulent foil-roasted chicken falls off the bone, leave us dreaming of old Havana. Puerto Rican friends introduced us to the combination of plantain and pine nuts nestled next to a rice and corn succotash with tender bits of chicken. We have carried these Caribbean combinations into a taco, minus the rice.

3. *If grilling,* prepare a charcoal fire and allow the coals to burn until they are mostly covered with white ash and a few red spots show through here and there. This will take about 40 minutes. When the fire is ready, place the chicken breasts on the grill rack directly above the coals. Cook until no longer pink but still moist in the center, about 1½ minutes on each side.

If frying, pour 1 tablespoon of the oil in each of 2 large frying pans and set over medium-high heat until the oil begins to smoke. (You can use 1 frying pan to save on dishes and cook the fajitas in several rounds.) Add as many chicken breasts as will fit in one uncrowded layer. Cook until no longer pink but still moist in the center, about 1½ minutes each side. Remove and drain off any liquid from the pan. Continue cooking another round until all of the breasts are cooked.

4. When all of the fajitas are cooked, heat 2 tablespoons oil in one or two large frying pans (the same ones you used for the chicken if you fried it). Add the plantain or banana pieces and stir over medium-high heat for 2 minutes for plantains, 1 minute for bananas.

5. Cut the chicken breasts into thin strips.

6. To assemble, place about ⅓ cup of chicken in the middle of a tortilla. Top with plantains or bananas, sour cream, Orange-Onion Salsa, and lettuce. Fold and serve.

VARIATIONS

▼

■ For other tropical fruit combinations try chicken with tamarind, feijoa, or fried papaya.

■ For non-tropical fruit combinations use fresh or dried apricots; dried pears; fresh figs; or dried figs, lightly sautéed in a little oil to soften.

SPICY SESAME CHICKEN FAJITAS

Serves 4 to 6
Takes less than 20 minutes

2½ pounds skinless, boneless chicken breasts
¼ cup sesame seeds
¼ teaspoon cayenne
Salt, to taste
2 tablespoons olive oil, if frying
18 corn or 12 flour tortillas, warmed or crisped just before
serving

TOPPINGS
2 cups chopped avocado
4 cups shredded lettuce
Mango-Jalapeño Salsa (page 51)
2 cups sour cream (optional)

1. Place a piece of waxed paper or plastic wrap on a countertop or cutting board. Place one chicken breast on top and cover with another piece of waxed paper or plastic wrap. With a mallet, hammer, or other pounding device, pound the chicken breast ⅛ inch thick. Continue in the same way until all the breasts are flattened. Set aside until ready to cook, or cover and refrigerate for up to 2 days.

2. When ready to cook the chicken breasts, remove the waxed paper or plastic wrap. Sprinkle both sides of the chicken breasts with the sesame seeds, cayenne, and salt. Set aside while preparing the grill or frying pan.

3. *If grilling,* prepare a charcoal fire and allow the coals to burn until they are mostly covered with white ash and a few red spots show through here and there. This will take about 40 minutes. When the fire is ready, place the chicken breasts on the grill rack directly above the coals. Cook until no longer pink but still moist in the center, about 1½ minutes on each side.

▲▲▲▲▲▲▲▲▲▲▲▲▲▲▲▲

Manuel, the chef at the Manila Bar and Grill in the Washington, D.C. area, sings to his dishes as he cooks. Sometimes he sings in Tagalog, sometimes Spanish, sometimes English. Back with the banyan trees he learned to mix chicken with exotic spices, the sweet fruits, seeds, and nuts of his native islands. He does the same things now, with chicken fajitas. We encountered Manuel during a trip to Washington. Our cab driver steered us to him. "The best chicken fajitas around," he said. He was right. Manuel's songs tell the story of his cooking. For this dish he sings, "Lying under the mango tree I dreamed of a sesame rain. A chicken walked by; I went in the house and cooked dinner." When we asked for his recipe, we copied down his lyrics, too. They often strike us when looking over the chicken in the market, and then we have to cook his fajitas and wrap them in tortillas.

▼▼▼▼▼▼▼▼▼▼▼▼▼▼▼▼

If frying, divide the oil between 2 large frying pans and set over medium-high heat until the oil begins to smoke. (You can use 1 frying pan to save on dishes and cook the fajitas in several rounds.) Add as many chicken breasts as will fit in one uncrowded layer. Cook until no longer pink but still moist in the center, about 1½ minutes on each side. Remove and drain off any liquid from the pan. Continue cooking another round until all of the breasts are cooked.

4. Cut the chicken into thin strips.

5. To assemble, place about ¼ cup of chicken in the center of a tortilla. Top with chopped avocado, lettuce, Mango-Jalapeño Salsa, and sour cream. Fold and serve.

CHICKEN FAJITAS WITH PICKLED BEETS AND PICKLED ONIONS

The union of beets with every other ingredient in our chicken fajita recipe—from the onions to the sour cream—is as old as the hills, save one. The combination of beets with tomatillos is new and super.

Serves 4 to 6
Takes 20 to 40 minutes

2½ pounds skinless, boneless chicken breasts
4 teaspoons dried oregano
Salt, to taste
2 tablespoons olive oil, if frying
18 corn or 12 flour tortillas, warmed or crisped just before
*   serving*

TOPPINGS
Pickled Beets (recipe follows)
Pickled Onions (page 72)
4 cups shredded lettuce
2 cups sour cream
Sweet and Hot Tomatillo Sauce (page 54)

1. Place a piece of waxed paper or plastic wrap on a countertop or cutting board. Place one chicken breast on top and cover with another piece of waxed paper or plastic wrap. With a mallet, hammer, or other pounding device, pound the chicken breast ⅛ inch thick. Continue in the same way until all the breasts are flattened. Set aside until ready to cook, or cover and refrigerate for up to 2 days.

2. When ready to cook the fajitas, remove the waxed paper or plastic wrap. Sprinkle both sides of each breast with oregano and salt. Set aside while preparing the grill or frying pan.

3. *If grilling*, prepare a charcoal fire and allow the coals to burn until they are mostly covered with white ash and a few red spots show through here and there. This will take about 40 minutes. When the fire is ready, place the chicken breasts on the grill rack directly above the coals. Cook until no longer pink but still moist in the center, about 1½ minutes on each side.

If frying, divide the oil between 2 large frying pans and set over medium-high heat until the oil begins to smoke. (You can use 1 frying pan to save on dishes and cook the fajitas in several rounds.) Add as many chicken breasts as will fit in one uncrowded layer. Cook until no longer pink but still moist in the center, about 1½ minutes each side. Remove and drain off any liquid from the pan. Continue cooking another round until all of the breasts are cooked.

4. Cut the chicken into thin strips.

5. To assemble, place about ⅓ cup of chicken in the middle of a tortilla. Top with Pickled Beets, Pickled Onions, shredded lettuce, sour cream, and Sweet and Hot Tomatillo Salsa. Fold and serve.

▲▲▲▲▲▲▲▲▲▲▲▲▲▲▲

If you are grilling your chicken fajitas on a small hibachi, there's a way to manage without the chicken fat causing the coals to flame and turning the chicken meat to cinders. Make sure the coals are well coated with ash. Put the chicken on the grill rack as far above the coals as possible. Turn the pieces every 30 seconds so that they don't burn. Have a spray bottle handy to douse flames caused by the dripping fat. You do have to stand there, but the chicken turns out perfectly browned on the outside and moist inside, just as if you had a larger grill with a cover.

▼▼▼▼▼▼▼▼▼▼▼▼▼▼

B eet juice is a renowned dye, that in Mexico is used to turn onions and other companion vegetables cheery pink. When making pickled beets and onions, we like to mix them together for just such a ruddy effect. Should you accidently stain your clothes while working with beets, apply cold water or white vinegar to the disconcerting spot or soak it in milk before laundering.

PICKLED BEETS

Makes about 2½ cups
Takes 20 to 40 minutes

2 pounds beets, tops removed
⅓ cup water
1 cup red wine vinegar
1 tablespoon sugar

1. Rinse the beets; cut lengthwise into quarters if medium-size, eighths if large. Place the beet wedges in a medium saucepan; add water to cover by 1 inch. Bring to a boil. Reduce the heat and simmer until soft enough for a knife to pass through, but not mushy, about 15 minutes. Drain and set aside to cool.

2. In a nonreactive small saucepan, combine the water, vinegar, and sugar. Bring to a boil. Remove from the heat.

3. When the beets are cool enough to handle, peel and cut the wedges into thin slices. Place the slices in a bowl and pour the vinegar mixture over. Set aside to marinate for 15 minutes, or cover, refrigerate, and use within 2 weeks.

TIPS

▶ You can pickle the beets right along with the onions when you do the Pickled Onions recipe.

▶ It's somewhat hard to cut raw beets into wedges, but it's worth the time saved in cooking small pieces rather than whole bulbs.

CHICKEN FAJITAS WITH GREEN OLIVE-CILANTRO SALSA

Serves 4 to 6
Takes 20 to 40 minutes

2½ pounds skinless, boneless chicken breasts
¼ medium onion
2 cups fresh orange juice
4 teaspoons soy sauce
2 tablespoons olive oil, if frying
18 corn or 12 flour tortillas, warmed or crisped just before
  serving

TOPPINGS
4 cups shredded lettuce
2 cups sour cream
Green Olive-Cilantro Salsa (see page 47)

1. Place a piece of waxed paper or plastic wrap on a countertop or cutting board. Place one chicken breast on top and cover with another piece of waxed paper or plastic wrap. With a mallet, hammer, or other pounding device, pound the chicken breast ⅛ inch thick. Continue in the same way until all the breasts are flattened. Set aside until ready to cook, or cover and refrigerate for up to 2 days.

2. When ready to cook the fajitas, finely grate the onion. In a large nonreactive dish, mix the onion and its juice with the orange juice and soy. Remove the waxed paper or plastic wrap, and place the chicken in the onion-orange-soy mixture. Turn to coat both sides. Set aside to marinate for at least 15 minutes and up to 45, turning once or twice.

3. *If grilling,* prepare a charcoal fire and allow the coals to

▲▲▲▲▲▲▲▲▲▲▲▲▲▲▲▲

We prefer olive oil as the frying medium for the chicken fajitas because of the grassy, fruity flavor it imparts. Olive oil reaches a smoking point at a lower temperature than most vegetable oils (though much higher than animal fats), so be prepared for it to be hot and ready faster than the others. We generally save our more expensive and flavorful extra virgin olive oil for salad dressing and sauces and use a less expensive virgin or pure grade olive oil for frying.

▼▼▼▼▼▼▼▼▼▼▼▼▼▼▼▼

burn until they are mostly covered with white ash and a few red spots show through here and there. This will take about 40 minutes. When the fire is ready, place the chicken breasts on the grill rack directly above the coals. Cook until no longer pink but still moist in the center, about 1½ minutes on each side.

If frying, divide the oil between 2 large frying pans and set over medium-high heat until the oil begins to smoke. (You can use 1 frying pan to save on dishes and cook the fajitas in several rounds.) Add as many chicken breasts as will fit in one un-crowded layer. Cook until no longer pink but still moist in the center, about 1½ minutes on each side. Remove and drain off any liquid from the pan. Continue cooking another round until all of the breasts are cooked.

4. Cut the chicken into thin strips.

5. To assemble, place about ⅓ cup of chicken in the middle of a tortilla. Top with some shredded lettuce, sour cream, and Green Olive-Cilantro Salsa. Fold and serve.

CHICKEN MOLE

D electable bits of savory roast chicken give rise to some of the most tantalizing and tender well-filled tortillas. Here we offer one of Mexico's traditional chicken dishes, Chicken Mole, turned taco. To save cooking time, we suggest roasting the chicken in pieces or quarters. For the most flavorful taco, be sure to use a combination of dark and white meat, and for the most classic rendition, use corn tortillas.

Serves 4 to 6
Takes 40 to 60 minutes

4 to 5 pounds chicken pieces, a combination of breasts,
   thighs, and legs, or 1½ chickens, quartered
2 dried ancho chilies, stemmed, seeded, and cut into ¼-inch-
   wide strips
3 garlic cloves, coarsely chopped
2 cups canned crushed tomatoes in purée or canned whole
   tomatoes, coarsely chopped and juices reserved
1 ounce bittersweet chocolate, coarsely chopped
¾ teaspoon dried oregano
½ teaspoon salt
1¼ cups water
18 corn or 12 flour tortillas, warmed or crisped just before
   serving

TOPPINGS
Avocado-Pumpkin Seed Salsa (page 44)
1 cup heavy (whipping) cream

1. Heat the oven to 450°F.

2. Place the chicken pieces in a large nonreactive baking dish. Distribute the chili strips and garlic around the chicken. Spread the tomatoes and chocolate pieces over the top of the chicken. Add the oregano, salt, and water.

3. Bake, uncovered, for 15 minutes. Turn the chicken pieces over and stir the chocolate into the sauce. Bake, turning one more time, until the meat is cooked through and pulls away from the bones, about 35 minutes more. Remove the chicken from the oven and transfer to a platter to cool.

4. Separate the chicken meat; discard the skin and bones. Return the meat to the baking pan and mix into the sauce.

5. To assemble, spoon about ⅓ cup of chicken and sauce into the middle of a tortilla. Top with Avocado-Pumpkin Seed Salsa and dribble on some cream. Fold and serve.

TIP

▶ The chicken mole filling may be prepared up to a day in advance and reheated over low heat just before serving.

You may ask, what is a *mole*? But the more pertinent question is, what's *in* a *mole*? The word *mole* comes from the Toltec word *molli* meaning "mixture" or "concoction." And that's what a *mole* is, a thick, paste-like concoction of mixed spices, a pastiche of many flavors. The *mole* we are most familiar with contains chocolate, as does this chicken *mole* dish. But chocolate *mole* is not only chocolate. It contains garlic, tomato, oregano, and often cinnamon, vanilla, or cumin. Other kinds of *moles* combine ground achiote seeds or ground pumpkin seeds mixed with other ingredients or a miscellany of puréed fresh or stewed chilies. In Mexican markets you can find blocks of various prepared *moles* to use as sauce and soup bases. Occasionally a *mole* is a dish in itself, such as in guaca-mole, a paste of avocado.

MENU

▼

*BE MY VALENTINE
PARTY*

———

*Red Chicken Enchiladas
with Two Red Hot Chili-
Garlic Salsas*

———

*Beet Salad with Orange
Vinaigrette*

———

*Sweet Ricotta and
Candied Fruit Flautas*

RED OR GREEN CHICKEN

A traditional red- or green-sauced enchilada is unbeatable. To make red enchiladas, merely sauce the chicken-filled, rolled tortillas in Ancho Chili Sauce. To make delicious green enchiladas—Enchiladas Verdes—blanket the rolled tortillas in Salsa Verde made from little green tomatillos. A few minutes in the oven finishes the dish.

Serves 4 to 6
**Takes 1½ hours if using fresh chicken, 20 to 40 minutes if using
    cooked chicken meat**

*4 to 5 pounds chicken pieces, a combination of breasts,
    thighs, and legs, or 1½ chickens, quartered, or 2½
    pounds cooked chicken meat (5 to 6 cups)*
1½ teaspoons dried oregano
Salt and freshly ground black pepper, to taste
3 medium onions, halved lengthwise and thinly sliced
3 tablespoons olive oil
Vegetable oil
18 corn or 12 flour tortillas

TOPPINGS
Ancho Chili Sauce (page 59) or Salsa Verde (page 52)
*1 cup grated or crumbled cheese, such as Cheddar, Jack,
    feta,* or *queso fresco*
2 cups sour cream

1. *If using fresh chicken,* heat the oven to 450°F. Place the chicken pieces, skin side up, in a roasting pan. Sprinkle with the oregano and salt and pepper. Arrange the onions over the chicken; drizzle the oil over the top. Bake until the juices are no longer pink, about 45 minutes. Remove from the oven and let cool enough to handle. Shred the meat; discard the skin and bones. Mix the chicken meat with the onions in the pan.

If using precooked chicken, heat the olive oil in a frying pan over medium heat. Add the onions, oregano, and salt and pepper to taste. Stir until the onions are soft, about 15 minutes. Stir in the cooked chicken and remove from the heat.

2. In a frying pan, heat enough vegetable oil to coat the bottom. Fry the tortillas over medium heat just until soft and pliable, a few seconds per side.

3. To assemble, fill each tortilla with about ⅓ cup of the warm chicken and onions and roll into a tube. Place the enchiladas in a single layer in a baking dish. Spread the sauce over the top and sprinkle on the cheese. Cover the baking dish with foil and place in a 350°F oven until the cheese melts, about 10 minutes. Served topped with sour cream.

TIP

▶ You needn't limit leftovers to roasted chicken. Leftover stewed or fried chicken works equally well for this taco, and leftover roast or ground beef makes a good beef enchilada taco.

ROAST CHICKEN AND PLANTAINS

Ancho Chili Sauce, avocado, and pumpkin seeds turn spicy roast chicken into a rich seductive taco.

Serves 4 to 6
Takes 1½ hours

In the depths of downtown Oakland, California, across from the city jail, sits the Mexicali Rose Restaurant. Open until 3 A.M., it's long been a haven for students studying late. When the original jail stood, it lay low and humble, painted pink outside, with murals of Mayan and Aztec scenes right on the inside plaster walls. Then in 1976, much to our dismay, it was razed to make way for the new medieval-style slammer with fortress walls and narrow slit windows. We all feared it would change. But no. The owners erected the Mexicali Rose just across the street again, still painted pink, still facing the corner diagonally. The only difference was the murals are now framed on canvas should the jail wander again. With men in blue ensconced every few booths, the place is a safe and comfortable lounge clear until its wee-hour closing. The plates of food are huge. To many a regular, the best dish offered is the green enchiladas: chicken wrapped in tortillas, covered with salsa verde, baked piping hot, and topped with cheese and sour cream. For others, it's the red enchiladas: the same rolled chicken stuffed tortillas, this time covered with a grainy, pungent, Northern-style dried chili sauce. Long beyond our student years, we haven't outgrown the place. After a late night working, you'll find us down there waiting for our green and red enchiladas.

Ancho Chili Sauce (page 59)
4 to 5 pounds chicken pieces, a combination of breasts,
*   thighs, and legs, or 1½ medium chickens, quartered*
Salt, to taste
3 large plantains or 4 green bananas, peeled, halved
*   lengthwise, and cut into ¼-inch-thick pieces*
18 corn or 12 flour tortillas, warmed or crisped just before
*   serving*

TOPPINGS
Toasted Pumpkin Seeds (page 75)
2 cups chopped avocado
2 cups sour cream
2 cups cilantro sprigs (optional)

1. Heat the oven to 450°F.

2. Spread ¼ cup of the Ancho Chili Sauce on the bottom of a roasting pan. Place the chicken pieces, skin side up, in the roasting pan. Spread another ¼ cup Ancho Chili Sauce over the top of the chicken and salt lightly. Place in the oven and bake for 20 minutes. Baste the chicken pieces with the pan juices and bake for 10 minutes more. Baste the chicken again. Add the plantains to the pan. Bake until the chicken is cooked through and the meat is beginning to pull away from the bones, 20 to 25 minutes more. Remove from the oven and let cool enough to handle.

3. Shred the chicken; discard the skin and bones.

4. To assemble, place about ⅓ cup of the chicken and plantains in the center of a tortilla. Top with some of the remaining Ancho Chili Sauce, Toasted Pumpkin Seeds, chopped avocado, sour cream, and cilantro sprigs. Fold and serve.

ROAST CHICKEN IN GOLDEN RAISIN SAUCE

Chicken swimming in tomatoes, sausage, and perky sweet and sour raisins—it's too thick and saucy to fold taco style. So, we mound the filling in a packet with sour cream and cilantro burrito style. Delicious.

Serves 4 to 6
Takes 1½ hours

4 to 5 pounds chicken pieces, a combination of breasts,
*   thighs, and legs, or 1½ chickens, quartered*
Salt and freshly ground black pepper, to taste
3 tablespoons olive oil
12 flour tortillas, warmed just before serving
Golden Raisin Sauce (recipe follows)

TOPPINGS
2 cups sour cream
3 cups cilantro leaves

1. Heat the oven to 450°F.

2. Place the chicken pieces, skin side up, in a roasting pan. Sprinkle with salt and pepper, then drizzle the oil over the top. Bake until the chicken is cooked through and the meat is beginning to fall away from the bones, 45 to 55 minutes. Remove from the oven and let cool enough to handle.

3. Shred the chicken meat; discard the skin and bones.

4. To assemble, place about ⅓ cup of the chicken in the center of a tortilla. Spread ¼ cup or so of the Golden Raisin Sauce over the chicken and top with sour cream and cilantro. Fold envelope style, tucking in the ends well, and serve.

M E N U
▼

A WINTER DINNER
WITH FRIENDS

———

Roast Chicken in
Golden Raisin Sauce in a
Taco

Carne Asada Tacos
Genghis Khan

Garlic-Sautéed Eggplant
in a Fried Tortilla

———

Coconut Milk Ice Cream
with Pineapple-Anisette
Sauce
in a Tostada Sundae

GOLDEN RAISIN SAUCE

Makes about 3 cups
Takes about 1 hour

¼ pound spicy sausage, such as chorizo, linguica, sweet
*　　Italian, or a mixture of all three*
½ tablespoon olive oil
½ medium onion, finely chopped
¼ cup golden raisins
½ teaspoon pure chili powder
1 medium tomato, coarsely chopped
½ cup canned whole tomatoes, drained
½ cup canned crushed tomatoes in purée
¼ cup dry red wine

1. Coarsely chop the sausage. In a large ungreased frying pan set over medium heat, cook the sausage until cooked through but not too browned, about 10 minutes. Remove to drain on paper towels.

2. In a large nonreactive frying pan or saucepan, heat the oil over medium heat. Add the onions, raisins, and chili powder and cook until the onions are wilted, about 5 minutes. Add the fresh tomato, canned tomatoes, tomatoes in purée, wine, and sausage. Bring to a boil, then reduce the heat and simmer for 45 minutes.

TIP

▶ The sauce can be made up to 5 days in advance. Store it in the refrigerator; reheat before serving.

▲▲▲▲▲▲▲▲▲▲▲▲▲▲▲▲▲

Our payback list of dinners we'd enjoyed at the hands of others had grown large enough for guilt to set in. On the spur of the moment, we decided to take care of everyone together at one party. We picked up the phone and called our neglected comrades. That done, we jerryrigged Susanna's old brick barbecue with an oven rack. Then we turned to the market. We found both chorizo and linguiça, golden raisins, fresh tomatoes and a brace of fresh plump chickens. Next day, we placed a galvanized tub in the empty fishpond and filled it with ice, beer, sodas, and wine. We stoked up the fire, got the tortillas, and a juicy, spicy feast was had by all.

▼▼▼▼▼▼▼▼▼▼▼▼▼▼▼▼

INDIAN-STYLE CURRIED CHICKEN

Hot flat chapatis, plain or onioned, puffed up like tortillas and filled with stews of lamb, vegetable, or chicken—India offers another taco-type cuisine. Here we turn to India for a highly seasoned stewed chicken chimichanga. Curry makes the dish pungent. Potatoes, carrots, and corn make it filling.

Serves 4 to 6
Takes 40 to 60 minutes

4 pounds chicken pieces, a combination of breasts, thighs,
*   and legs, or one 4-pound chicken, quartered*
½ medium onion, cut in half and sliced thin
1 large carrot, peeled, and cut into ¼-inch dice
1 yellow wax chili pepper, stemmed and coarsely chopped
½ teaspoon dried marjoram
1½ teaspoons curry powder
¾ teaspoon salt
2 cups chicken stock or broth
1 cup dry white wine
8 ounces potatoes, cut into small dice
¾ cup fresh corn kernels (about 1 medium ear)
18 corn or 12 flour tortillas

TOPPINGS
2 cups crumbled sharp white cheese, such as feta, hard
*   chèvre, or cotija*
2 cups grated mild cheese, such as white Cheddar or gouda
2 cups sour cream
Dressed Cilantro (page 76)

Vegetable oil

The heat of curry comes on dense and long-smoldering, rather than fast and fiery like the heat of chilies. As a fire extinguisher, we suggest you counter Indian-Style Curried Chicken tacos with Avocado and Grapefruit Salad, Mexican Fruit Salad, or side bowls of Pear-Lime Salsa, Mango-Jalapeño Salsa (going easy on the jalapeño), or Orange-Onion Salsa (see Index for recipe page numbers). A bowl of minted yogurt will also quench the heat.

1. Place the chicken, onion, carrot, chili, marjoram, curry powder, salt, stock, and wine in a large nonreactive pot. Bring to a boil. Partially cover, reduce the heat, and simmer for 20 minutes. Add the potatoes and simmer until the chicken pulls away from the bones, about 15 minutes more. Turn off the heat, remove the chicken pieces. Set aside to cool enough to handle.

2. When the chicken is cool, shred the meat; discard the skin and bones. Return the meat to the pot, along with the corn. Heat just to the boiling point.

3. To assemble, spread about ⅓ cup of the chicken and vegetables in the center of a tortilla. Top with some of each kind of cheese, sour cream, and Dressed Cilantro. Fold and continue until all the chimichangas are assembled.

4. In a large frying pan set over high heat, heat enough oil to coat the bottom. A few at a time, place the folded tacos in the pan and fry until browned, about 30 seconds per side. Serve hot.

▲▲▲▲▲▲▲▲▲▲▲▲▲▲▲

A lthough a powder and not a sauce or paste, curry is in essence a *mole*—a compound of many flavors, in which curry leaves are sometimes, though rarely, one element. The variety of curry mixtures is vast, but in general there are two styles. The main ingredient of one style—and the one that imparts the yellow color— is turmeric. The foundation of the other is well-roasted and pounded cardamom seed. Where curry is common, like *mole* it livens stewed dishes often devoured taco style. In India, Pakistan, and Sri Lanka folks dip and fill hand-patted flat breads with their curried stews. In Indonesia and Burma they fill crisp pancakes or edible leaves. Here we use tortillas, but chapatis, pita, or lettuce would do as nicely.

▼▼▼▼▼▼▼▼▼▼▼▼▼▼▼

STEWED CHICKEN WITH ALMONDS AND ANCHOS

During stewing, chicken sops up flavors and aromas like a beauty queen soaks up flattery. At the same time, the meat cooks to such a moist tenderness, it practically shreds itself. That's why we particularly like to stew chicken, and why stewed chicken fillings make some of the most outstanding tacos. Below we offer a rich, dense, stewed chicken filling with a counterpoint of crunchy toasted almonds. It can be prepared a day or two in advance and gently reheated. A chicken filling becomes all the more mellow while resting in its sauce.

Serves 4 to 6
Takes 40 to 60 minutes

4 to 5 pounds chicken pieces, a combination of breasts,
    thighs, and legs, or 1½ chickens, quartered
½ teaspoon ground allspice
Small pinch of ground cinnamon
4 whole cloves
2 dried ancho chilies, stemmed and seeded
½ teaspoon salt
2 cans (14 ounces each) crushed tomatoes in purée
3½ cups water
1 teaspoon oil
½ cup almond slivers
18 corn or 12 flour tortillas, warmed or crisped just before
    serving

TOPPINGS
2 cups heavy (whipping) cream, whipped to soft peaks
2 cups cilantro leaves

You might think heavy cream is an unusual ingredient for a well-filled tortilla, but there is a reason for it. Stewed chicken yields an abundance of savory juices that cream thickens. We also find that heavy cream adds a sweetness and gloss to the muskiness of the ancho chilies, whereas sour cream adds an undesirable tartness. We simply wouldn't have this filling any other way than with heavenly soft peaks of heavy cream.

1. In a large nonreactive pot, combine the chicken, allspice, cinnamon, cloves, chilies, salt, tomatoes, and 3½ cups water. Bring to a boil. Partially cover, reduce the heat, and simmer until the meat pulls away from the bones, 35 to 45 minutes. Remove the chicken and chilies and set aside. Continue to simmer the sauce for 15 minutes while the chicken cools.

2. Heat the oil in a frying pan over medium heat, add the almonds, and stir until browned, 2 to 3 minutes. Set aside.

3. When cool enough to handle, shred the chicken; discard the skin and bones. Scrape the pulp off the chili skins. Return the chicken and chili pulp to the pot.

4. To assemble, spread about ⅓ cup of the chicken and sauce in the center of a tortilla. Top with the whipped cream, toasted almonds, and cilantro. Fold and serve.

CHICKEN AND PORK STEW

▲▲▲▲▲▲▲▲▲▲▲▲▲▲▲

F or another mixed meat stew, check the Index for Spanish-Style Ground Beef and Pork. And next time you cook up one of the beef stew fillings, consider adding a piece of pork or sausage to it too.

▼▼▼▼▼▼▼▼▼▼▼▼▼▼▼

T here is a beauty to the tasty mingled flavors of a mixed meat stew, both as a tortilla filling or simply on its own, ladled steaming into a bowl. Here we call for a combination of chicken and pork, though rabbit could replace the chicken and veal replace the pork.

Serves 4 to 6
Takes 40 to 60 minutes

1 pound boneless pork butt, loin end, or stew meat
2 tablespoons olive oil
3 garlic cloves, pressed or minced
3½ pounds chicken pieces, or 1 medium chicken,
    quartered
4 medium tomatoes, coarsely chopped
1½ teaspoons grated orange zest
½ teaspoon dried marjoram
½ teaspoon ground cumin
¾ teaspoon salt
2 cups water
1 teaspoon vegetable oil
½ cup pine nuts
18 corn or 12 flour tortillas, warmed or crisped just before
    serving

TOPPINGS
Breaded Chili Strips (page 71)
4 cups shredded lettuce
2 cups sour cream

From the Rock of Gibraltar to the rocks of Galilee, people of the Mediterranean make stews of mixed meat, often flavored with orange from the groves of native trees. In Lebanon you might find an *oleo* of goat and lamb. In Greece a favorite *stifatho* combines beef and hare. In sunny Mallorca, on different journeys, we each came across orange-flavored stews of chicken and pork. Jeeping along the back roads of the island, you have to make way for unfettered pigs and flocks of free-ranging chickens. Marjoram grows wild, citrus blossoms scent the sunsets, and orange and lemon slices flavor the evening sangria. We think a fruit-infused wine perfectly complements our taco rendition of a mutually remembered Mallorca stew.

1. Cut the pork into very thin strips, trimming off excess fat as you go.

2. Heat the olive oil in a large pot set over medium-high heat until the oil begins to smoke. Add the pork and garlic and stir-fry until the pork is lightly browned, about 5 minutes. Add the chicken, tomatoes, orange zest, marjoram, cumin, salt, and water. Bring to a boil. Partially cover, reduce the heat, and simmer until the chicken is cooked through and the meat pulls away from the bones, 35 to 40 minutes. Remove the chicken; set aside to cool. Simmer the other ingredients for 20 minutes.

3. Heat the vegetable oil in a frying pan over medium-high heat. Add the pine nuts and stir until browned, 2 to 3 minutes. Set aside.

4. Shred the chicken; discard the skin and bones. Return the meat to the pot with the pork.

5. To assemble, spread about ⅓ cup of the chicken and pork stew in the center of a tortilla. Top with Breaded Chili Strips, shredded lettuce, sour cream, and pine nuts. Fold and serve.

TURKEY

The New World bestowed more than its glorious vegetables upon the rest of the world's cuisines. It also sent its native "big bird," the turkey. Indeed, although other parts of the globe at first looked skeptically at tomatoes, corn, potatoes, and such, they instantly adopted our gawky fowl. Now the bird is raised in Africa, Europe, South America, and the Pacific Islands. Since it rarely flies—never more than a few hundred feet—and its little-used muscles require little oxygen, it offers mounds of white meat. And except for the leg, even the dark meat is crossed with few tough tendons.

Still, wherever the turkey traveled, despite its enthusiastic reception (and perhaps because of its appearance), its name became synonymous with "fool." *Pavo* means both turkey and dolt in Spanish, and turkey to us means . . . well, a turkey. But, turkey is low in cholesterol, available year round, and in the new cuts, quick and easy to cook. We think anyone who eats turkey tacos, therefore, is no fool.

ALL-AMERICAN GROUND TURKEY

To our bemusement and happy surprise, ground turkey tacos have become almost our hallmark dish. Their evolution began one Thanksgiving. Faced with a mound of leftover turkey and not having the desire for one more cold turkey platter, turkey croquettes, and definitely not turkey à la king, we opted for a new idea, turkey tacos. Very soon we found ourselves besieged by a loud and raucous demand for more. A run to the supermarket, where we spied the quick cooking ground turkey, turned the idea to its present, even more tantalizing form. Ground turkey works splendidly for the lean zesty taco filling. Virtually any salsa and topping works with this filling.

Serves 4 to 6
Takes 30 minutes

3 tablespoons peanut or olive oil
2 large onions, finely chopped
2 to 4 garlic cloves, pressed or minced
2½ pounds ground turkey
1¼ cups fresh corn kernels (about 2 medium ears)
Fresh Tomato Salsa (page 37) or Salsa Verde (page 52)
⅔ cup dry white wine
¾ teaspoon salt
*18 corn or 12 flour tortillas, warmed or crisped just before
    serving*

TOPPINGS
2 cups chopped tomatoes
4 cups shredded lettuce
3 cups shredded cheese
2 cups sour cream

▲▲▲▲▲▲▲▲▲▲▲▲▲▲▲▲

We introduced turkey tacos at the Good and Plenty Cafe shortly after it opened. We had been racking our brains over something new to serve. Our mostly student clientele had already gone through Corsican lasagne, Chinese chicken salad, tuna Capri, and eggplant pie. Many of the students, if not outright vegetarians, shun red meat, and the pocketbooks of most are thin. We knew turkey tacos were good enough to infatuate the family, why not the cafe, too? They are fast, lean, inexpensive, filling, and fun. Now we turn 30-plus pounds of ground turkey into turkey tacos (converted into burritos for carry-out purposes and quick reheating) every week. We start with 15 pounds of turkey, 8 jumbo onions, and a bottle and a half of white wine on Monday and repeat the process on Wednesday. Our supplier asked us what we do with all the ground turkey. We offered him a sample, and now he orders them to take out.

▲▲▲▲▲▲▲▲▲▲▲▲▲▲▲

Along the sun-blanched coast of Turkey, tiny grapes we know as dried currants grow along terrace walls. Centuries-old almond trees break up the acres and acres of olive groves, and the earth is so fertile, vegetables of every type fill the markets. Each town sports a spice bazaar with its perfumes, especially of cumin, a Turkish favorite, wafting through the corridors, under the arches, up the alleyways, and into every nook and cranny. The Turkish people use pita as their tortilla and wrap any and everything inside—*donners* of ground meats, lamb chunks grilled on skewers, goat, chicken. Perhaps the only food they don't have, ironically enough, is the bird early American settlers thought were Turkish Guinea Hens. We still call the awkward, dewlapped gobblers "turkeys," and do they blend well with all the ingredients of Turkish cooking!

▼▼▼▼▼▼▼▼▼▼▼▼▼▼

1. Heat the oil in a large frying pan set over medium-high heat. Add the onions and garlic and stir until the onions are wilted, about 5 minutes. Add the turkey and cook, stirring occasionally to break up any chunks, until browned thoroughly, about 10 minutes. Add the corn, 3 to 6 tablespoons of the Fresh Tomato Salsa or Salsa Verde, the wine, and salt. Cook until most of the liquid has been absorbed, 10 to 15 minutes.

2. To assemble, spread about ⅓ cup of the turkey filling in the middle of a tortilla. Top with some of the remaining salsa, chopped tomatoes, shredded lettuce, cheese, and sour cream. Fold and serve.

TIPS

▶ You can also make these tacos, or for that matter Turkish-Style Ground Turkey tacos, with leftover holiday turkey. Use about 6 cups diced roasted turkey meat and add a little extra wine for more moisture.

▶ Turkey tends to dry out easily, so when reheating this filling, add a little more wine or some water.

TURKISH-STYLE GROUND TURKEY

In Istanbul, restaurants offer spicy ground meat fillers such as the one below enclosed in pita bread, but you often see the restaurateurs and their staff enjoying the same dish wrapped in a lettuce leaf. Theirs are of beef and lamb. Our version is with turkey, and we suggest trying it on a leaf of spinach or romaine when you're in a salad mood.

Serves 4 to 6
Takes 20 minutes

3 tablespoons peanut or olive oil
2 large onions, finely chopped
¾ cup slivered almonds
⅔ cup currants
2½ pounds ground turkey
¾ teaspoon ground cumin
¾ teaspoon salt
⅔ cup dry red wine
18 corn or 12 flour tortillas, warmed or crisped just before
*   serving*

TOPPINGS
1 cup sliced jalapeño chili peppers
4 cups shredded lettuce
2 cups sour cream
1 cup thinly shredded fresh mint leaves

1. Heat the oil in a large frying pan set over medium-high heat. Add the onions, almonds, and currants and stir until the onions are wilted and the almonds browned, about 5 minutes. Stir in the turkey, cumin, salt, and red wine. Cook until most of the liquid has been absorbed, about 15 minutes.

2. To assemble, spread about ⅓ cup of the turkey filling in the middle of a tortilla. Top with sliced jalapeños, shredded lettuce, sour cream, and mint. Fold and serve.

TIP

▶ For the jalapeño topping, fresh rather than canned jalapeños give Turkish-Style Ground Turkey more spark and added crunch. Of course, canned will do in a pinch.

▲▲▲▲▲▲▲▲▲▲▲▲▲▲▲▲▲

In Susanna's early college days she lived in Estes Park, Colorado. She commuted down the mountains to school every day, raised Siberian huskies, and first started cooking tacos. One evening she heard a knock on the door of the cabin where she was huddled with her books for the night. Outside stood a young, but already craggy and taciturn, Colorado mountain dweller. "This your dog?" he asked, pointing to the most mischievous husky of the pack. "Yes," replied Susanna. "Well, I got to tell you, ma'am, your dog just killed all my turkeys."

Now this was serious. Turkey farming is big business in Colorado. Many farmers on both plains and hills rear large flocks and supply the nation's Thanksgiving fare, not to mention year-round taco fillings and fajitas. Dogs that kill livestock of any sort are game for quick execution, in the eyes of the law, the community, and with the authority of shotguns agreeing. The dog owner is also liable for any damage a dog causes. "All of them?" a stunned Susanna responded, her mind quickly counting the potential cost of tens or even hundreds of turkeys. "Yep," he replied. "Both of 'em." Luckily, he did not have dog killing on his mind. He merely wanted to report the incident. Nor would he take any compensation for his two turkeys. Since the denizens of Estes Park are taco eaters, we hope he finds this recipe and takes his due in wonderful turkey tacos.

BASIC TURKEY FAJITAS

Thin cutlets of turkey breast, seared tender and moist over high heat, make delicious, versatile, and lean fajitas. You can buy the cutlets already cut and prepackaged or you can slice your own from a whole breast just as you would carve a cooked turkey breast. Turkey fajitas, unlike beef and chicken, are too delicate and spare for the grill, and should be pan-fried. When you introduce the turkey cutlets to the skillet, it is important to have the pan very hot with wisps of smoke rising. This way the cutlets brown quickly without losing succulence.

Serves 4 to 6
Takes less than 20 minutes

18 turkey cutlets (about 2¼ pounds)
1½ teaspoons dried marjoram
2½ teaspoons paprika, preferably Hungarian sweet
Salt and freshly ground black pepper, to taste
Olive or peanut oil
18 corn or 12 flour tortillas, warmed or crisped just before
    serving

TOPPINGS
Avocado-Pumpkin Seed Salsa (page 44)
2 cups sour cream
1 cup sliced jalapeño chili peppers (optional)

1. Sprinkle both sides of the turkey cutlets with the marjoram and paprika. Lightly salt and pepper both sides.

2. Coat the bottom of 1 or 2 heavy frying pans with oil and set over high heat until the oil begins to smoke. Add as many turkey cutlets as will fit in one uncrowded layer and fry for 30

VARIATIONS

Basic Turkey Fajitas, like their cousin Basic Chicken Fajitas, mingle harmoniously with all kinds of flavors. One rule prevails, though. Since turkey lacks much juiciness of its own, the combinations you create need to provide some moisture.

If you add Basic Fried Potatoes (see Index), a wonderful pairing with turkey, be sure to keep the sour cream or add a second moist salsa along with the Avocado-Pumpkin Seed Salsa. Or, instead of the Avocado-Pumpkin Seed Salsa, try lettuce and Fried Chili Strips or Greek Salsa. Ancho Chili or Pasilla, Mint, and Pickled Red Onion Sauces go well with turkey—but be sure also to serve the sour cream and perhaps add Pickled Carrots.

You can also coat Turkey Fajitas in ground pine nuts. Garnish them with Mango-Jalapeño Salsa and top them with Dressed Cilantro. (See Index for page numbers.)

seconds on each side. Remove to a platter and keep warm. Continue cooking another round until all the cutlets are cooked.

3. Slice the cutlets crosswise into thin strips.

4. To assemble, place about ⅓ cup of the turkey in the center of a tortilla. Top with Avocado-Pumpkin Seed Salsa, sour cream, and chopped fresh jalapeños. Fold and serve.

TURKEY FAJITAS WITH BACON AND ORANGE-ONION SALSA

Serves 4 to 6
Takes 40 minutes

¼ cup tequila, preferably gold
¼ cup fresh lime juice
2 jalapeño chili peppers, stemmed and minced
18 turkey cutlets (about 2¼ pounds)
1 pound sliced bacon
Olive or peanut oil
Salt, to taste
18 corn or 12 flour tortillas, warmed or crisped just before
    serving

TOPPINGS
4 cups shredded lettuce
Orange-Onion Salsa (see page 49)

▲▲▲▲▲▲▲▲▲▲▲▲▲▲▲▲

E d Kagen drives no mean pickup, but a big, black powerful GM workhorse. On the back bumper near the trailer hitch flashes a sticker reading, "It's hard to soar with eagles when you work with turkeys." Ed should know. Living out near Modesto, California, a sleepy agricultural town that discovered its farms were Eden and its climate heaven for poultry, Ed surrounds himself with 30,000 of the feathered, caruncled birds. Highly active in the turkey industry, which produces its own newspaper, "California Turkey Talk," Ed has been one of the people responsible for bringing to our daily tables turkey meat in parts—ground turkey, turkey tenderloin, breasts, and thighs. The cutlets sliced from the breast offer us another juicy fajita meat and for that, we are grateful.

▼▼▼▼▼▼▼▼▼▼▼▼▼▼▼▼

VARIATIONS

Wake up a turkey fajita with the addition of other piquant meats and salsas.
- In place of the bacon substitute: Canadian bacon, fried and diced; ham bits; or crumbled fried sausage.
- Instead of the Orange-Onion Salsa try: Pear-Lime Salsa or Mango-Jalapeño Salsa.
- Double up on the salsas by adding to the Orange-Onion with: Peanut-Garlic Salsa; Pasilla, Mint, and Pickled Red Onion Sauce; or the Deviled Peanuts and Coconut Topping.

1. In a large nonreactive dish, mix together the tequila, lime juice, and chili peppers. Add the turkey cutlets, turn to coat, and let marinate for 10 minutes or so.

2. Cut the bacon slices crosswise into ¼-inch pieces. Place the bacon in a large heavy skillet set over medium-low heat, and fry until crisp, about 25 minutes. Stir occasionally to brown evenly. Using a slotted spoon, remove and drain on paper towels.

3. To cook the turkey, coat 1 or 2 large frying pans with oil and set over high heat until the oil begins to smoke. Lightly salt the turkey cutlets and add as many as will fit in one uncrowded layer to the frying pan. Fry for 30 seconds on each side. Remove to a platter and keep warm. Continue cooking another round until all of the cutlets are cooked.

4. Slice the turkey cutlets crosswise into thin strips.

5. To assemble, place about ⅓ cup of the turkey in the center of a tortilla. Top with shredded lettuce, Orange-Onion Salsa, and bacon bits. Fold and serve.

TURKEY FAJITAS WITH PEAR AND GORGONZOLA

In Central America pumpkin seeds, ground fine, become a *mole* paste and a sauce thickener. They make a fine breading as well. Pulverized and toasted, the rich nutty flavor of pumpkin seeds coats the turkey in a most accommodating way, as Montezuma surely knew when he served turkey and pumpkin seeds to the *conquistadores.*

Serves 4 to 6
Takes less than 20 minutes

1½ cups shelled pumpkin seeds
18 turkey cutlets (about 2¼ pounds)
Salt, to taste
Olive or peanut oil
3 ripe but firm pears
¼ cup fresh lime juice
18 corn or 12 flour tortillas, warmed or crisped just before
serving

TOPPINGS
Fresh Red Hot Chili-Garlic Salsa (page 39)
4 cups shredded lettuce
¾ pound Gorgonzola, Bavarian blue, or other soft blue
cheese, crumbled

1. Mince the pumpkin seeds in a food processor or using a chef's knife. Spread out on a large plate. Place the turkey cutlets on the pumpkin seeds and turn to coat both sides. Lightly salt the cutlets.

2. Coat the bottom of 1 or 2 large heavy frying pans with oil and set over high heat until the oil begins to smoke. Add as many turkey cutlets as will fit in one uncrowded layer and fry for 30 seconds on each side. Remove to a platter and keep warm. Continue cooking another round until all the cutlets are cooked.

3. Remove the stems and cores from the pears and thinly slice. Place the pear slices in a bowl and toss gently with the lime juice.

4. Slice the turkey cutlets crosswise into thin strips.

5. To assemble, place about ⅓ cup of the turkey in the center of a tortilla. Top with pear slices, Fresh Red Hot Chili-Garlic Salsa, and shredded lettuce. Crumble the blue cheese over all. Fold and serve.

▲▲▲▲▲▲▲▲▲▲▲▲▲▲▲▲

S eed and nut coatings give turkey fajitas an appealing toasty crust. Here we use pumpkin seeds, which is very Mexican, but you may wish to try ground almonds, pine nuts, cashews, pistachios, or hazelnuts.

▼▼▼▼▼▼▼▼▼▼▼▼▼▼▼▼

TURKEY FAJITAS WITH PICKLED CORN

C ombining turkey and corn harks back to the early days of the Iroquois Indians. The Iroquois were Siouan speakers who intruded on the Algonquins of the East. They attempted to migrate as far as Montreal, but the Algonquins balked at giving up such a gem and pushed them back.

Great agriculturists that they were, the Iroquois were happy to settle and be among the first to "take New York." The forests and rivers teemed with fish. Ducks, abundant turkeys, and flocks of now extinct passenger pigeons—so thick men could knock them from trees with poles—filled the air. The Iroquois women, whose childbearing power was thought magically to transfer to the crops, did all the farming except for slashing new fields. Their corn stretched for miles on both sides of irrigating streams. The culinary year culminated in the fall with men hunting turkey, women husking the ripe corn, and a joyous festival to celebrate the bounty.

Serves 4 to 6
Takes less than 20 minutes

2 tablespoons achiote paste or pure chili powder
¼ cup fresh lime juice
18 turkey cutlets (about 2¼ pounds)
Salt, to taste
Olive or peanut oil
1 cup heavy (whipping) cream
Ancho Chili Sauce (page 59)
18 corn or 12 flour tortillas, warmed or crisped just before
    serving

TOPPINGS
4 cups shredded lettuce
Pickled Corn (page 73)
¾ pound feta cheese or queso fresco, crumbled

1. Sprinkle the achiote and lime juice evenly over both sides of the turkey cutlets. Lightly salt both sides.

2. Coat the bottom of 1 or 2 heavy frying pans with oil and set over high heat until the oil begins to smoke. Add as many turkey cutlets as will fit in one uncrowded layer. Fry for 30 seconds on each side. Remove to a platter and keep warm. Continue cooking another round until all the cutlets are cooked.

3. With paper towels, wipe any excess oil out of one of the frying pans. Add the cream and cook over medium-high heat until just beginning to boil. Add the Ancho Chili Sauce and stir. Remove from the heat. Slice the turkey crosswise into thin strips.

4. To assemble, place about ⅓ cup of the turkey in the center of a tortilla. Smooth about 2 tablespoons of the Ancho Cream Sauce over the turkey. Top with shredded lettuce, Pickled Corn, and crumbled cheese. Fold and serve.

SHREDDED ROAST TURKEY WITH TWO SALSAS

Roast turkey, shredded and seasoned with a complement of nutty and peppery salsas, makes a copious
tortilla filling. You can roast a small, tender 12-pounder—
available almost all year round now—and satisfy those who
prefer white meat and those who prefer dark in one fell
swoop. Or, you can buy a turkey breast fillet and some
thighs to suit the same purpose, with the cooking done
in less time.

Serves 4 to 6
Takes 2 hours

1½ teaspoons achiote paste or pure chili powder
1 tablespoon fresh lime juice
1 tablespoon olive oil
3 pounds turkey breast and/or thighs
Salt, to taste
18 corn or 12 flour tortillas, warmed or crisped just before
    serving

TOPPINGS
Peanut-Garlic Salsa (page 50)
Roasted Red Pepper, Chili, and Pine Nut Sauce (page 57)
4 cups shredded lettuce

   1. Heat the oven to 375°F.

   2. In a small bowl, mix together the achiote, lime juice, and
olive oil. Place the turkey in a nonreactive baking pan and spread
the achiote mixture over the top of the meat. Salt lightly.

M E N U

▼

*A SPECIAL
THANKSGIVING*

———

*Crispy Crab and Breaded
Chili Strip Tacos*

———

*Shredded Roast Turkey
Tacos with Two Salsas*

*Fried Sweet Potato, Chili,
and Cream Cheese Melt
Tacos*

*Avocado and Grapefruit
Salad with Lime-
Jalapeño Vinaigrette*

———

*Sweet Ricotta and
Candied Fruit Flautas*

▲▲▲▲▲▲▲▲▲▲▲▲▲▲▲▲

Holiday season was rolling around, and as we were having a joint family Thanksgiving, we decided to splurge on a big 25-pound Willy Bird. Willies are our favorite local brand of broad-breasted, grain-fed, moist turkey. We like to roast them in garlic paste, stuff them with chili corn bread, and savor their delicious falling-off-the-bone leftovers for days. We ordered our bird from the butcher and picked it up Thanksgiving eve. On Thanksgiving morning, we lovingly opened the wrap on our Willy Bird. Lo and behold, the breast had no skin. Bare, forlorn, and almost embarrassed looking, at least it was still plump. We popped it into the sink and took a Polaroid, then saved the bird for eating by slathering its flesh with the garlic paste and roasting it upside down. Next day we took the picture to the butcher, who, amused and appalled at the same time, said he would investigate the matter. Several days later we received a handwritten, not typed, not computerized, letter from the Willy Bird company. It seems they had opened a new processing plant and a misguided packaging device had pulled off the skin instead of wrapping the bird. They were chagrined and offered us another 25-pound turkey, gratis. We forgave all on the spot. The turkey chapter for our book was next on our agenda, and there was no better material for shredded roast turkey filling than another Willy Bird.

3. Roast the turkey, basting once or twice, until an instant reading thermometer registers 155° to 160°F in the center of the meat, about 1½ hours for breasts, about 45 minutes for thighs. Remove and set aside for at least 10 minutes to allow juices to settle.

4. Shred the turkey; discard the skin and bones. Moisten the meat with the juices from the baking pan.

5. To assemble, spread about ⅓ cup of the turkey meat in the center of a tortilla. Top with Peanut-Garlic Salsa, Roasted Red Pepper, Chili, and Pine Nut Sauce, and shredded lettuce. Fold and serve.

TIPS

▶ Since turkey meat, especially the breast, tends to dry out while roasting, be sure to baste the meat with the pan juices from time to time.

▶ If you decide to roast a whole 12-pound turkey, it will take about 2 hours. Place the turkey in a 450°F oven. After 30 minutes, reduce the heat to 375°F and roast for 1 hour more. Raise the temperature back to 450°F and continue roasting until an instant reading thermometer inserted in the thigh registers 155° to 160°F, about 30 minutes more. This filling, along with the ground turkey fillings, offers creative uses for the leftover meat. Dice the meat (you'll need 6 cups for 12 to 18 tortillas) and place it in a frying pan. Add double the olive oil, along with the achiote and lime, and stir over medium heat until the meat is warmed through. Proceed as above.

DUCK

From the upper reaches of the Nile River to the fruited plains of the New World, in fall skeins of wild ducks pepper the horizon and entice hunters to the game. Here and now we usually eat our long-since-domesticated duck roasted. But consider the history and the taste. The ancient Ethiopians ate simmered pieces of the bird with chick-peas and millet served atop platter-size thin breads. The Cherokee prepared duck with pounded corn. The Aztecs were so avid for duck meat they husbanded pens of Muscovies to go with their tortillas. Duck and pan breads go together, dare we say, better than a duck takes to water.

In Mexico, as in Europe, chevrons of duck wing over cool mountain highlands and families of the bird hide among marsh reeds. And in Mexico, as in Europe, besides being a savored dish, duck appears as a frequent motif in art. Perhaps the most well known decorative pottery from Mexico, certainly the most whimsically designed and sweetly colored—with deer, owls, cockatoos, flowers, suns, and moons in mystic pinks, blues, and buffs—comes from Tonalá, a village of craftspeople near Guadalajara.

The signature piece of the village ware is the famous Tonalá duck. No matter which family of potters crafts the bird, it always sits smooth and compact on its belly, its small head perked up, slightly turning as if listening to some noise. Every Tonalá duck is painted with fantastic breast feathers across the chest, while pin feathers of different eerie tones decorate the back and dot the head. Our friend May Diaz, who did her anthropology field work in Tonalá and wrote a lyrical book about the village, tells us that when eaten, duck in Mexico, like in Europe, is commonly stewed in a rich broth and served with beans. If you want to try this dish Mexican style, make the beans pintos and the sauce Tomato-Pumpkin Seed Salsa.

DUCK AND WHITE BEANS

Not long ago we were served delicate little tacos of duck and white beans at a gourmet festival. The duck was grilled separately, and served in rare slices. The beans were firm, swimming in clear juices. They were good, those tacos. But for home cooking, our taste runs more to duck and beans cooked together country style as in the cassoulets of southern France, or the way Mexicans have cooked duck with beans for centuries. Cooked along with the duck, the beans attain an incomparable and mouth-watering flavor.

Serves 4 to 6
Takes 2½ hours

1½ cups white beans, such as Navy, Great Northern, or
*   Italian cannelini*
1 tablespoon peanut oil
3 ducks (about 4½ pounds each), quartered (see first Tip,
*   page 177)*
8 garlic cloves, pressed or minced
1½ tablespoons tomato paste
1 tablespoon fresh thyme leaves or 1 teaspoon dried
1 teaspoon salt
1 teaspoon freshly ground black pepper
1 cup dry white wine
2 quarts chicken stock or broth
18 corn or 12 flour tortillas, warmed or crisped just before
*   serving*

TOPPINGS
Leek, Feta, and Sour Cream Salsa (page 48)
Dressed Cilantro (page 76)

1. Place the white beans in a medium-size saucepan and add water to cover by 2 inches. Bring to a boil. Cook for 1 minute, and remove from the heat. Set aside to soak for 1 hour; drain.

2. Heat the oil in a large nonreactive pot set over medium-high heat. Add as many duck quarters, skin side down, as will fit in one uncrowded layer. Cook until browned, about 10 minutes. Continue cooking another round until all of the duck is browned.

3. Return all of the duck to the pot, along with the beans, garlic, tomato paste, thyme, salt, pepper, wine, and stock. Bring to a boil. Reduce the heat to a simmer; partially cover the pot. Cook until the duck meat easily pulls away from the bones, about 1¼ hours. Remove the duck pieces; set aside to cool. Drain the beans, reserving the liquid for another dish. Set the beans aside.

4. When the duck is cool enough to handle, shred the meat; discard the skin and bones.

5. To assemble, place about ⅓ cup of the duck meat in the middle of a tortilla. Arrange some beans over the duck. Top with Leek, Feta, and Sour Cream Salsa and Dressed Cilantro. Fold and serve.

DUCK WITH POBLANO CHILIES AND WALNUTS

D uck hot from the oven with walnuts roasted, saturated, and imbued with duck juices. A touch of nutmeg and just enough chili pepper give the dish a slight zing. Yet this duck is destined for a tortilla, not a silver serving platter.

~~~~~~

VARIATIONS

▼

For other south-of-the-border duck fillings, trim the
bird with pumpkin seeds
instead of walnuts, or substitute squab for the duck,
Or top the duck with a
combination of Orange-
Onion Salsa and shredded
lettuce or Roasted Garlic,
Tomato, and Anchovy Sauce
and cilantro sprigs. (See
Index for recipe page numbers.)

Serves 4 to 6
Takes 2 hours

3 ducks (about 4½ pounds each), quartered (see Tips)
3 tablespoons pure chili powder
¾ teaspoon grated nutmeg
¾ teaspoon salt
2 tablespoons fresh lemon juice
3 cups dry white wine
6 poblano chili peppers (about ¾ pound), stemmed, seeded,
    and cut into thin strips
1½ cups walnut halves or pieces (about 3 ounces)
18 corn or 12 flour tortillas, warmed or crisped just before
    serving

TOPPINGS
Yucatan Sauce (page 61)
2 cups chopped avocado
2 cups cilantro leaves

1. Heat the oven to 450°F.

2. Wash the duck and pat dry. With a fork, prick each quarter
in several places through the skin but not into the meat.

3. In a small bowl, mix together the chili powder, nutmeg,
salt, lemon juice, and wine. Rub the skin sides of each duck
quarter with the mixture.

4. Arrange the chili strips and walnuts in the bottom of a
large roasting pan. Set the duck pieces, skin side up, in one layer
in the roasting pan. Roast until the meat easily separates from
the bone when pulled with a fork, about 1½ hours. Remove and
let cool.

5. When cool enough to handle, shred the duck meat; discard
the skin and bones.

6. To assemble, spread about ⅓ cup of the duck meat in the
center of a tortilla. Arrange some chili strips and walnuts over
the duck. Top with the Yucatan Sauce, chopped avocado, and
cilantro sprigs. Fold and serve.

TIPS

▶ To cut ducks, which are very strong-boned, into quarters, first use a boning knife or chef's knife to cut down one side of the backbone, severing the joint where the thigh meets the backbone. Open the duck out flat, skin side down. Holding a chef's knife in one hand, place it at the center of the wishbone. Cover the top of the blade with a folded kitchen towel to protect your hand, and rap sharply on the blade with your other hand to cut through the bone. Using the towel technique to protect your hand again, cut each duck half into half again between the bottom of the breast and top of the thigh.

▶ Be sure to tuck the chili strips under the duck pieces in the roasting pan so they won't burn.

▲▲▲▲▲▲▲▲▲▲▲▲▲▲▲▲

There's Mille Lacs, Leech Lake, Lower Red Lake, Upper Red Lake, Rainey Lake, and Lake of the Woods just to mention the large ones. All of them, along with a plethora of smaller lakes, plus the wing of one huge one, fall in the state of Minnesota. All of them harbor havens for ducks. Duck eating thrives in Minnesota. There are fine restaurants in Duluth and Minneapolis that serve divine domestic duck. We have attended barbecues and parties in St. Paul and Rochester where duck starred. The duck at these affairs has been both domestic and feral, with the wildest duck yet above the snow line on the reservation at Bemidji. In this filling, we offer duck American- and sort of Minnesota-style. Walnuts grow throughout the state. Tortillas, at least corn ones, have been seen in stores. White wine and avocados have crept into gatherings. We didn't add a salsa of apples, but we couldn't resist a touch of poblano chili.

▼▼▼▼▼▼▼▼▼▼▼▼▼▼▼▼

FISH

Chalchihutlicue, goddess of lakes, oceans, rivers, and water travelers, was a busy Aztec goddess for Mexico has coastlines that stretch thousands of miles, rivers like long, winding snakes, and many glistening fish-filled lakes. The finny animals that populate the waters are so varied and abundant that fish markets all along her shoreline gleam with jewel-like hues of gray, blue, green, red, and yellow.

The warm gulfs and cold rocky reaches of North America, too, brim with fish: abundant salmon, snapper to be blackened, catfish hovering in the mud silts up and down the Mississippi River, and lake bass.

Pick almost any bright-eyed and firm-fleshed fish from the market, and you have the makings of some of the best possible tortilla fillings. Bake the fish, stew it, fry it, or grill it, then savor it simple or return it to a sea of salsa and let it swim in spice. Whatever the fish, we offer a tangy hint: Bathe it in lime and salt or another marinade for a few minutes prior to cooking. This treatment firms the texture and adds a spark of flavor, especially important for blander fish.

SEATTLE SALMON IN A DIPPED TORTILLA

Seattle and points north are the lucky recipients of a lush salmon run every year. Salmon is so plentiful you can even get it fish-and-chips style from vendors, in the fresh food markets by the water's edge. For tacos we like salmon baked Seattle-style—clean and fresh, with just a touch of cucumber, a dash of Salsa Verde, tequila, and a gossamer coating of cream. The tacos burst with the unparalleled flavor that only salmon has.

Serves 4 to 6
Takes less than 20 minutes

2 teaspoons pure chili powder
2¼ pounds salmon steaks, fillets, or chunks, cut ¾- to 1-inch
    thick
¼ cup tequila
1 tablespoon fresh lime juice
Salt, to taste
1½ cups heavy (whipping) cream
½ cup sour cream
18 corn or 12 flour tortillas
Salsa Verde (page 52)

TOPPINGS
2 medium cucumbers, cut into matchstick strips
2 cups cilantro leaves

    1. Heat the oven to 375°F.

    2. Rub the chili powder evenly over both sides of the fish. Place the fish in a nonreactive baking dish, sprinkle on the tequila and lime juice, and salt lightly. Set aside while the oven heats.

▲▲▲▲▲▲▲▲▲▲▲▲▲▲▲▲

Down in the industrial section close to the bay, not too far from our homes, sits one of the best kept secrets of the East San Francisco Bay, Sportsman's Cannery. Inside the low and humble building labors a team of experts who will smoke fish, duck, venison, or whatever you catch or bag. Mostly they smoke salmon, for San Francisco marks the southern boundary of the great North Coast salmon runs. Every year starting in May, people like us head happily out of the bay to fish our own salmon. Our take has run from 7 pounds to 20, but the real fun isn't the weight of the catch, it's the number of fish we catch. The more fish we reel in, the more the different kinds of smoking we can try. Sportsman's offers a Nova Scotia-style smoke, a smokier English kipper smoke, and a dry, dense Indian smoke, and you can choose mild, medium, or heavy for each. They cut the fish in halves, quarters, or eighths, as you like, and vacuum-pack it to freeze perfectly. Whether we've netted our limit or less, we always save one salmon for Seattle-style salmon tacos.

3. Bake the fish until white curds are beginning to form on the top or an instant reading thermometer registers 112°F, 8 to 10 minutes for chunks, 12 to 14 minutes for steaks or fillets, depending on the thickness. Remove from the oven and set aside to allow the juices to settle for a few minutes.

4. In a small bowl, whisk together the cream and sour cream until smooth.

5. Just before serving, dip the tortillas in the Salsa Verde. Heat in a frying pan or in the oven.

6. Break the salmon into bite-size pieces, removing any bones.

7. To assemble, place about ⅓ cup of the salmon in the center of a tortilla. Top with cucumber strips, cilantro leaves, some of the remaining Salsa Verde, and a dollop or two of the cream mixture. Fold and serve.

TIPS

▶ Steaks that are ½- to ¾-inch thick take 8 to 10 minutes.

▶ If the cucumbers have large seeds, remove them. For a more pronounced cucumber flavor, lightly sprinkle the cut cucumber with salt. Set aside to wilt. Squeeze out the excess liquid before serving.

SAVORY BAKED FISH

When contemplating cooking fish, many of us think of frying or grilling. But baking is easy and has great advantages. While the fish bakes in the oven, you are free to roam. You need add no oil, which keeps the dish lean. Lay the fish in a tortilla and spread on toppings subtle or fancy. You can use fish chunks or whole fish, steaks or fillets for a baked fish filling.

Serves 4 to 6
Takes less than 20 minutes

2¼ pounds meaty fish steaks, fillets, or chunks, such as
*   snapper, rock cod, sea bass, shark, tuna, cut ¾- to 1-inch*
*   thick*
½ teaspoon pure chili powder
2 tablespoons fresh lime juice
2 tablespoons dry white wine
1 medium-size red onion, thinly sliced
Salt, to taste
18 corn or 12 flour tortillas, warmed or crisped just before
*   serving*

TOPPINGS
4 cups shredded lettuce
Fresh Tomato Salsa (page 37)

1. Heat the oven to 375°F.

2. Meanwhile, place the fish in a nonreactive baking dish. Sprinkle evenly with the chili powder, lime juice, and wine. Arrange the onion on top and season lightly with salt. Set aside while the oven heats.

3. Bake the fish until white curds are just beginning to form

VARIATIONS
▼

FOR THE TOPPINGS
Many toppings also complement a simple baked fish. In addition to shredded lettuce, heap on:
■ Chopped tomatoes—especially if you aren't using Fresh Tomato Salsa.
■ Basic Fried Potatoes—a tablespoon or so adds up to the perfect combination, fish and chips.
■ Pepper strips—raw, fried, grilled, or baked chili or bell peppers.
■ Sliced jalapeños—sliced very thin.
■ Feta cheese—especially in combination with canned jalapeños.

FOR THE SALSA
Many salsas finish Savory Baked Fish with gusto. We particularly like: Chive Salsa; Greek Salsa; Red Bell Pepper-Tomatillo Salsa; South American Jalapeño-Parsley Salsa; Roasted Garlic, Tomato, and Anchovy Sauce; and Pasilla, Mint, and Pickled Red Onion Sauce (see Index for recipe page numbers).

on the top or an instant reading thermometer registers 115°F, 8 to 12 minutes for chunks, 10 to 13 minutes for steaks or fillets, depending on the thickness. Remove the fish and set aside to allow the juices to settle for a few minutes.

4. Break the fish into bite-size pieces, removing any bones.

5. To assemble, spread about ⅓ cup of the fish in the center of a tortilla. Top with shredded lettuce and Fresh Tomato Salsa. Fold and serve.

FRESH GRILLED FISH

In Spain the cook places the fish over the fire encaged in a fish-shaped wire basket. That way the fish can be turned over, basket and all, and there is no problem of its breaking. In Greece they have cup-shaped, clay charcoal braziers that hold just enough fire over which to grill a small offering from Poseidon's realm. The Hawaiians skewer the fish on a stick and arch it over glowing coals to cook. In backyards here we use a wide variety of grills large and small, and when winter comes we resort to indoor broilers to grill our trout, tuna, swordfish, or salmon. Whatever the technique, grilling fish is a surefire delight. Toast the tortillas on the grill alongside and you have dinner with no pots and pans.

Serves 4 to 6
Takes less than 20 minutes (not including preparing grill)

¾ cup olive oil
2 garlic cloves, pressed or minced
1 tablespoon fresh marjoram leaves or 1 teaspoon dried
2¼ pounds firm fish steaks, fillets, or chunks, such as tuna,
     swordfish, shark, angler, or salmon, cut ½ inch thick
18 corn or 12 flour tortillas, warmed or crisped just before
     serving

TOPPINGS
4 cups shredded lettuce
Pickled Onions (page 72)
Avocado-Pumpkin Seed Salsa (page 44)

1. Prepare a charcoal fire for grilling, allowing the coals to burn until they are mostly covered with white ash but a few red spots show through here and there. This will take about 40 minutes.

2. Meanwhile, place the olive oil, garlic, and marjoram in a large nonreactive pan or dish. Add the fish and turn to coat all over. Set aside until the fire is ready.

3. When the coals are hot, lift the fish out of the marinade. If using fish chunks, string them on skewers. Arrange the fish on the grill rack directly above the coals. Grill for 2 minutes. Turn and grill just until the flesh springs back when poked with a finger, about 2 minutes more. Remove and set aside to allow the juices to settle, a few minutes.

4. Break the fish into bite-size pieces, removing any bones.

5. To assemble, spread about ⅓ cup of the fish in the middle of a tortilla. Top with lettuce, Pickled Onions, and Avocado-Pumpkin Seed Salsa.

VARIATIONS

▼

FOR THE MARINADE
To perk up the marinade for grilled fish, stir in:
■ ½ tablespoon fresh lemon juice or red wine vinegar with the olive oil mixture.
■ Mix 1 tablespoon Dijon mustard into the olive oil mixture.
■ Vary the herbs with dill, rosemary, thyme, bay leaf, parsley, or cilantro in place of the marjoram.

FOR THE TOPPINGS
■ A tablespoon or so of chopped tomatoes goes well with both the fish and the Avocado-Pumpkin Seed Salsa.
■ Pickled carrots are good with any fish and any of the topping variations.
■ Cut fresh mild Anaheims, spicier poblanos, or pasillas into ½-inch-thick strips and grill along with the fish.

FOR THE SALSAS
Any and all the salsas in this book work well with grilled fish with the exception of Pear-Lime, Orange-Onion, and Yucatan Salsas. The particular perfumes of these salsas fight the flavor of fish.

PORTUGUESE-STYLE GRILLED FISH

▲▲▲▲▲▲▲▲▲▲▲▲▲

During the age of discovery, the Portuguese were intrepid seafarers. On their journeys, they collected all manner of spices and fruits—cloves, oranges, cayenne. They happily incorporated their exotic edible treasures into the fish dishes of their cuisine. Here we use a Portuguese-style marinade to produce a zesty and unique fish taco. The result is a seductive combination of familiar ingredients.

▼▼▼▼▼▼▼▼▼▼▼▼▼

Sea bass is particularly delicious grilled, but any good white meat grilling fish, such as swordfish, shark, angler, or mahimahi will do nicely.

The fish should not marinate longer than 15 or 20 minutes, or it will become too sweet from the infusion of the orange flavor. Coordinate the grill preparation with the step of marinating the fish by preparing the fish about 20 minutes after you start the fire.

Serves 4 to 6
20 to 40 minutes

⅔ cup fresh orange juice
¼ cup dry white wine
½ tablespoon paprika, preferably
    Hungarian sweet
Small pinch of cayenne
Small pinch of ground cloves
2 tablespoons fresh thyme leaves or
    2 teaspoons dried
2¼ pounds sea bass fillets, cut ½- to ¾-inch thick
24 scallions (green onions), trimmed
18 corn or 12 flour tortillas, warmed or
    crisped just before serving

TOPPING
Roasted Red Pepper, Chili, and Pine Nut
    Sauce (page 57)

1. Prepare a charcoal fire for grilling, allowing the coals to burn until they are mostly covered with white ash but a few red spots show through here and there. This will take about 40 minutes.

2. Fifteen or 20 minutes before the fire is ready, mix together the orange juice, wine, paprika, cayenne, cloves, and thyme in a nonreactive dish. Place the fish fillets in the mixture and turn to coat all sides. Set aside to marinate.

3. When the coals are hot, arrange the fish fillets on the grill rack directly above the coals. Grill for 4 minutes. Turn and grill until white curds begin to form on top, about 4 minutes more, depending on the thickness. Remove the fish and set aside to allow the juices to settle for a few minutes.

4. While the fish rests, grill the scallions. Place them on the rack directly above the coals and cook for 2 minutes. Turn and cook until lightly charred, 1 to 2 minutes more.

5. Break the fish into bite-size chunks, removing any bones.

6. To assemble, spread about ⅓ cup of the fish in the middle of a tortilla. Top with 2 scallions and some Roasted Red Pepper, Chili, and Pine Nut Sauce. Fold and serve.

SOLE AND FRIED POTATOES WITH ANCHO CHILI SAUCE

Flaky and quick to cook, low-fat sole is one of the most available and popular fish fillets. It lends itself to a wide variety of condiments and flavor enhancements. Since sole is so mild, we like to spunk it up with Basic Fried Potatoes and earthy Dressed Cilantro topping, then serve the combination in a crunchy chimichanga.

Serves 4 to 6
Takes less than 20 minutes

2½ pounds sole fillets
1½ cups fresh lemon juice
Salt, to taste
Peanut oil
18 corn or 12 flour tortillas

TOPPINGS
Basic Fried Potatoes (page 210)
Ancho Chili Sauce (page 59)
Dressed Cilantro (page 76)

1. Place the sole fillets in a nonreactive dish. Pour the lemon juice over the fillets and sprinkle on salt to taste. Set aside to marinate for a few minutes but no longer than 15, so the fish doesn't pickle.

2. Pour enough oil into a large nonreactive frying pan to reach ¼ inch up the sides. Set over high heat until the oil begins to smoke. Add as many fillets as will fit in one uncrowded layer. Fry for 1 minute. Turn and fry for 1 minute more. Drain the fillets on paper towels. Add more oil to the pan if necessary, and continue with another round until all the fish is cooked.

3. Break the fish into bite-size pieces, removing any bones.

4. To assemble, spread about ⅓ cup of the fish in the middle of a tortilla. Top with the Basic Fried Potatoes, Ancho Chili Sauce, and Dressed Cilantro. Fold envelope style and continue until all the chimichangas are assembled.

5. In a large frying pan, heat enough oil to coat the bottom and set over high heat. A few at a time, place the folded chimichangas in the pan and fry until browned, about 30 seconds per side. Serve hot.

VARIATIONS

▼

Besides the Ancho Chili Sauce, you might try Ranchero Sauce; Pasilla, Mint, and Pickled Red Onion Sauce; Fresh Tomato Salsa; or Leek, Feta, and Sour Cream Salsa (see Index for recipe page numbers).

STEWED FISH WITH TOMATO, SAFFRON, AND GARLIC SAUCE

F ish, stewed and smothered in its own sauce, turns blander varieties, such as some of the rock cods, into rich, distinctive fillings.

Serves 4 to 6
Takes 20 to 40 minutes

2¼ pounds meaty white fish fillets or chunks, such as
    snapper, cod, sea bass, halibut, cut ½- to ¾-inch thick
2 tablespoons fresh lime juice
Salt
3 pounds fresh tomatoes, coarsely chopped,
    juices reserved
10 garlic cloves, cut into thin slivers
Large pinch of saffron threads or ½ teaspoon
    powdered saffron
1 cup chopped parsley leaves
1½ cups chicken stock or broth
4 tablespoons (½ stick) butter
18 corn or 12 flour tortillas, warmed or crisped
    just before serving

TOPPING
Dressed Cilantro (page 76), or 4 cups shredded lettuce

1. Place the fish in a large nonreactive baking dish. Sprinkle the lime juice over it and salt lightly. Set aside while preparing the sauce.

2. To make the sauce, divide the tomatoes, garlic, saffron, parsley, stock, butter, and ½ teaspoon salt between 2 large nonreactive skillets or stew pots. (Or use one pan, cook the fish in

VARIATIONS
▼

FOR THE TOPPINGS
■ Basic Fried Potatoes make a hearty dish even more filling.
■ Crumbled feta or *cotija* cheese adds a pleasing sharp taste.
■ Sour cream smooths out the sauce.
■ Ancho Chili Sauce imparts an earthy depth to the stewing sauce.

several rounds, and allow more time for reducing the sauce at the end.) Bring to a boil. Cook over medium heat until the tomatoes are soft but still hold their shape, about 10 minutes.

3. Divide the fish fillets between the pans, keeping them in one layer. (Don't overlap or stack them or they won't cook evenly.) Simmer for 2 minutes. Turn and simmer just until the fish begins to flake when prodded with a wooden spoon, about 2 minutes more.

4. Break the fish fillets into bite-size pieces, removing any remaining bones.

5. To assemble, spread about ⅓ cup of the fish in the middle of a tortilla. Spoon a few tablespoons of the sauce over the fish, top with Dressed Cilantro or lettuce. Fold and serve.

CALIFORNIA-STYLE FISH CHUNKS IN A DIPPED TORTILLA

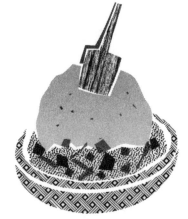

Although often chided for its sometimes rarefied delicacies, California cuisine nonetheless generally presents fresh and simple foods combined in intriguing ways. Here we take a bow to California cuisine in a union of fish chunks with fanciful elements. The trimmed parts often sold as chunks are much less expensive and often tastier than whole fish fillets or steaks. If you can't find fish chunks, you can always cut some from larger pieces.

Serves 4 to 6
Takes 20 to 40 minutes

2¼ *pounds fish chunks, such as swordfish,*
  shark, salmon, or tuna
¼ *cup fresh lemon juice*
½ *cup soy sauce*
2 *jalapeño chili peppers, stemmed and*
  minced
½ *medium Napa cabbage (see* Tip *below)*
Olive oil
18 *corn or* 12 *flour tortillas*
Pasilla, Mint, and Pickled Red Onion Sauce
  (page 60)

1. If the fish chunks are large, cut them into bite-size pieces, about 1-inch square.

2. In a large bowl, mix together the lemon juice, soy sauce, and chili peppers. Add the fish chunks and turn to coat all over. Set aside to marinate for 10 to 20 minutes.

3. Halve the cabbage half lengthwise and remove the core from each piece. Cut the leaves crosswise into very thin shreds.

4. Coat the bottom of a large frying pan with olive oil. Set over high heat until the oil begins to smoke. Add as many fish chunks as will fit in one uncrowded layer. Fry for 3 minutes. Turn and fry until flaky but still moist in the centers, 3 to 5 minutes more. Remove to a platter and keep warm. Continue cooking another round until all of the fish is cooked.

5. Add more oil to the pan. Add the cabbage and stir-fry until the cabbage is barely wilted, about 2 minutes.

6. Just before serving, dip the tortillas in ½ cup of the Pasilla, Mint, and Pickled Red Onion Sauce. Heat in a frying pan or the oven.

7. To assemble, spread about ⅓ cup of the fish chunks in the middle of a tortilla. Top with some of the wilted cabbage and remaining Pasilla, Mint, and Pickled Red Onion Sauce. Fold and serve.

TIP

▶ If you don't have Napa cabbage, sometimes called Chinese cab-

N appa or Napa—two *ps* or one? And did Napa valley have anything to do with the cabbage? We were on our way to a food society gathering in the wine country with one wine expert, one food critic, and one fine chef, all of whom had excellent taste, none of whom knew what we, the caterers, were going to cook. "What's for dinner?" they asked. Oh, something California style. "What's in it?" they asked. Duck eggs, sun-dried tomatoes, sourdough bread, they guessed. No, we replied. A sort of flat bread well known to early California settlers. Fish, well known to Italian California coastal fishermen. Napa cabbage, well known to Asian-California farmers. That's when the argument started about the *ps* and geography of Napa cabbage among our backseat gourmets and erudites. It kept them busy almost until mealtime, when we stirred up this taco. Two servings each, with California wine, our companions voted the taco three stars.

P.S. By the way, the cabbage has one *p* and nothing to do with the county.

bage, rather than substituting regular green cabbage, use a lettuce. The mild taste and soft curly leaves of Napa cabbage more closely resemble a crunchy lettuce, such as romaine, than they do their closer *brassica* kin. If you use lettuce, though, don't fry it. Strew it on as a topping.

BRAZILIAN-STYLE FISH

Fish Brazilian style—green, white, flecked with good black olives—makes some of the quickest, easiest, most festive looking *and* tasting tacos. This dish is one of our best, unbelievably good, and we frequently make it for parties.

Serves 4 to 6
Takes less than 20 minutes

*2¼ pounds white fish fillets, such as snapper, cod, halibut,
    sea bass, cut about ½ inch thick*
2 tablespoons fresh lime juice
Salt, to taste
8 tablespoons (1 stick) butter
Salsa Verde (page 52)
3 cups fresh corn kernels (about 3 medium ears)
*18 corns or 12 flour tortillas, warmed or crisped just before
    serving*

TOPPINGS
2 cups sour cream
*4 ounces black olives, preferably Calamata, pitted and
    coarsely chopped*

While we make and serve every recipe we create numerous times, when one turns out so delicious that we find ourselves making it over and over again, perhaps even once a week, it becomes one of our "Five Easy Pieces," a term we borrowed from the movie of the same name. Every cook has his or her "five easy pieces" as well: those family and company favorites that are well memorized and always delightful. That is the case for us with Brazilian-Style Fish. Once developed, it instantly became part of our show. It is spectacular.

1. Place the fish fillets in a large nonreactive baking dish. Sprinkle the lime juice over them and salt to taste. Set aside while preparing the sauce.

2. To make the sauce, divide the butter between 2 large non-reactive frying pans or stew pots. Melt over medium heat. (Or use 1 pan, cook the fish in several rounds, and allow more time for reducing the sauce at the end.) Add the Salsa Verde. Bring to a boil. Add the fish fillets, keeping them in one layer. (Don't overlap or stack the fillets or they won't cook evenly.) Reduce the heat and simmer for 2 minutes. Turn and simmer until the fish flakes when prodded with a wooden spoon, about 2 minutes more. Stir the corn kernels into the sauce. Remove the pan from the heat.

3. Break the fish fillets into bite-size pieces.

4. To assemble, spread about ⅓ cup of the fish in the middle of a tortilla. Spoon a few tablespoons of the sauce over the fish. Top with sour cream; sprinkle on the olives. Fold and serve.

SNAPPER VERA CRUZ

Snapper Vera Cruz with whole fresh fillets of Caribbean snapper in a tomato sauce fragrant with capers and olives is famous not only in its coastal province of origin, but throughout Mexico and in Mexican restaurants in the United States. It's traditionally served accompanied by a side of rice. We learned to turn this succulent dish into a burrito and offer it that way here.

Serves 4 to 6
Takes 20 to 40 minutes

2¼ pounds red snapper fillets, cut ½- to ¾-inch thick
2 tablespoons fresh lime juice
Salt, to taste
Vera Cruz Sauce (recipe follows)
12 flour tortillas, warmed just before serving

TOPPING
1 cup chopped fresh parsley leaves

1. Place the snapper fillets in a large nonreactive dish. Pour the lime juice over it and season with salt. Set aside for 15 minutes.

2. Divide the Vera Cruz Sauce between 2 large nonreactive frying pans. (Or use 1 pan, cook the fish in several rounds, and allow more time for reducing the sauce at the end.) Over low heat, bring the sauce to simmering.

3. Divide the snapper fillets between the pans, keeping them in one layer. (Don't overlap or stack the fillets or they won't cook evenly.) Simmer for 2 minutes. Turn and simmer until the fish begins to flake when prodded with a wooden spoon, about 2 minutes more.

4. Break the fish into bite-size pieces.

5. To assemble, spread about ⅓ cup of the fish in the middle of a tortilla. Spoon a few tablespoons of the sauce over the fish, and sprinkle with parsley over the top. Fold burrito style, and serve.

VERA CRUZ SAUCE

Makes 6 cups
Takes 15 minutes

4 tablespoons olive oil
2 medium onions, finely chopped
8 garlic cloves, minced
2½ pounds tomatoes, coarsely chopped
6 jalapeño chili peppers, stemmed and minced
15 large or other good Sicilian-style green olives, pitted and
    coarsely chopped
¼ cup capers, drained
1 large bay leaf
1 teaspoon salt
1½ cups water

1. Place the olive oil in a nonreactive medium-size saucepan and set over medium heat until the oil begins to smoke. Add the onions and garlic, and cook until wilted but not browned, about 5 minutes. Add the tomatoes, chili peppers, olives, capers, bay leaf, salt, and water. Bring to a boil, then reduce the heat and simmer until the tomatoes are soft but still hold their shape, about 15 minutes.

2. Remove the pan from the heat and fish out the bay leaf. Set the sauce aside until ready to use, or refrigerate for up to 2 weeks.

▲▲▲▲▲▲▲▲▲▲▲▲▲▲▲▲

A team of archeologist friends digging in the jungle near Vera Cruz came upon the treasure every archeologist longs to uncover—not gold, but an ancient site complete with hieroglyphics and four highly important pieces of statuary. Almost at the same moment, they endured another experience not unfamiliar to archeologists. They were set upon by bandits who after compelling our friends to dig out the statues and load them onto a truck, absconded with the treasure. The officials of Vera Cruz joined with the archeologists to chase down the poachers. They located the varmints in an obscure cantina, forced them to reload the statues and replant them at the site exactly as they had lain for centuries. In the midst of this action our poor friends had no time to eat until the local workers brought them fresh fish simmered with tomatoes, green olives, and capers as they cook it in Vera Cruz, only wrapped in portable tortillas rather than on plates. Back home they entertained us with the tale of their adventure and with the classic Red Snapper Vera Cruz in taco form. It was so good, we offer our variation here, and suggest while savoring it, you look at pictures of Olmec statuary.

SHELLFISH

Along the Atlantic coast of Colombia and the Pacific coast of Equador and Peru rise mounds of shells, refuse from devoured shellfish left by ancient peoples. The mounds date back as far as 800 B.C. at Momil and 3000 B.C. at Puerto Hormiga (both in Colombia), the oldest place in the New World where pottery is found. Near the huge piles of shells are systems of earthen levees and channels where maize, potatoes, and manioc were planted and settlements rose.

Prehistoric mounds filled with the shells of clams, lobsters, and scallops also lie across the southeastern seaboard of the United States where the great corn-growing tribes of American Indians, the Chickasaw, Choctaw, Cherokee, and Creek, lived. And along the coasts of California the shell mounds date back to at least 1300 A.D., giving homage to the Chumash, Miwak, Yoruk, and others who gathered over 45 varieties of clams, squid, crabs, and abalone.

To this day the coasts of the Americas proliferate with shellfish. And shellfish fillings abound along with the shellfish. They vary with the catch—chunks of abalone, lobster tail, shrimp in many sizes—and with the country. Argentinians munch lobster and crab tarts; fat squid steaks garlicked in *mojo de ajo* fill piping hot homemade tortillas and are enjoyed from Honduras to Costa Rica; and now—if you haven't before—you can enjoy them, too.

SHRIMP WITH LEMON-CHILI CREAM SAUCE

*C*amarones is Spanish for shrimp. They range from tiny bay shrimp to medium transparent ones with tails that swing up in the air to ones as big as your fist—the giant *camarones* of Mexico. Shrimp find their way into tortillas in more forms than you can count—fried, breaded, steamed, in garlic, in butter, in Ranchero Sauce, and in Salsa Verde. We find the flavor of shrimp so subtly delicious unadorned, we avoid anything that would overwhelm the shrimp itself. In our basic shrimp taco, we merely finesse the delicate flesh with a few strips of mild yellow bell pepper and a light lemon-chili cream we have created just for shrimp.

Serves 4 to 6
Takes less than 20 minutes

3½ pounds uncooked medium shrimp, peeled, tails removed, and deveined
¼ cup olive or peanut oil
Salt, to taste
18 corn or 12 flour tortillas, warmed or crisped just before serving

TOPPINGS
2 cups Lemon-Chili Cream Sauce (recipe follows)
3 large yellow bell peppers, stemmed, seeded, and cut into very thin 1½-inch-long strips
4 cups shredded lettuce

1. Rinse the shrimp and pat them dry.

2. Place half of the oil in a large frying pan and set over medium-high heat until the oil begins to smoke. (Or use 2 pans

VARIATIONS
▼

■ If you can't find yellow bell peppers, use red, or mild Anaheim chili peppers, instead.
■ Use tangy Lemon-Chili Cream Sauce—a gem of speed and versatility—on all kinds of shellfish, pork, chicken, lamb, turkey, duck, or blanched vegetables.

and cook the shrimp in 1 round.) Add half of the shrimp and salt liberally. Stir just until the shrimp are white in the centers, 3 to 5 minutes. Remove the shrimp from the heat and set aside in a warm place. Repeat with the remaining shrimp.

3. To assemble, place about ⅓ cup of the shrimp in the center of a tortilla. Top with Lemon-Chili Cream Sauce, yellow bell pepper strips, and shredded lettuce. Fold and serve.

LEMON-CHILI CREAM SAUCE

Makes 2 cups
Takes 15 minutes

1 yellow wax chili pepper, stemmed and minced
2 cups heavy (whipping) cream
2 tablespoons pure chili powder
3 tablespoons fresh lemon juice
¼ teaspoon salt

1. Combine all of the ingredients in a nonreactive medium saucepan. Bring to a boil and cook over medium heat until thick enough to coat a spoon, about 5 minutes.

2. Use right away, or cover and refrigerate for up to 1 week. May be reheated to serve warm, or serve chilled.

▲▲▲▲▲▲▲▲▲▲▲▲▲▲▲

One weekend, several years ago, we all—kids and mates included—took a trip to San Diego to see their splendid zoo. Unfortunately it was February and the rains came in torrents. So much for sunning on the beach or strolling past the pen of Gregory Peccary. We had to view the zoo from a canopied trolley. Looking for other diversions, Susanna remembered an obscure Italian restaurant that lay hidden behind a grocery store she had found once before. We rented a car and combed the district street by street until we passed a window displaying rows of olive oil, boxes of salt cod, and bins of dry pasta. There it was, the hidden *ristorante.* The special of the day was fresh shrimp served in a simple lemon cream. The plate was garnished with some mildly hot pickled peppers and flat Italian rosemary bread. The seven of us basked in the warmth of the dish, if not the sun. Now when the February rains prevail, and we are cold, we bask in the dish taco style.

▼▼▼▼▼▼▼▼▼▼▼▼▼▼▼

SPICY SHRIMP WITH SPINACH

Lightly dressed, topped with Deviled Peanuts and Coconut, wrapped in a spinach leaf, then a tortilla, shrimp turns into a sublime hand food.

Serves 4 to 6
Takes less than 20 minutes

3½ pounds uncooked medium shrimp, peeled, tails removed, and deveined
¼ cup olive or peanut oil
Salt, to taste
1 tablespoon cider vinegar
24 large spinach leaves, washed and patted dry
18 corn or 12 flour tortillas, warmed or crisped just before serving

TOPPINGS
Deviled Peanuts and Coconut (page 77)
3 limes, cut into 8 thin wedges each

1. Rinse the shrimp and pat them dry.

2. Place half of the oil in a large frying pan. Set over medium-high heat until the oil begins to smoke. (Or use 2 pans and cook the shrimp in 1 round.) Add half of the shrimp to each pan and salt liberally. Stir just until the shrimp are white in the centers, 3 to 5 minutes. Pour half of the vinegar into the pan and cook, stirring until the liquid evaporates. Remove the shrimp from the heat and set aside in a warm place. Repeat with the remaining shrimp.

3. To assemble, place 1 or 2 spinach leaves on top of a tortilla. Arrange 2 or 3 shrimp in the center of the spinach. Top with Deviled Peanuts and Coconut and squeeze on some lime juice. Roll up and eat.

▲▲▲▲▲▲▲▲▲▲▲▲▲▲▲▲

Susanna was on the island of Corfu when she had the best shrimp she ever ate. She was distantly daydreaming on a beautiful crescent-shaped beach when a cordial man approached her. Pointing to the small taverna at the far end of the beach and hesitant that this American wouldn't understand his Greek, he said he had just caught some shrimp and was she interested. All it took was the word *garides* to smack Susanna back to reality and its pedestrian pleasures, especially eating. She jumped up with a bold "Most certainly!" and off they strode. Taverna owner and cook as well as fisherman, he dumped his catch in a frying pan with just some olive oil and garlic, sautéed them in a flash, and spilled them onto a plate. He placed a spinach salad to the side and propped a glass of retsina wine above the dish. The taste was poetry. Who could ask for anything more artless, more artful, or more unforgettable?

▲▲▲▲▲▲▲▲▲▲▲▲▲▲

We love them at baseball games, serve them with cocktails, relish them in candy bars, eagerly await them on airplane rides, eat tons of them puréed as a butter, but we rarely take them seriously. Peanuts are another New World food scarcely acknowledged as western, though now one of the 15 most important crops worldwide. A native of South America, probably of Peru, the peanut is actually a legume (like peas, beans, and lentils) that pushes its seed-filled pod underground to ripen. Though it's our own, we have largely ignored the peanut as a staple food. Recently other peoples, such as the Thais and the Ethiopians, have shown us what they do with peanuts. They serve peanuts as a porridge, peanuts in rich meat-like patties, peanuts as a thickener, a topping, a dressing, and a flavor enhancer on other foods.

▼▼▼▼▼▼▼▼▼▼▼▼▼▼

THAI-STYLE SHRIMP

Shrimp are a staple of Southeast Asian cooking. The abundant, flavorful coral flesh and even the shells go into a paste that is the basic seasoning of the cuisine. The shrimp themselves, pink and prim, are lavished over cucumbers, burnished with peanuts, fretted with mint or coconut, or dotted with cashews, and served with a chilied vinegar dip. From that cuisine and its crown element, we offer this Thai-Style Shrimp in a taco.

Serves 4 to 6
Takes less than 20 minutes

3½ pounds uncooked medium shrimp, peeled, tails removed, and deveined
¼ cup peanut or olive oil
Salt, to taste
Chive Salsa (page 45)
1 tablespoon cider vinegar
1 teaspoon vegetable oil
1 cup roasted peanuts
18 corn or 12 flour tortillas, warmed or crisped just before serving

TOPPINGS
4 cups shredded lettuce
2 medium cucumbers, peeled and coarsely grated
½ cup fresh mint leaves

1. Rinse the shrimp and pat them dry.

2. Place half of the oil in 1 large frying pan. Set over medium-high heat until the oil begins to smoke. (Or use 2 pans and cook the shrimp in 1 round.) Add half the shrimp and salt liberally. Stir just until the shrimp are white in the centers, 3 to 5 minutes.

Add ⅛ cup of the Chive Salsa and the vinegar; stir to mix well. Remove from the heat; set aside in a warm place. Repeat with the remaining shrimp.

3. Heat the vegetable oil in a small frying pan over medium-high heat. Add the peanuts and stir until browned, about 4 minutes. Coarsely chop the peanuts in a food processor or with a chef's knife.

4. To assemble, place about ⅓ cup of the shrimp in the center of a tortilla. Top with the shredded lettuce, grated cucumber, mint leaves, remaining Chive Salsa, and roasted peanuts. Fold and serve.

CRABMEAT WITH LEMON-GARLIC BUTTER

Blessed as we are in San Francisco with crab-filled waters, a flotilla of crab boats, and a crab market, we can testify that crabmeat makes marvelous tacos. Saucing crab with traditional garlic and butter, even in taco form, is still one of the best ways to exalt the already rich and flavorful meat. We like to round out the crab, lemon, and garlic with the velvety smoothness of avocado. The pumpkin seeds are a frill, it's true, but one that adds bite, flair, and gusto.

Serves 4 to 6
Takes less than 20 minutes

MENU
▼

RING IN THE NEW YEAR

Crabmeat with Lemon-Garlic Butter in a Dipped Tortilla

Mock Tamales

Jicama-Pomegranate Christmas Salad

Baked Yam Flautas with Pine Nuts and Sesame Seeds

▲▲▲▲▲▲▲▲▲▲▲▲▲▲▲▲

In the early days of American history, distinguished souls from George Washington on down to unknown colonists prized the tiny oyster crabs that have almost disappeared from our shores. Only 1½ centimeters across at full growth, the oyster crab finds itself an oyster, crawls inside the pearly home, and without doing harm to its landlord, stays for free shelter. The little crabs were fried up in batches, floated like crackers on fish soups, and used to stuff canapés. Now we rarely eat the smallest crabs, but seek out the abundant meat of big ones, or at least the claws, bellies, and sometimes soft-shell variety of blue ones. Dungeness crab from the Pacific is available nationwide, and the huge King crabs of Alaska provide us bountiful meat for crab tacos all year long and in every location, if not fresh then via your freezer. The tiny oyster crabs, once practically extinct, are now returning. Perhaps someday they will be readily available for great tortilla fillings.

▼▼▼▼▼▼▼▼▼▼▼▼▼▼▼▼

½ pound (2 sticks) butter
1 tablespoon fresh lemon juice
2 garlic cloves, pressed or minced
1½ pounds cooked crabmeat, picked over to remove any
    remaining shell
18 corn or 12 flour tortillas
Salsa Verde (page 52)

TOPPINGS
2 cups chopped avocado
Toasted Pumpkin Seeds (page 75)
1 cup shredded fresh basil leaves

1. Place the butter, lemon juice, and garlic in a large non-reactive frying pan set over medium heat until the butter foams. Add the crabmeat. Stir and remove from the heat.

2. Just before serving, dip the tortillas in ½ cup of the Salsa Verde. Heat in a frying pan or in the oven.

3. To assemble, place about ⅓ cup of the crab in the center of a tortilla. Top with additional Salsa Verde, chopped avocado, Toasted Pumpkin Seeds, and shredded basil. Fold and serve.

CRISPY CRAB AND BREADED CHILI STRIPS

Serves 4 to 6
Takes less than 20 minutes

12 tablespoons (1½ sticks) butter
1 tablespoon dry white wine
2 garlic cloves, pressed or minced
1½ pounds cooked crabmeat, picked over to remove any
     remaining shell
18 corn or 12 flour tortillas, crisped just before serving

TOPPINGS
Breaded Chili Strips (page 71)
Pasilla, Mint, and Pickled Red Onion Sauce (page 60)
4 cups shredded lettuce

1. Place the butter, wine, and garlic in a large nonreactive frying pan. Set over medium heat until the butter foams. Add the crabmeat. Stir and remove from the heat.

2. To assemble, place about ⅓ cup of the crab in the center of a tortilla. Top with Breaded Chili Strips, Pasilla, Mint, and Pickled Red Onion Sauce, and shredded lettuce. Fold and serve.

SCALLOPS WITH SAUCE BELIZE

Extraordinarily tender, large or tiny, calico, *conchitas,* or *coquilles,* scallops turn a soft hot tortilla into a taco for the gods and goddesses. Scallops go with many accompaniments. Rich in the flavors of the tiny nation of Belize, land of many ancient Mayan ruins, we offer our Sauce Belize. Be sure not to overcook the scallops. Tender enough to eat raw, long cooking makes them tough and chewy.

Serves 4 to 6
Takes less than 20 minutes

2½ pounds bay or sea scallops
4 tablespoons plus 1 teaspoon olive oil
2 tablespoons fresh lemon juice
Salt, to taste
2 cups fresh parsley leaves, preferably Italian flat-leaf
1 teaspoon cider vinegar
18 corn or 12 flour tortillas, warmed or crisped just before
*   serving*

TOPPINGS
Sauce Belize (recipe follows)
1 tablespoon finely chopped lemon zest

1. Pat the scallops dry. If you have large sea scallops, cut them into ½-inch pieces.

2. Pour 2 tablespoons of the olive oil in a large frying pan. Set over high heat until the oil begins to smoke. Add half of the scallops, half of the lemon juice, and salt liberally. Stir until the scallops are just firm, about 1 to 1½ minutes. Remove to a platter and keep warm. Using 2 tablespoons of the oil, the remaining 1 tablespoon lemon juice, and additional salt, repeat the process with the remaining scallops. (Or use 2 skillets and cook the scallops in 1 round.)

3. Place the parsley in a bowl. Add vinegar, the remaining 1 teaspoon olive oil, and a light sprinkling of salt; toss well.

4. To assemble, spread about ⅓ cup of the scallops in the middle of a tortilla. Top with the Sauce Belize, some of the dressed parsley, and a little lemon zest. Fold and serve.

SAUCE BELIZE

Makes 2 cups
Takes less than 20 minutes

〜〜〜〜〜〜〜〜〜〜〜〜〜〜〜〜〜〜〜〜〜〜

4 medium-size ripe tomatoes, cut into eighths
2 dried ancho chili peppers, stemmed, seeded, and torn into
    3 or 4 pieces each
2 large garlic cloves, coarsely chopped
¼ teaspoon salt
Scant ¼ teaspoon cayenne
1½ cups water

1. Place all of the ingredients in a small nonreactive saucepan. Bring to a boil. Reduce the heat to a simmer and cook until the chilies and garlic are soft, about 10 minutes.

2. Purée the mixture in a food processor, blender, or food mill until quite smooth. Use right away, cover and refrigerate for up to 1 week, or freeze.

GUAYMAS SQUID OR ABALONE
MOJO DE AJO

〜〜〜〜〜〜〜〜〜〜〜〜〜〜〜〜〜〜〜〜

The intriguing, pleasing Spanish phrase for garlic is *mojo de ajo.* It also describes a Mexican way of cooking fish, especially shellfish. First chopped or slivered garlic is browned to perfection in butter and oil. This must be done with some patience over medium-low heat or the garlic will burn and become bitter. Then the fish is slipped into the pan and quickly turned in the aromatic butter. In Guaymas where the squid steaks are as big as a plate and thick as your thumb, and where the abalone shells with their rich meat can be grabbed by hand with a dive from a glass-bottomed dinghy, *mojo de ajo* ranks as the supreme cooking style.

▲▲▲▲▲▲▲▲▲▲▲▲▲▲

Mojo de ajo was a New World favorite even before Europeans brought bulbous heads of garlic to the Americas. In fact, the Americas had native wild garlic and pre-Columbians ate it bulb and shoots together, like a vegetable.

▼▼▼▼▼▼▼▼▼▼▼▼▼▼

▲▲▲▲▲▲▲▲▲▲▲▲▲▲▲
HOW TO PREPARE SQUID

To prepare the squid, separate the head from the body. Cut off the tentacles from the head just above the eyes (discard the head). Push out the hard ball from the center of each set of tentacles as you go. Remove the pen from inside the body and discard it. Next slit the bodies open lengthwise and scrape away the insides. Cut the bodies into 2 or 3 sections, each about 1½ inches long. Rinse the prepared squid and pat dry.

▼▼▼▼▼▼▼▼▼▼▼▼▼▼▼

Serves 4 to 6
Takes less than 20 minutes

2¼ pounds squid steaks or abalone steaks, cut about ⅛ inch thick
4 tablespoons fresh lime juice
Salt, to taste
2 tablespoons olive oil
6 tablespoons (¾ stick) butter
18 garlic cloves, coarsely chopped or slivered
18 corn or 12 flour tortillas, warmed just before serving

TOPPINGS
4 cups shredded lettuce
1 cup sliced fresh jalapeño chili peppers
1 cup cilantro leaves

1. Place the squid or abalone steaks in a large nonreactive dish. Moisten with 1 tablespoon of the lime juice and salt liberally.

2. In a nonreactive large frying pan, combine 1 tablespoon of the oil, 3 tablespoons of the butter, and half of the garlic. Set over medium-low heat until the butter foams and the garlic turns golden, about 2 minutes. (Or use 2 pans and cook the steaks in 1 round.) Add half the steaks and cook over medium-low heat, for 1½ minutes. Turn and cook the other side for 1½ minutes. Remove the steaks and garlic from the heat and set aside in a warm place. Place the remaining oil, butter, and garlic in the pan and repeat the process. Remove the second round of steaks. Stir the remaining 3 tablespoons lime juice into the pan and remove it from the heat.

3. Cut the steaks into ½-inch squares. Coat one side of each heated tortilla with the garlic butter that remains in the pan.

4. To assemble, spread about ⅓ cup of the squid in the center of the tortilla. Drizzle on a little of the garlic butter. Top with shredded lettuce, sliced jalapeños, and cilantro leaves. Fold and serve.

TIP

▶ For squid and abalone steaks, it's important to watch the timing. Seconds more and the steaks are overcooked and tough.

SQUID AND OLIVES WITH ORANGE-ONION SALSA

Ten arms, all seemingly extending out of a chin, fins on backs like sideways boat rudders, movements that shoot them forward and backward in gusts of propelled water. Odd and humorous as they appear, squid make a great catch. Squid with black olives and orange is both Portuguese and Brazilian in origin, and the best way not to lose a drop is to wrap the mixture in a tortilla envelope.

Serves 4 to 6
Takes less than 20 minutes

4 tablespoons olive oil
4 pounds cleaned squid (see How to Prepare Squid, page 204)
1 tablespoon chopped fresh oregano leaves or 1 teaspoon dried
Salt, to taste
8 ounces Calamata or other good black olives, pitted and coarsely chopped
2 jalapeño chili peppers, stemmed and finely chopped
½ cup dry white wine
12 flour tortillas, warmed or crisped just before serving

TOPPINGS
Orange-Onion Salsa (page 49)
4 cups shredded lettuce

1. Pour 2 tablespoons of the oil into a large frying pan and set over high heat until the oil begins to smoke. (Or use 2 pans and cook the squid in 1 round.) Add half of the squid and oregano to the hot oil and sprinkle generously with salt. Cook, stirring,

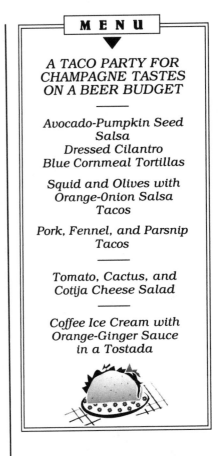

MENU
▼

A TACO PARTY FOR CHAMPAGNE TASTES ON A BEER BUDGET

Avocado-Pumpkin Seed Salsa
Dressed Cilantro Blue Cornmeal Tortillas

Squid and Olives with Orange-Onion Salsa Tacos

Pork, Fennel, and Parsnip Tacos

Tomato, Cactus, and Cotija Cheese Salad

Coffee Ice Cream with Orange-Ginger Sauce in a Tostada

just until the squid pieces are white in the center, about 1½ minutes. Remove the squid and their juices to a bowl. Add the remaining 2 tablespoons oil to the pan. Heat the oil, then cook the remaining squid as before.

2. Remove the second batch of squid and leave the juices in the pan. Pour the juices that collected from the first batch back into the pan. Add the remaining oregano, and the olives, chili peppers, and wine. Bring to a boil. Cook over medium-high heat, reducing the sauce in the pan until bubbles break from the bottom of the pan, about 2 minutes. Remove from the heat. Return the squid to the pan and stir to mix with the sauce.

3. To assemble, spread about ⅓ cup of the squid and some of its sauce in the center of a tortilla. Top with the Orange-Onion Salsa and shredded lettuce. Fold up envelope style and serve.

LOBSTER WITH AVOCADO-LIME CREAM

There's hummer and langoustine, astakos, rarog, and iseebi, all names for that decapod crustacean we call lobster. As an edible, we deem them all elegant. As an animal they are not so refined. They come with their claws banded, not so they won't pinch you, but so they won't devour each other. In a taco, the lobster reaffirms its sophisticated reputation, especially when topped with asparagus and a dazzle of delicate Avocado-Lime Cream.

Serves 4 to 6
Takes 20 to 40 minutes

4 *live lobsters (about 1¼ pounds each), or 2 pounds lobster
    tails*
1 *pound medium to large asparagus spears*
18 *corn or 12 flour tortillas, warmed or crisped just before
    serving*

TOPPINGS
Avocado-Lime Cream (recipe follows)
Dressed Cilantro (see page 76)
2 *bunches of scallions (green onions), trimmed and sliced
    into very thin rounds*

1. Bring 2 large pots of water to a boil. (Or use 1 pot and cook the lobsters one at a time.) Drop in the lobsters or lobster tails and cook for 11 minutes for whole lobster or 6 to 8 minutes for lobster tails. Drain and let cool enough to handle.

2. While the lobster cools, bring a medium-size pot of water to a boil. Snap off the ends of the asparagus spears at the point where they break easily. Cut the asparagus spears into ⅛-inch-thick rounds. Drop the asparagus rounds into the boiling water and cook for 1 minute. Drain in a colander; set aside.

3. *If using live lobster,* pull off the small legs and set aside to use in another dish. Pull off the large front claws and crack the shells with a nutcracker, hammer, or mallet. Break the lobster body in half crosswise at the joint between the tail and upper body. Using a knife, split the shell down the center of the underside of the tail. Remove the meat from the claws and tail.

If using lobster tails, remove the meat from the tails as described above.

4. Cut the lobster meat into ½-inch chunks.

5. To assemble, spread about ⅓ cup of the meat in the center of a tortilla. Arrange a layer of asparagus rounds over the lobster. Top with Avocado-Lime Cream, Dressed Cilantro, and scallions. Fold and serve.

TIP

▶ There are several steps in this recipe, but a little kitchen coordination makes the execution quite easy. Plan to boil the water

While we recommend our great American Maine lobster for this filling, still we have to give a nod to frozen lobster when making tacos for many. Most of our frozen lobsters come from South America and Australia. These iced visitors are usually spiny lobsters, a little smaller, and clawless, though equally tasty as the great cold-water American variety. Spiny lobsters are thin shelled, like the langoustine of France. When South Americans simmer them into soup and seafood stews—their usual practice—they toss in the shells too to make the flavor of the broth all the better. If you are in the mood for a less creamy and smooth sauce than the Avocado-Lime Cream in this recipe, you might try lobster tacos in Sauce Belize (see Index). Should you have a spiny lobster, simmer the shells in the sauce. But do remove them before biting into the taco!

for the asparagus at the same time you start the water for cooking the lobster. The asparagus rounds cook very quickly, and when they are done, you can turn your attention to preparing the Avocado-Lime Cream while the lobster finishes cooking and cooling. This way, everything will be ready at about the same time.

AVOCADO-LIME CREAM

Makes a bit more than 2 cups
Takes about 10 minutes

1 cup heavy (whipping) cream
2 tablespoons sour cream
¼ cup fresh lime juice
2 ripe but still firm avocados, peeled and pitted
1 jalapeño chili pepper, stemmed
½ teaspoon salt

Place all of the ingredients in the bowl of a food processor and purée until smooth. Or, to make by hand, place the cream, sour cream, and lime juice in a bowl and whisk until smooth. Mash the avocado with a fork and add to the bowl. Mince the jalapeño and add to the bowl. Add the salt and whisk until the ingredients are well blended. Use right away, or cover and refrigerate for up to several hours.

There are two easy ways to remove an avocado pit. Either quarter the avocado and pull away three of the quarters from the pit. The seed will remain with the last quarter and is easy to remove. Or halve the avocado and remove one half from the pit with a gentle twist. With the cutting edge of a chef's knife, give the pit a solid whack that is strong enough to lodge the blade in the pit. The pit will pull away with the knife, leaving the second half ready for scooping.

POTATOES, BEANS, AND VEGETABLES

Beans of almost every hue—white to black, pink to maroon—full of protein, pulpy and satisfying. Potatoes—red, white, brown, purple, and golden. Spinach, squash, onions—far more than with meat, poultry, or fish, the people who traditionally well-fill tortillas and other flat breads, stuff them with beans and vegetables.

Rarely do we see a purely vegetable taco in the cafes and homes north of the Rio Grande, but nothing quite matches a crisp tortilla wrapped around piping hot, crunchy potatoes or a soft burrito filled with black beans and sour cream. We invite you to bypass the beef and curtail the chicken.

~~~~~~

VARIATIONS
▼

FOR THE TOPPINGS
Along with one of the salsas and perhaps some cheese, add: Deviled Peanuts and Coconut, Dressed Cilantro, Pan-Grilled Scallions, Breaded Chili Strips, and Well-Filled Guacamole.

FOR THE SALSAS
Try: Tomato, Pumpkin Seed, and Scallion Salsa; Orange-Onion Salsa; Roasted Garlic, Tomato, and Anchovy Sauce; Leek, Feta, and Sour Cream Salsa. (See Index for recipe page numbers.)

FOR THE FILLINGS
Almost every other vegetable goes with potatoes.
■ Reduce the amount of potatoes to 2 pounds (about 4 cups diced) and add 2 cups coarsely chopped red and/or green bell peppers while frying the potatoes.
■ Reduce the amount of potatoes to 2 pounds (about 4 cups diced) and add 2 cups corn kernels in the last 5 minutes of frying.
■ Reduce the amount of potatoes to 2 pounds (about 4 cups diced) and add 2 cups plantains or green bananas, cut into ¼-inch-thick slices, during the last 10 minutes of frying.

BASIC FRIED POTATOES

~~~~~~

English chips, *pommes frites, frittos,* cottage fries, shoestrings—it's hard to imagine anything could improve on simple fried potatoes, whatever the national cut. But there is something better—fried potato tacos. In a taco, that mound of fried potatoes doesn't lie on a cold plate or in a limp piece of paper. It reposes in an edible, hot, soft or crisp tortilla. Ketchup gives way to salsa and any number of other toppings, and fried potatoes take on elements of the ecstatic. Be warned: Once you have a taste, you'll want them for breakfast, lunch, and dinner.

Serves 4 to 6
Takes 20 to 40 minutes

½ cup peanut oil
3 pounds red- or white-skinned potatoes, cut into ¼-inch dice
1 medium onion, cut into ¼-inch dice
Salt, to taste
18 corn or 12 flour tortillas, warmed or crisped just before
  serving

TOPPINGS
Fresh Tomato Salsa (page 37), Salsa Verde (page 52),
  Ranchero Sauce, (page 55), or Ancho Chili Sauce
  (page 59)
4 cups shredded lettuce
2 cups sour cream

1. Divide the oil between 2 large frying pans and set over medium-high heat until the oil begins to smoke. (Or use 1 skillet and fry the potatoes in 2 rounds.) Add the potatoes and onions and stir to coat with the oil. Pat the potatoes into an even layer and cook for 10 minutes. Turn the potatoes over and pat into a flat layer. Continue cooking until the potatoes are browned on both sides, about 10 minutes more. Stir once or twice at the end. Drain on paper towels; sprinkle lightly with salt.

2. To assemble, spread about ⅓ cup of the potatoes and onions in the middle of a tortilla. Top with a salsa, the shredded lettuce, and sour cream. Fold and serve.

TIPS

▶ It's important to resist stirring the potatoes often. If you stir them before they are thoroughly browned on the bottom, they become oil-logged and soggy.

▶ You can fry the potatoes in advance and reheat them in the same frying pan just before serving, but don't refrigerate them. In the refrigerator they develop a thick hide and do not crisp up again.

POTATOES PLUS WITH TOASTED ALMOND-GARLIC TOPPING

Serves 4 to 6
Takes 20 to 40 minutes

1 batch Basic Fried Potatoes filling (facing page)
3 pounds fresh spinach (about 4 bunches)
Vegetable oil
8 ounces lightly smoked ham, cut into thin strips
Ancho Chili Sauce (page 59)
18 corn or 12 flour tortillas

VARIATIONS
▼

MEATS AND POTATOES
■ Fry ½ to 1 pound bacon, cut crosswise into thin strips. Drain and stir into the potatoes as they are done.
■ Using ½ to 1 pound, crumble bulk or patty sausage, or cut links into thin slices, then cut slices in half. Fry separately and stir into the potatoes as they are done.
■ Stir in 1 to 2 cups ham strips or chunks, depending on how meaty you want your taco, to the potatoes for the last 10 minutes of frying.

TOPPINGS
Toasted Almond-Garlic Topping (recipe follows)
2 cups sour cream

1. Place the fried potatoes in a large nonreactive frying pan over very low heat.

2. Cut the spinach leaves crosswise into thin shreds. Plunge into plenty of water, allow the grit and sand to settle to the bottom, and then carefully lift the spinach into a colander. Shake to remove excess water; set aside to drip dry.

3. In a second large nonreactive frying pan, heat enough oil to coat the bottom. Set over medium-high heat and add the ham. Stir until lightly browned, about 5 minutes. Add the ham to the fried potatoes.

4. Add the spinach to the same pan you fried the ham in. Stir over medium-high heat until completely wilted, 2 to 3 minutes. Drain the spinach and stir it into the potatoes and ham.

5. Just before serving, dip the tortillas in ½ cup of the Ancho Chili Sauce. Heat in a frying pan or in the oven.

6. To assemble, spread about ⅓ cup of the potato, ham, and spinach mixture in the middle of a tortilla. Top with sour cream, some of the remaining Ancho Chili Sauce, and the Toasted Almond-Garlic Topping. Fold and serve.

TOASTED ALMOND-GARLIC TOPPING

Fragrant Toasted Almond-Garlic Topping is best warm and fresh out of the pan. To prepare it in advance or to have a stock on hand, cover and store in the freezer. Reheat just before serving.

Makes 1 cup
Takes 10 minutes

1 cup blanched almonds
12 garlic cloves
1 tablespoon peanut oil
⅛ teaspoon cayenne
¼ teaspoon salt

1. Coarsely chop the almonds and garlic in a food processor or with a chef's knife.

2. Pour the oil into a large frying pan and set over medium-high heat until it begins to smoke. Add the almonds, garlic, cayenne, and salt. Stir until lightly browned, about 3 minutes.

TIP

▶ If you find yourself out of almonds, use pine nuts, walnuts, or pecans instead.

▲▲▲▲▲▲▲▲▲▲▲▲▲▲▲▲

Although South America, the native home of potatoes, once had over 400 varieties, they were not the ones we see today. Most were small and bleak, and it's no wonder that it took a while for Europeans to like them. When Europeans and Africans did take to them, they developed wonderful fat and fully developed potatoes, but they let pass into obscurity many of the original varieties. Then modern grocery stores cut us further down to two or three varieties. Now the tide has reversed. We are beginning to see Finnish yellows, purples, ruby crescents, fingerlings. Like differing beans or peas, each has different assets in cooking. Little reds and purples are irresistible for boiling, butter, and parsley. Russets are great for baking or deep-fat, double frying but tend to collapse in pan-frying. Whites and yellows fry wonderfully—so we recommend them most for fried potato tacos. Since the skins of most frying potatoes—and even baking russets—are thin and the nutrients are mainly in the skin, we also recommend not peeling the potatoes. Besides, the skin gives added crispness to the taco.

▼▼▼▼▼▼▼▼▼▼▼▼▼▼▼▼

POTATOES AND PAPAYA

Papaya slices heated to a honey brown lend the potatoes a mellow tropical accent. Dressed with Ancho Chili Sauce, these tacos assume a deep smoky flavor. With Salsa Verde they become more piquant.

Serves 4 to 6
Takes 20 to 40 minutes

3 firm, just ripe, papayas
3 tablespoons butter
3 tablespoons pure chili powder or achiote paste
1 batch Basic Fried Potatoes filling (page 210), heated
18 corn or 12 flour tortillas, warmed or crisped just before
  serving

TOPPINGS
4 cups shredded lettuce
2 cups sour cream
Ancho Chili Sauce (page 59) or Salsa Verde (page 52)

1. Using a paring knife, peel the papayas and cut them in half. Scoop out the seeds. Cut each half into thin slices.

2. Melt the butter in a large frying pan over medium-high heat. Add as many papaya slices as will fit in one uncrowded layer. Fry until lightly browned on both sides, about 3 minutes per side. Remove to a plate and continue with another round until all of the papaya is browned. Sprinkle the papaya slices with the chili powder.

3. To assemble, spread about ⅓ cup of the fried potatoes in the middle of a tortilla. Place a layer of papaya over the potatoes and top with lettuce, sour cream, and Ancho Chili Sauce or Salsa Verde. Fold and serve.

POTATO MELT

F estooned with melted cheese, the already splendid potato taco becomes extraordinary. This simple trick lifts your spuds to banquet status. See the Potato and Roquefort Melt with Pear-Lime Salsa and the Fried Sweet Potato, Chili, and Cream Cheese Melt with Orange-Onion Salsa for two very special variations.

Serves 4 to 6
Takes 20 to 40 minutes

1 batch Basic Fried Potatoes filling (page 210)
2 cups shredded or crumbled cheese, such as sharp
    Cheddar, Jack, or queso fresco
18 corn or 12 flour tortillas, warmed or crisped just before
    serving

TOPPINGS
Fresh Tomato Salsa (page 37)
2 cups sour cream

1. Fry the potatoes as in the Basic Fried Potatoes recipe. Spread the cheese over the top. Cover the pan and cook over medium heat until the cheese melts, 2 to 3 minutes.

2. To assemble, spread about ⅓ cup of the potato-cheese mixture in the middle of a tortilla. Top with Fresh Tomato Salsa and sour cream. Fold and serve.

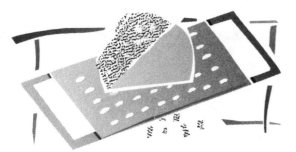

A t the Good and Plenty Cafe, the rush for melted cheese on fried potatoes, dash of salsa, hit of sour cream in a hot tortilla starts at 7:30 A.M. when we open our doors. We need so many fried potatoes so fast as a breakfast item, that we bake potatoes to cut and refry just before the crowd arrives. The call for potato melts resurges around 11:30 A.M. and persists until 1:00 while we fry up more batches, with green pepper, with onion, with chili powder, with paprika, until Dale, our manager and potato cook, cries, "Batches, batches, I won't cook no more batches." Frequently the last item sold at 7:00 P.M., before we let down the screen that turns the cafe into an after-hours student lounge, is yet one final potato melt. If we could bag them like cheese-flavored potato chips, we'd sell a million. Should your crowd get as hooked on them as ours, you can, like us, use leftover potatoes or bake a bunch to have ready for the frying pan, cheese, and a soft tortilla.

■ A number of vegetables blend well with Roquefort cheese and can be added to the potatoes during the last 5 minutes of cooking. Try: Asparagus, trimmed and sliced into 1-inch lengths; water-packed artichoke hearts, diced; mushrooms, especially shiitakes, chanterelles, and oyster mushrooms, sliced; yellow string beans, cut into ½-inch lengths; water chestnuts, sliced.

■ Several kinds of nuts also combine well with potatoes and Roquefort. Toast, chop, and add them to the potatoes for the last 5 minutes: pine nuts, macadamia nuts, pecans, and walnuts.

■ Vary the lettuce with some of the more lacy, flavorful greens. Try: Arugula, chicory, and frisée.

POTATO AND ROQUEFORT MELT WITH PEAR-LIME SALSA

I f you love blue cheese sprinkled on salads, stuffed in celery ribs, spread on crackers, or melted on burgers, this is the filling for you. You can top it deliciously with Pear-Lime Salsa, as we do here, or vary the topping with the more tropical Mango-Jalapeño Salsa. We are particularly fond of Roquefort for this melt, but you can also use Gorgonzola, Danish Blue, or any other semisoft blue cheese.

Serves 4 to 6
Takes 20 to 40 minutes

1 batch Basic Fried Potatoes filling (page 210)
12 ounces Roquefort cheese
18 corn or 12 flour tortillas, warmed or
*   crisped just before serving*

TOPPINGS
4 cups shredded lettuce
Pear-Lime Salsa (page 51)

1. Fry the potatoes as in the Basic Fried Potatoes recipe. Crumble the cheese and spread it over. Cover the pan and cook over medium heat until the cheese melts, 2 to 3 minutes.

2. To assemble, spread about ⅓ cup of the potato-cheese mixture in the middle of a tortilla. Top with shredded lettuce and Pear-Lime Salsa. Fold and serve.

FRIED SWEET POTATO, CHILI, AND CREAM CHEESE MELT

Serves 4 to 6
Takes 20 to 40 minutes

½ cup peanut oil
2 pounds sweet potatoes, peeled
and cut into ¼-inch dice
2 yellow wax chili peppers, stemmed and
coarsely chopped
8 ounces cream cheese, at room temperature
18 corn or 12 flour tortillas, warmed or
crisped just before serving

TOPPINGS
2 cups cilantro leaves
Orange-Onion Salsa (page 49)

1. Divide the oil between 2 large frying pans and set over medium-high heat until the oil begins to smoke. Add the potatoes and stir to coat with the oil. Pat them into an even layer and cook for 10 minutes. Turn the potatoes over, add the chilies, and pat into a flat layer. Continue cooking, stirring once or twice at the end, until the potatoes are browned on both sides, about 10 minutes more. Dollop the cream cheese over the top of the potatoes and cover the pans. Cook over medium heat until the cheese melts, 2 to 3 minutes.

2. To assemble, spread about ⅓ cup of the potato-cheese mixture in the middle of a tortilla. Top with cilantro leaves and Orange-Onion Salsa. Fold and serve.

▲▲▲▲▲▲▲▲▲▲▲▲▲▲▲▲

N o one knows exactly when sweet potatoes reached the Pacific islands, but South Americans had seaworthy boats from about 100 A.D. Sweet potatoes also reached Africa along with many other New World crops— kaffir corn, Livingstone potatoes, pumpkins, sweet and bitter manioc, and ground nuts. Now in both places sweet potatoes are staples, as "native" as the Irish potato and Italian tomato. Sweet potatoes are nibbled out of hand as people wander from home to garden, town to city, chore to chore. We've added the tortilla.

▼▼▼▼▼▼▼▼▼▼▼▼▼▼▼▼

BASIC BLACK BEANS

White beans are undeniably good. Made brown with molasses and served with brown bread they comprise a sort of Back Bay Boston taco. Pinto beans are the Mexican classic. Refried they are the heart of burritos and come as a side dish on every Mexican platter. But—and although we know opinions on this will differ as much as they do for favorite cars—we think of black beans as the Cadillac of beans. We have reason beyond the nutty flavor and integral texture. Like a quick starting and smooth running vehicle, they don't require warming up, in short, no soaking. They cook up from dry to done in about 1½ hours, and come out still sleek and classy. We also like their other name, turtle beans. In order not to lose a single delicious bite, we usually wrap these beans up burrito style, tucking in the ends of the tortilla.

Serves 4 to 6
Takes 2 hours

1½ pounds black beans (about 3½ cups)
1½ medium onions, finely chopped
6 garlic cloves, minced
3 jalapeño chili peppers, stemmed and finely chopped
½ cup canned crushed tomatoes in purée
⅛ teaspoon pure chili powder
12 cups water
½ teaspoon salt
18 corn or 12 flour tortillas, warmed or crisped just before
*   serving*

TOPPINGS
2 cups cilantro leaves
2 cups sour cream
Fresh Tomato Salsa (page 37)

1. Place the black beans, onions, garlic, chili peppers, to-matoes, chili powder, and water in a large pot. Bring to a boil. Reduce the heat to maintain a gentle boil (see Tips), and cook for 1½ hours. Stir in the salt and cook a little longer if the beans are not tender; remove from the heat if they are.

2. To assemble, use a slotted spoon to remove about ½ cup of the beans from the pot and place them in the center of a tortilla. Top with cilantro leaves, sour cream, and Fresh Tomato Salsa. Fold and serve.

TIPS

▶ If you buy black beans in bulk, place them on a baking sheet and sort through them to discard any stones or pebbles. Packaged black beans from the supermarket are presorted and don't require this step.

▶ It's important to cook the beans at a gentle boil—more than a simmer but not a full boil—so they become tender through to the centers.

▶ If you would like your black bean filling more compact (and less liable to spill out the ends of the taco), you can purée half the beans with the cooking liquid and stir in the remaining whole beans. This makes a filling more in the *frijoles refritos* style.

▶ Basic Black Beans can be used as a taco topping. Try them on: Pork Tacos, Egg Tacos, Quesadillas.

BLACK BEANS WITH MANGOS AND FRIED LEMONS

In the wide area in which they are a staple, black beans appear in many presentations. Since they are such a canon in Puerto Rican, Cuban, Bahamian, and Haitian cuisine, we sometimes lean toward a Caribbean variation for our tacos. A little fried lemon and a sliced mango make up our preferred sort of Bermuda Triangle.

Serves 4 to 6
Takes 2 hours

2 teaspoons peanut oil
2 lemons, rinsed and sliced very thin, each slice
    cut into quarters
1 batch Basic Black Bean filling (page 218),
    heated through
18 corn or 12 flour tortillas, warmed or crisped
    just before serving

TOPPINGS
3 mangos, peeled and coarsely chopped
2 cups cilantro leaves
2 cups sour cream

1. Heat the oil in a large nonreactive frying pan set over high heat. Add the lemons and fry, turning once, for 1 minute. Transfer to a plate.

2. To assemble, place about ½ cup of the black beans in the center of a tortilla. Top with the fried lemons, chopped mango, cilantro, and sour cream. Fold and serve.

▲▲▲▲▲▲▲▲▲▲▲▲▲▲

Cielo from Colombia, all mysticism, tarot cards, palm reading, spirits, and vegetarianism, and Claudio from Cuba, all business, managing, papers, accounts, and meat, met over the produce section in an Oakland, California, supermarket. It was a marriage of opposites, but one of the things they do have in common is their love of black beans. In their kitchen they stew black beans and pile them on tortillas. Claudio adds lemon, a touch from the citrus groves of Cuba. Cielo deftly dices mango and heaps it over the beans and lemon. We met them at the California College of Arts and Crafts, when Cielo was Susanna's anthropology student, long before the Good and Plenty Cafe. We thank them for their capital Pan American version of black bean tacos.

▼▼▼▼▼▼▼▼▼▼▼▼▼▼

INDIAN-STYLE LENTILS

Serves 4 to 6
Takes 20 to 40 minutes

1 pound lentils (about 2½ cups)
6 cups chicken stock or broth
½ teaspoon ground turmeric
¼ teaspoon ground coriander
⅛ teaspoon pure chili powder
⅛ teaspoon ground cumin
⅛ teaspoon cayenne
Pinch of ground cloves
¾ teaspoon salt
4 medium red- or white-skinned potatoes,
    cut into ¼-inch dice
3 tablespoons fresh lime juice
12 flour tortillas, warmed or crisped just
    before serving

TOPPINGS
2 cups chopped tomatoes
1½ cups shredded fresh mint leaves
2 cups sour cream
Pickled Carrots (optional, page 74)

1. Place the lentils, chicken stock, turmeric, coriander, chili powder, cumin, cayenne, cloves, and salt in a large pot. Bring to a boil. Add the potatoes, and reduce the heat. Simmer until the lentils and potatoes are tender but still hold their shape, about 20 minutes. Remove from the heat. Stir in the lime juice.

2. To assemble, spread about ½ cup of the lentils and potatoes in the center of a tortilla. Top with chopped tomatoes, mint, sour cream, and Pickled Carrots. Fold and serve.

▲▲▲▲▲▲▲▲▲▲▲▲▲▲▲▲

Lentils—the famous "peas" of "pease porridge hot, pease porridge cold"—were a staple of the Middle East, Near East, and Europe long before upstart potatoes arrived. Lentils are nutritious both for people and for soil. On every medieval manor in Europe, the large communally worked field was divided into three parts. Each year one section was planted with grain, one with lentils, and the third left to rest fallow. Each year the order rotated. Overworked fields in India, the Near East, and southern Europe are still seeded with lentils as a restorative crop. Meanwhile, the tillers have the benefit of rich thick porridge or flat breads stuffed with the steaming savory legume, as in this taco.

▼▼▼▼▼▼▼▼▼▼▼▼▼▼▼▼

▲▲▲▲▲▲▲▲▲▲▲▲▲▲

S ince tamales have been a theme running like a ribbon through both our lives, we were delighted when our Los Angeles friends, Terry and Elva, made them for us during one of our visits. First cousins, the two women make tamales only at Christmas, but when they do, there's no cutting corners, it's from the corn husks up. We also found frequent excuses to lunch at Melrose Avenue's Border Grill where sweet corn-filled Oaxacan tamales star on the menu. We each used to construct tamales at home, but who has the time these days? So we took a shortcut with the tapa format. Now with a little hominy, onion, cream, and sometimes bits of tender chicken, pork, or barbecued beef, we still often have a *tamal* or two, taco style.

▼▼▼▼▼▼▼▼▼▼▼▼▼▼

MOCK TAMALES

A long with tacos, burritos, and enchiladas, the most widespread and beloved dish throughout Mexico and Central America is the *tamal. Masa,* the same dough that is patted into corn tortillas, is spread upon a softened corn husk or banana leaf. This dough is filled with meats, fowl, game, seafood, beans, nuts, sweetened corn, or even left unfilled like a soft bread, then the whole composition is wrapped into a tight package and steamed. The Aztecs offered tamales of all different sorts to their gods during the holiday season of their year. They are still a favorite holiday dish, but tamales are a lot of work. To avoid the labor, we simplify the process by wrapping a typical tamale filling in a corn tortilla, envelope style.

We like to mix southern and northern types of tamales together using both cream and dried red chili sauce to flavor a simple corn and hominy filling. Olé, a tamale tapa!

Serves 4 to 6
Takes 20 to 40 minutes

Peanut oil
1 medium-size red onion, finely chopped
4 red serrano or yellow wax chili peppers, stemmed and finely chopped
4 cups fresh corn kernels (4 to 5 medium ears)
4 cups drained canned hominy
2 cups heavy (whipping) cream
18 corn tortillas

TOPPINGS
Ancho Chili Sauce (page 59)
4 cups shredded lettuce
2 cups chopped avocado
2 cups sour cream

1. Heat 2 tablespoons of peanut oil in a large pot or frying pan set over medium-high heat. Add the onion and chili peppers and stir until the onion begins to wilt. Add the corn and hominy. Cook, stirring occasionally, until the mixture begins to brown on the bottom, about 5 minutes. Stir in the cream. Bring to a boil. Cook until the mixture is thickened and most of the liquid is absorbed, about 8 minutes more.

2. To assemble, heat the tortillas in a frying pan lightly coated with peanut oil. Spread a tablespoon or so of Ancho Chili Sauce on a tortilla. Place about ½ cup of the corn and hominy mixture in the center; top with lettuce. Fold up envelope style. Continue until all the tortillas are filled and folded.

3. Coat the bottom of a frying pan with peanut oil and set over medium-high heat until smoking. Add as many tortilla envelopes as will fit in one uncrowded layer and fry for 30 seconds. Turn and fry until golden, about 30 seconds more. Remove to a plate or platter. Top with chopped avocado and sour cream. Serve.

VARIATION
▼

Non-vegetarian northern-style tamales with meat centers or southern-style tamales with poultry can also be mocked in a tamale tapa. Place 2 tablespoons of any stewed meat or chicken in the middle of the corn-hominy tamale filling. Fold the tortilla and fry.

PLANTAINS WITH SUNFLOWER SEEDS AND AVOCADOS

Plantains sweeten and round out chicken and pork fillings, but they also stuff tacos substantially and satisfactorily on their own. Fry them and wrap them, they're a glorious hot snack or an elegant meatless meal. Pairing them with avocado, similar in texture but contrasting in flavor, makes them sublime. The only thing missing is some crunch, which a topping of sunflower seeds provides.

▲▲▲▲▲▲▲▲▲▲▲▲▲▲▲

Strange as it seems, bananas are America's favorite fruit (for bananas outsell even oranges). First cultivated in India, where Alexander the Great sampled them, and Malaysia, bananas eventually made their way to the Americas by the 16th century. Of the 120 varieties that exist throughout the world, about half are eaten raw and half are eaten cooked. The kind seen in most American markets and sliced into many cereal bowls is a sweet dessert variety, usually eaten raw. More common in the places where bananas are an integral part of cooking are the less sweet, starchier sort called plantains. They are often roasted, here fried.

▼▼▼▼▼▼▼▼▼▼▼▼▼▼▼

Serves 4 to 6
Takes less than 20 minutes

2½ pounds plantains (4 to 5 plantains depending on size)
4 tablespoons (½ stick) butter
¾ cup shelled, roasted, salted sunflower seeds
18 corn or 12 flour tortillas, warmed or crisped just before serving

TOPPINGS
2 cups chopped avocado
Pasilla, Mint, and Pickled Red Onion Sauce (page 60)
4 cups shredded lettuce
2 cups sour cream

1. Peel the plantains and cut them into ¼-inch dice.

2. Divide the butter between 2 large frying pans and set over medium-high heat until the butter foams. (Or use 1 pan and cook the plantains in 2 rounds.) Add the plantains and sunflower seeds and sauté until golden brown, about 3 minutes.

3. To assemble, place about ⅓ cup of the plantains and sunflower seeds in the center of a tortilla. Top with chopped avocado, Pasilla, Mint, and Pickled Red Onion Sauce, shredded lettuce, and sour cream. Fold and serve.

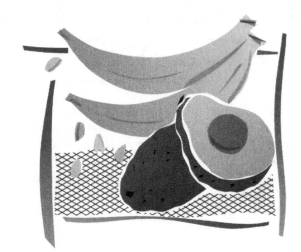

FRIED TOMATILLOS WITH ONIONS AND CREAM

Tomatillos are more tart and less juicy than their cousins, unripe tomatoes, but you can use tomatoes picked green off the vine as well.

Serves 4 to 6
Takes less than 20 minutes

2¼ pounds tomatillos
¼ cup olive or peanut oil
2 medium onions, quartered, then sliced thin
1 teaspoon salt
⅔ cup heavy (whipping) cream
18 corn or 12 flour tortillas, warmed or crisped just before
*   serving*

TOPPINGS
Breaded Chili Strips (page 71)
2 cups cilantro leaves

1. Remove the papery husks from the tomatillos. Rinse the tomatillos; halve and cut into thin slices.

2. Pour the oil in a large nonreactive frying pan set over medium heat until the oil begins to smoke. Add the onions and stir to coat well. Add the tomatillos and salt and cook until the tomatillos are soft, about 5 minutes. Add the cream, and bring to a boil. Immediately remove from the heat.

3. To assemble, spoon about ½ cup of the tomatillo mixture in the middle of a tortilla. Top with Breaded Chili Strips and cilantro leaves. Fold and serve.

Tomatillo means "little tomato" in Spanish. They look a lot like tomatoes, and like early tomatoes, their color ranges from vivid green to golden yellow. Still, when wearing their papery husks, they resemble the little white eggplants of India as much as they do tomatoes, and it figures. Despite their Spanish name, tomatillos aren't tomatoes. They are, along with tomatoes, a separate member of the nightshade family, which includes eggplant and potatoes.

▲▲▲▲▲▲▲▲▲▲▲▲▲▲

To this day Hank and Ruth Jenanyan, Victoria's parents, keep up the family's Saturday Lunch tradition—breaded eggplant in white bread sandwiches. They started the custom long ago as a way to have Hank's soulfood, eggplant, in Ruth's meal of choice, a sandwich. Over the years, they introduced the countless friends of their four daughters to the unusual Saturday lunch, Though they were often faced with grimaces and skepticism, they won over countless converts. Now the four daughters carry on the legacy, with a modern interpretation. The eggplant is still batter-fried, but the bread has become a tortilla, and instead of mayo, there's salsa.

▼▼▼▼▼▼▼▼▼▼▼▼▼▼

BREADED EGGPLANT

Eggplant, so "meaty" and substantial, serves as a meat substitute better than almost any other vegetable. It takes to as many flavors as meat and here provides the base of a hearty tortilla filling.

Serves 4 to 6
Takes less than 20 minutes

¾ cup milk, or 2 eggs mixed with ¾ cup water
2 cups cornmeal
4 pounds eggplant (2 to 3 eggplants depending on size), cut
*   into ½-inch cubes*
1 cup olive or peanut oil
Salt, to taste
18 corn or 12 flour tortillas, warmed or crisped just before
*   serving*

TOPPINGS
4 cups shredded lettuce
3 cups shredded cheese
Tomato, Pumpkin Seed, and Scallion Salsa (page 42)

1. Place the milk or eggs and water in a bowl. Spread the cornmeal on a plate. Dip the eggplant first in the liquid and then in the cornmeal, coating all sides.

2. Divide the oil between 2 large frying pans and set over medium-high heat until smoking. (Or use 1 pan and cook the eggplant in 2 rounds.) Add as much of the eggplant as will fit in one uncrowded layer to each pan, and salt lightly. Fry, turning once or twice, until the eggplant is soft to the touch and golden, about 8 minutes. Drain on paper towels; continue cooking more rounds until all the eggplant is cooked.

3. To assemble, place about ½ cup of the eggplant in the center of a tortilla. Top with lettuce, cheese, and Tomato, Pumpkin Seed, and Scallion Salsa. Fold and serve.

GARLIC-SAUTEED EGGPLANT IN A FRIED TORTILLA

At one time North Americans thought that eggplants caused tremors and fever. Now we enjoy them even in tacos. If you like your eggplant herby and more like *ratatouille*, add a pinch of oregano, thyme, or marjoram while sautéeing. Also a touch of chopped onion or shallot adds some tang.

Serves 4 to 6
Takes less than 20 minutes

1 cup olive oil, plus extra for heating the tortillas
4 pounds eggplant (2 to 3 eggplants depending on size), cut
 into ½-inch cubes
8 garlic cloves, pressed or minced
Salt, to taste
18 corn or 12 flour tortillas

TOPPINGS
3 cups shredded or crumbled sharp cheese, such as sharp
 Cheddar or feta
Roasted Red Pepper, Chili, and Pine Nut Sauce (page 57)
Dressed Cilantro (page 76)

1. Pour ½ cup of oil in each of 2 large frying pans. Set over medium-high heat until smoking. (Or use 1 pan and cook the eggplant in 2 rounds.) Add half of the eggplant and half of the garlic to each pan. Salt lightly and stir to coat the eggplant pieces with oil. Cook until soft, about 8 minutes.

2. Wipe out one of the pans. Add enough oil to coat the bottom of the pan and set over medium-high heat. Add a tortilla to the pan and fry until it puffs up, about 30 seconds. Turn and fry until golden on the second side, about 30 seconds more.

3. To assemble, place about ⅓ cup of the eggplant in the center of a fried tortilla. Top with the cheese, Roasted Red Pepper, Chili, and Pine Nut Sauce, and Dressed Cilantro. Fold and serve.

▲▲▲▲▲▲▲▲▲▲▲▲▲▲▲▲

The term "chop suey" originated in San Francisco with the 49ers, those tough-and-tumble miners who dug for the elusive lodes of gold in the California hills. At mealtime, they would spill into the nearest camptown demanding food. If the cook was Chinese, he would chop up whatever vegetables he could find, add meat if he could muster any, stir-fry it all together, and ladle it up to soothe the savage sourdough. Chop suey can, accordingly, be almost any vegetable combination—sprouts, cabbages, carrots, peppers— quickly sautéed with soy sauce, and made more tasty with a splash of sherry. When the refrigerator is bare but for scattered vegetables, and the hungry campers are about to burst in the door, we call on our San Francisco heritage and quickly chop up chop suey tacos.

▼▼▼▼▼▼▼▼▼▼▼▼▼▼▼

VEGETABLE CHOP SUEY

Rice isn't the only "platter" for a Chinese stir-fry. Pancakes are, too. The most familiar stir-fry in a pancake, mu shu pork, comes with thin tortilla-size crêpes, a scattering of scallions, and a swish of special sauce. In a more homespun vein, we offer this chop suey filling, a vegetable combination that can include almost anything in the larder. Ancho Chili Sauce serves in place of the mu shu hoisin sauce, cilantro or lettuce in place of the scallions. We often add ham for flavor, but using vegetables alone is fully satisfying, and the filling—should any be leftover—makes a great salad the next day.

〰〰〰〰〰〰〰〰〰〰〰〰〰〰〰〰〰〰〰〰〰〰〰〰〰〰〰〰〰〰〰〰

Serves 4 to 6
Takes less than 20 minutes

4 tablespoons peanut oil
2 medium carrots, cut lengthwise into quarters,
  then sliced thin
5 large celery ribs, thinly sliced
1 large red bell pepper, cored, seeded, and
  cut into thin strips
1 jalapeño chili pepper, stemmed, seeded, and
  finely chopped
1 bunch of scallions (green onions), trimmed
  and cut into ½-inch pieces
5 to 6 ounces cooked ham, cut into
  thin strips (optional)
12 ounces bean sprouts
2½ tablespoons soy sauce
2½ tablespoons dry sherry or white wine
½ cup sesame seeds
18 corn or 12 flour tortillas, warmed or crisped
  just before serving

TOPPINGS
Ancho Chili Sauce (page 59)
2 cups cilantro leaves

1. Pour the oil into a large frying pan or wok and set over high heat until the oil begins to smoke. Add the carrots, celery, bell pepper, chili pepper, scallions, and ham, if using it. Stir-fry until the vegetables begin to wilt, about 3 minutes. Add the bean sprouts, soy, and sherry. Stir until the bean sprouts are just wilted, about 2 minutes more. Remove from the heat.

2. Place the sesame seeds in a small ungreased frying pan and stir over medium-high heat until the sesame seeds are browned, about 2 minutes.

3. To assemble, on a tortilla spread a tablespoon or so of the Ancho Chili Sauce. Place about ½ cup of the chop suey mixture in the center. Sprinkle on some sesame seeds, and top with cilantro leaves. Fold and serve.

VARIATIONS
▼

In the tradition of chop suey, you can use just about any herb, vegetable, or meat tidbit at hand. Especially good are:
■ Basil: As a topping in place of cilantro.
■ Bok Choy: Sliced crosswise into thin strips.
■ Egg: Lightly beaten and stirred in with the bean sprouts.
■ Ginger: Peel and mince 1 tablespoon fresh ginger. Marinate it in 1 tablespoon rice or white wine vinegar mixed with 1 teaspoon sugar for 15 minutes. Drain and stir in with the vegetables.
■ Mushrooms: Any kind, but especially shiitakes, sliced thin.
■ Napa Cabbage: Sliced crosswise into thin strips.
■ Peanut-Garlic Salsa (see Index): In place of the toasted sesame seeds.
■ Shrimp: Stirred in with the bean sprouts.
■ Snow Peas: Cut in half or thirds to match the size of the other vegetables.

MENU

▼

VEGETARIAN FIESTA

———

*Good and Plenty
Wine-Simmered
Vegetable Tacos*

*Black Beans with Fried
Lemon and Mango Tacos*

———

Mexican Fruit Salad

———

*Sweet Banana Tacos
with Toasted Almonds*

GOOD AND PLENTY WINE-SIMMERED VEGETABLES

The secret and distinction of this filling comes from simmering the vegetables in white wine only, using no oil, stock, or water at all. The vegetables absorb so much flavor and become so enticing, you will want to serve them both as a taco filling and as a dinner side dish. Try these wine-simmered vegetables with salsas and cheese as well as sour cream. Strew them over fajitas. Swirl them into a scrambled egg filling. Or have them just the way they are.

**Serves 4 to 6
Takes 20 to 40 minutes**

5 medium red- or white-skinned potatoes, cut
　　into ¼-inch dice
6 medium tomatoes, cut into ½-inch dice
1 large or 2 medium onions, cut into
　　½-inch dice
3 medium zucchini, cut into ½-inch dice
1 jalapeño chili pepper, stemmed and
　　minced
2 cups frozen lima beans (10-ounce
　　package)
1 teaspoon dried oregano
1½ teaspoons salt
¾ cup dry white wine
¼ cup chopped cilantro leaves
18 corn or 12 flour tortillas, warmed or
　　crisped just before serving

TOPPING
2 cups sour cream

1. Place the potatoes, tomatoes, onions, zucchini, chili pepper, lima beans, oregano, salt, and wine in a large nonreactive pot. Bring to a boil. Simmer over medium-high heat until the potatoes are done, 15 to 20 minutes. Remove from the heat; stir in the cilantro.

2. To assemble, spoon about ½ cup of the vegetables in the center of a tortilla. Top with sour cream. Fold and serve.

Susanna created this "Americana" mixed vegetable taco filling out of the blue, the larder, and a quick run to the basement for a bottle of white wine when she discovered just before a dinner party that her guests included three vegetarians. Every last morsel, except the cupful she saved for Victoria to sample, was eaten by vegetarian and carnivore alike. Next day upon receiving her taste, Victoria declared the filling her favorite and has made it regularly ever since. Wine-Simmered Vegetables has become one of our signature dishes, demanded by guests, customers, and audiences. We make it often for cooking demonstrations, catering events, and parties.

EGGS

An egg wrapped in a tortilla is a mouthwatering parcel. A sunny fried or poached yolk seeps onto the corn or flour blanket and tastes delicious. A fluff of scrambled curds luxuriates in sauce. With plenty of chili and crisp lettuce to provide the egg's only nutritional lack—vitamin C and roughage—egg tacos are light, delicious, and a complete food.

We recognize that minding cholesterol is a modern concern, and we can no longer wantonly consume eggs for breakfast everyday, whipped into mayonnaise, souffléed for dessert. But for an occasional indulgence, to make the best of that rare egg, make it an egg taco.

SUNNY FRIED EGGS

The first time Susanna tasted a fried egg taco was in a little mountain village in Mexico. The egg was straight from the nest, the tortilla was corn lightly crisped on a griddle, and the salsa was an absolutely fresh mixture of tomatoes and chilies. Victoria's first fried egg was in New Mexico in her aunt's kitchen. The egg was from the country market, the tortilla was flour, soft and warm, and the sauce was a typical New Mexico one of earthy puréed dried chili peppers. For both of us, it was love at first bite. We now have them Victoria's first way, Susanna's first way, and every other style, with every salsa.

Serves 4 to 6
Takes less than 20 minutes

4 tablespoons (½ stick) butter
12 large eggs
2 tablespoons water
12 corn or flour tortillas, warmed or crisped just before serving

TOPPINGS
4 cups shredded lettuce
Fresh Tomato Salsa (page 37) or Salsa Verde (page 52)

1. Divide the butter between 2 frying pans large enough to hold 6 eggs each. Set over medium heat. When the butter melts and bubbles, gently crack the eggs, and drop into the pans without breaking the yolks. Drizzle 1 tablespoon water all around the outside edge of the eggs in each pan. Cover the pans, reduce the heat to low, and cook until the whites are set and the yolks are firm, about 3 minutes.

2. To assemble, place a fried egg in the middle of a tortilla. Top with lettuce and Fresh Tomato Salsa or Salsa Verde. Fold and serve.

▲▲▲▲▲▲▲▲▲▲▲▲▲▲

Drizzle water around eggs as they fry, then cook them in a covered pan—that's the way to get them perfect, and you don't have to flip them over. The whites come out cooked through, but still tender. The yolks set, but still stay a little runny in the middle, just right for seeping into the lettuce topping and moistening the tortilla.

▼▼▼▼▼▼▼▼▼▼▼▼▼▼

VARIATIONS
▼

FOR THE TOPPINGS
Any of the toppings in this book can add dimension to Sunny Fried Egg tacos. Classic, of course, are Basic Fried Potatoes (see Index) and cheese. The cheese is especially good sprinkled over the top of the eggs as they cook so it melts all around.

FOR THE SALSAS
Vary the Sunny Fried Egg filling with almost any of the salsas in this book, including three special sauces from other chapters: Avocado-Lime Cream, Lemon-Chili Cream, and Sauce Belize (see Index for recipe page numbers).

VARIATIONS

▼

Huevos Rancheros Tacos can be built up with elements to suit your fancy of the moment. Layer a bed of shredded lettuce over the tortilla and under the egg. Sprinkle on *queso fresco* or Parmesan cheese in place of the more familiar Cheddar or Jack cheese. Douse with Salsa Verde, Sweet and Hot Tomatillo Sauce, or Ancho Chili Sauce in place of the Ranchero. Top with minced onion, Breaded Chili Strips, or Toasted Pumpkin Seeds (see Index for recipe page numbers).

HUEVOS RANCHEROS

We couldn't complete a tortilla book without including a rendition of *huevos rancheros,* one of the most famous and popular tortilla dishes. Fried to perfection in butter, quickly slipped onto a crisp tortilla, doused with Ranchero Sauce, and graced with shredded cheese, the simple egg is transformed.

Serves 4 to 6
Takes less than 20 minutes

12 Sunny Fried Eggs (page 233)
12 corn or flour tortillas, crisped just before serving

TOPPINGS
Ranchero Sauce (page 55)
3 cups shredded cheese, Cheddar, Jack, queso fresco, *or a*
* mixture*

1. Fry the eggs as in Sunny Fried Eggs.

2. To assemble the *huevos rancheros,* place 1 fried egg on a tortilla. Top with Ranchero Sauce and shredded cheese. Fold and serve.

TIP

▶ You can also poach the eggs for Huevos Rancheros. Follow the recipe for Salsa-Poached Eggs, using Ranchero Sauce. You will need 3 cups of sauce, half for poaching and half for topping.

SALSA-POACHED EGGS

Salsa has a little-exploited advantage: it's a spicy and zesty liquid perfect for poaching eggs. They take on flavor right in the pan and come out soft, never rubbery or crisped, from yolk to rim.

Serves 4 to 6
Takes less than 20 minutes

Fresh Tomato Salsa (page 37) or Salsa Verde (page 52)
½ cup water
12 large eggs
12 corn or flour tortillas, warmed or crisped just before
*   serving*

TOPPING
4 cups shredded lettuce

1. Place 1½ cups of the salsa and the water in a pan large enough to hold 12 eggs, or divide between 2 smaller pans. Heat until the liquid begins to bubble. Crack the eggs and drop them into the liquid without breaking the yolks. Poach over medium-low heat, keeping the liquid just below the boiling point to avoid disintegrating the whites, until done as you like, 3 to 5 minutes.

2. To assemble, carefully spoon an egg and some of the salsa onto a tortilla. Top with additional salsa and shredded lettuce. Fold and serve.

M E N U

▼

A SPICY WEEKEND BRUNCH

———

Spicy Shrimp with Spinach in Warm Homemade Hominy Tortillas

———

Salsa-Poached Egg Tacos

———

Mexican Fruit Salad

VARIATIONS

▼

FOR THE FILLINGS
Besides chili peppers and cheese, many other savories can be scrambled with the eggs including almost any herbs; spices, especially cumin, clove, or saffron; bacon and sausage, especially chorizo; crab or shrimp; and vegetables, such as chopped tomatillos, tomatoes, onions or green onions, black olives, bell pepper, corn kernels, zucchini or other summer squash.

FOR THE TOPPINGS
From sour cream to guacamole, potatoes to pumpkin seeds, almost all the toppings in this book can enrich scrambled egg tacos, excluding perhaps Pickled Onions, Pickled Carrots, Pickled Corn, and Dressed Cilantro (see Index for recipe page numbers).

FOR THE SALSA
Scrambled eggs are a mellow medium for many salsas, raw or cooked, puréed or chunky. Do be sure to try a variety of the ones offered in the Salsa chapter.

FLUFFY SCRAMBLED EGGS

Airy yet firm, or creamy and moist, however you like them, scrambled eggs pad a soft warm tortilla with a tempting filling. Start with chilies and cheese. Add bacon, herbs, onions, sausage, potatoes, as you relish. Whatever goes in or on scrambled eggs outside a tortilla, fits inside, too.

Serves 4 to 6
Takes less than 20 minutes

12 large eggs
½ medium poblano chili pepper, stemmed, seeded, and finely chopped
½ cup shredded cheese, such as Cheddar, Jack, gouda, or other semisoft melting cheese
¼ teaspoon salt
⅛ teaspoon freshly ground black pepper
2 tablespoons butter
6 corn or flour tortillas, warmed or crisped just before serving

TOPPINGS
Ancho Chili Sauce (page 59)
2 cups shredded lettuce

1. Break the eggs into a large mixing bowl. Add the chili pepper, cheese, salt, and pepper. Mix with a fork until the yolks are all broken but the mixture is not homogenized.

2. In a large heavy frying pan, melt the butter over medium heat until foaming. Add the egg mixture and cook, stirring with a wooden spoon and pushing the eggs down around the edges of the pan and into the middle, until the whites begin to turn opaque, about 5 minutes. Reduce the heat to medium-low and cook, stirring, until the whites and yolks are firm as you prefer them, 5 to 7 minutes more. Remove from the heat right away.

3. To assemble, spread about ½ cup scrambled eggs in the center of a tortilla. Top with Ancho Chili Sauce and shredded lettuce. Fold and serve.

TIP

▶ Scrambled eggs continue to cook and set for several minutes after you remove them from the heat. Treat them as you would a piece of meat, allowing time for them to finish cooking to the doneness you like as they rest off the heat while you finish assembling the tacos.

Victoria prefers her scrambled eggs scrambled with no added liquid at all. She turns the eggs into a pan with barely melted butter and cooks them slowly. She likes the eggs to emerge dense, yellow, still slightly runny. Susanna prefers to lighten the eggs with a little water—one half eggshell full for every two eggs. She waits until the butter in the pan is almost browning and has a nutty aroma, and cooks the eggs rather quickly to produce dry, fluffy curds. Both of us gently scramble the eggs by pushing the faster cooking outer edges into the creamy, still undone center with a wooden spoon. We also agree that never, never should you add milk to your scrambled eggs. It makes them hard.

QUESADILLAS

When cows and goats arrived with the great Spanish land grant holders, cheese became an integral part of Spanish-American cooking. Across the New World, there developed indigenous varieties of cheese that met and married with native foods such as corn and potatoes. In Mexico, little cheese turnovers wrapped in corn dough were created. Filled with *queso Oaxaca* or one of the other melting cheeses, the turnovers, called quesadillas, are easy to make for one or a gang of 20. Quesadillas suffice to quiet hungry children, whet the appetite at Margarita hour, and quell the pangs of hunger at any time of day.

BASIC WELL-FILLED QUESADILLAS

C heese enfolded in a corn or flour tortilla and fried till it melts—that's the basic quesadilla. Salsa and sour cream dolloped on the outside further enhance it.

Our Basic Well-filled Quesadilla is minimally seasoned with tomatillo, scallions, and slices of fresh jalapeño chili peppers. But, as with all well-filled tortillas, we often take great liberties. We embed onions, pickles, peppers, black beans, and papaya in the melted cheese. We use French, Dutch, Bulgarian, Italian, Wisconsin, Vermont, and English cheeses, and even several cheeses together. Feel free; you almost can't go wrong.

Serves 4 to 6
Takes less than 20 minutes

8 to 9 cups (about 2¼ pounds), shredded cheese, such as Cheddar, Jack, mozzarella, gouda, or other semisoft melting cheese
18 corn or 12 flour tortillas
12 ounces tomatillos, papery husks removed, tomatillos, rinsed and cut into ¼-inch dice
2 bunches of scallions (green onions), trimmed and very thinly sliced
1 cup sliced fresh jalapeño chili peppers
½ cup oil

TOPPINGS
Fresh Tomato Salsa (page 37)
2 cups sour cream

VARIATIONS
▼

FOR THE FILLINGS
Cook any of the following with the melting cheese (check the Index for recipe page numbers): Marinated or fresh cooked artichoke hearts; fresh or roasted bell peppers; Basic Black Beans; chili flakes; chili peppers, such as chopped fresh poblanos or Anaheims, canned roasted chili peppers, or Chili Strips, either Breaded or Pan-Grilled; Basic Fried Potatoes; nuts, such as chopped walnuts, almonds, or peanuts; chopped olives; finely chopped onion; peeled, seeded, and sliced papaya; pickled vegetables, such as pickled jalapeño peppers, pepperoncini, Pickled Carrots, Pickled Corn, or Pickled Onions; seeds, such as caraway, shelled sunflower, sesame, and especially shelled pumpkin seeds; chopped tomato, and chopped cooked eggplant, zucchini, broccoli, spinach, or chard.

FOR THE SALSAS
Sweet and fruity, hot, spicy, smooth, or chunky, any and all of the salsas and sauces in this book are superb on a quesadilla.

▲▲▲▲▲▲▲▲▲▲▲▲▲▲▲▲▲

T he traditional quesadilla is
made from a ball of *masa* dough
that is stuffed with cheese and
other bits, then cooked. You can
duplicate these original-style
quesadillas when you make your
own tortillas. Press the dough into
a fat oval about ¼ inch thick, fill it,
fold it, then press the edges
together and fry it a little longer
than a thin tortilla quesadilla.

▼▼▼▼▼▼▼▼▼▼▼▼▼▼▼

1. Spread ½- to ¾-cup shredded cheese on one half of each tortilla. Leave about ¼ inch between the cheese and the edge of the tortilla. Arrange tomatillos, scallions, and jalapeños over the cheese. Fold each tortilla in half.

2. Generously coat the bottom of a large frying pan or griddle with 1 to 2 teaspoons oil. Set over high heat. Depending on the size of the pan, place 1 or 2 quesadillas in the pan and fry until golden, about 1 minute. Turn and fry on the other side until golden and the cheese is melted, about 1 minute more.

3. Top each quesadilla with a dollop of salsa and sour cream and eat while still warm and the cheese is still runny.

TIPS

▶ Quesadillas can also be cooked in the oven. Assemble the quesadillas as above, spreading the ingredients over the entire tortillas. Don't fold the tortillas. Place them face up in a 450°F oven. Bake until the cheese is melted, 5 to 6 minutes. Fold and serve.

▶ If you are making many quesadillas, hold them in a low oven to keep warm until ready to serve.

QUESADILLAS WITH GOAT CHEESE AND DEVILED WALNUTS

G ood goat cheeses, often found locally, have become plentiful, across the United States, and the combination of goat cheese and dressed greens with nuts has become a popular menu offering countrywide. Like children following the Pied Piper, we love the theme and can't resist falling into line with our rendition. As usual we like our plate transportable, so we offer a goat cheese quesadilla in a crisp flour tortilla.

Serves 4 to 6
Takes 20 to 40 minutes

1 pound 2 ounces soft goat cheese, such as
    Montrachet, Boucheron, or
    one of the soft domestic goat cheeses,
    at room temperature
12 flour tortillas
3 cups Deviled Walnuts (recipe follows)
12 scallions (green onions), trimmed and
    thinly sliced
½ cup vegetable oil

TOPPINGS
2 cups fresh parsley leaves, preferably
    Italian flat-leaf
1 teaspoon cider vinegar
1 teaspoon olive oil
Salt, to taste
3 to 6 small fresh red chili peppers, stemmed
    and finely chopped

1. Spread about 1½ ounces goat cheese on one half of each tortilla. Leave about ¼ inch between the cheese and the edge of the tortilla. Sprinkle 3 tablespoons of the Deviled Walnuts and some scallions over the cheese. Fold each tortilla in half.

2. Generously coat a large frying pan or griddle with 1 to 2 teaspoons oil. Set over high heat. Depending on the size of the pan, add 1 or 2 quesadillas and fry until golden, about 1 minute. Turn and fry on the other side until golden and the cheese is melted, about 1 minute more.

3. Toss the parsley with the vinegar and olive oil; sprinkle lightly with salt. Tuck some chopped chili peppers and dressed parsley in the crisp quesadilla and eat while still warm and the cheese is still creamy.

▲▲▲▲▲▲▲▲▲▲▲▲▲▲▲▲

I n its early years, Berkeley's famed Chez Panisse restaurant had limited seating and the only offering was its still renowned fixed five-course dinner. As the restaurant began to make its mark, demand grew. More seats, please, and little meals so we can taste more things. Our friend Alice Waters, the inspiration behind the restaurant, had a brilliant idea. She turned the upstairs into a cafe while leaving the downstairs a dining room. She built a brick wood-burning pizza oven and designed a menu of whimsical pizzas, light pastas, and fresh garden green salads. On opening day, April Fool's, 1976, one of the dishes was a goat cheese calzone— sort of a pizza turnover. She has tried many times now to remove the dish from the menu, loving as she does innovation and change, but the protests ring too loud. Goat cheese calzone has become a standard we enjoy on our every return. Inspired by her innovation, here's our tortilla version.

▼▼▼▼▼▼▼▼▼▼▼▼▼▼▼▼

DEVILED WALNUTS

▲▲▲▲▲▲▲▲▲▲▲▲▲▲

In keeping with the myth that the devil likes things hot, deviling in cooking means spicing something up. Deviled ham is potted with cayenne pepper and deviled butter is made zesty with vinegar, mustard, and hot paprika. Nuts too take well to deviling. We like to spice up pine nuts and pumpkin seeds, and pat them on cream cheese to serve as appetizers. Here we devil walnuts to make our goat cheese quesadilla devilishly hot.

▼▼▼▼▼▼▼▼▼▼▼▼▼▼

Makes 3 cups
Takes about 5 minutes

2 teaspoons olive or peanut oil
3 cups (about 8 ounces) walnuts, finely chopped but not minced
2 tablespoons fresh thyme leaves or 1½ teaspoons dried
1 tablespoon pure chili powder

1. Heat the oil in a medium-size frying pan set over medium-high heat. Add the walnuts, thyme, and chili powder. Stir until the walnuts are lightly browned and exude a nutty aroma, about 2 minutes.

2. Serve right away, or store in an airtight container and refrigerate for up to 1 week.

TOSTADAS

Fried flat and used as a platter, tostadas are open-faced, salad-filled tortillas. On top of the tortilla, tostadas tower high with strata after edible strata: fresh greens, tomatoes, meats, cheeses, sour cream, often a layer of beans. The pyramid of delectables can be dressed with a salad dressing or not. We prefer undressed, but "salsa-fied" with a dousing of a zesty fresh salsa. The meat can be hot or cold—in most *taquerias* it's hot. The cheese can be in chunks or shredded, the pinnacle guacamole or sour cream, the decoration perhaps beet, egg, or olive. Piled high, it's hard to get a bite of the complete tostada all at once. Some people lift the whole heap to mouth and try. Others succumb to more civilized techniques and bring knife and fork into play. Still most tostada structures crumble and fall, so be prepared. You may have to resort to fingers.

VARIATIONS
▼

FOR THE FILLINGS
- Tostadas in Mexico and *tacquerias* everywhere often have a pile of pinto beans on the bottom layer. We prefer a lighter, beanless version, but for a heartier meal, spread pintos, red kidneys, or black beans over the crisp tortilla before mounding on the lettuce.
- Tostadas provide a viable vehicle for using up leftovers. The last cupful of stew, such as Chili Colorado, Chili Verde, or Wine-Simmered Vegetables (see Index for recipe page numbers), takes on new life as the substantive ingredient for a tostada. Also any of the grilled, baked, or roasted meats or poultry in this book, cut in small pieces or strips, can embellish a tostada in place of the chicken breast.
- Fish and shellfish make particularly tantalizing tostadas. You can use leftover fish or fry, bake, or grill fresh fish.
- Sprinkle toasted pine nuts, almonds, cashews, macadamias, shelled pumpkin or sunflower seeds over the top of the tostada.

TOWERING TOSTADAS

A basic tostada is just the beginning. You can vary the chilied cinnamon chicken with pork, beef steak, or leftover stew. Make a bottom layer of black or red beans. Add chick-peas, hard-cooked egg, green tomatoes, bell peppers, carrots, beets, capers. Use curly endive, red leaf lettuce, or escarole. Make a tapenade of chopped green olives. Add blue cheese instead of Jack. Turn the sour cream into a ranch-style dressing or splash the whole shebang with a vinaigrette. A tostada can have any salad ingredient you like and be different every time.

Serves 4 to 6
Takes 20 to 40 minutes

3 whole chicken breasts, split
Salt and freshly ground black pepper, to taste
2 tablespoons olive or peanut oil
1 tablespoon pure chili powder
¼ teaspoon ground cinnamon
1 teaspoon dried oregano
12 cups shredded lettuce
6 corn or flour tortillas, crisped hard or flat just before serving
6 medium tomatoes, sliced or coarsely chopped
4 cups shredded or crumbled cheese, preferably a mixture
4 avocados, peeled, pitted, and sliced or coarsely chopped
*1½ cups Calamata, oil-cured, or other good black olives
    (about ½ pound)*
2 cups sour cream
Fresh Tomato Salsa (page 37)

1. If you prefer, remove the skin from the chicken breasts. Salt and pepper both sides of each chicken breast.

2. In a large frying pan heat the oil over medium-high heat until it begins to smoke. Add the chicken breasts, skin side down, and cook for 15 minutes. Turn and cook until the juices run yellow, 5 to 10 minutes more. Remove and allow to cool enough to handle.

3. In a small bowl mix together the chili powder, cinnamon, and oregano.

4. Pull the chicken from the bones; cut the meat into thin strips. (Include the skin or not, as you like.) Toss the chicken with the chili powder mixture.

5. To assemble, spread about 2 cups shredded lettuce over each tortilla. Arrange about ¼ cup chopped tomatoes over the lettuce, then sprinkle about ⅓ cup cheese over the lettuce and tomatoes. Mound about ½ cup of the chicken breast strips in the center and top with avocado. Strew some olives over the lettuce; top with a large dollop of sour cream and a ladle of Fresh Tomato Salsa. Eat right away while still crunchy.

CRAB, WATERMELON, AND BREADED CHILI STRIPS

Does this summery tostada seem a little offbeat? Take our word. The sweet seedy melon adds an almost winy tang to the lush crabmeat. Breaded Chili Strips add some zip. Tomatillo Mayonnaise binds them all into the best of lazy, hot-day fare.

Serves 4 to 6
Takes 20 to 40 minutes

MENU
▼
A LUNCH WITH FRIENDS

———

Crab, Watermelon, and Breaded Chili Strips, in a Tostada with Tomatillo Mayonnaise

———

Fried Pineapple and Orange Tacos with Grated Chocolate

Watermelon is a fruit that does not ripen once off the vine. In order to enjoy one at the peak of perfection, you must choose carefully. If you are buying a whole watermelon, here are a few tips: A good, ripe, sweet watermelon gives off a hollow sound—almost an echo—when tapped with your knuckles. It feels light for its size when hefted. Its rind feels thinnish and has considerably white or yellow mottling; it's not solid dark green. Most importantly, where the stem once was, only a flat brownish-gray patch remains, showing the stem fell off or separated on its own. Any remaining stem means the watermelon was cut from the vine before its time.

12 cups shredded lettuce
6 corn or flour tortillas, crisped hard and flat just before
    serving
3 pounds watermelon, rind and seeds removed, pulp cut into
    small cubes
Breaded Chili Strips (page 71)
1¼ pounds cooked crabmeat, picked over to remove any
    remaining shell
Tomatillo Mayonnaise (recipe follows)
2 cups cilantro leaves

Spread about 2 cups of the lettuce over each tortilla. Arrange about ¾ cup watermelon cubes and several Breaded Chili Strips over the lettuce. Mound about ½ cup crabmeat in the center and top with a dollop of Tomatillo Mayonnaise. Strew cilantro leaves over all. Serve the remaining mayonnaise on the side. Eat right away while still crunchy.

TIP

▶ The new variety of seedless watermelon is delicious and makes melon preparation effortless. If they are available in your market, by all means try one.

TOMATILLO MAYONNAISE

Makes about 3 cups
Takes about 5 minutes

1½ cups Salsa Verde (page 52)
¾ cup mayonnaise, preferably homemade
¾ cup sour cream
1 tablespoon fresh lemon juice
½ teaspoon salt

Place all the ingredients in a mixing bowl and stir until well blended and smooth. Use right away, or cover and refrigerate for up to 3 days.

SHRIMP TOSTADAS WITH SWEET POTATOES

Here we top a fine seafood tostada of shrimp, diced sweet potato, cucumbers, and a Fresh Tomato Salsa-Sour Cream Dressing with a sprinkling of mildly licorice-tasting tarragon leaves.

Serves 4 to 6
Takes 20 to 40 minutes

1 pound sweet potatoes, peeled and cut into ½-inch cubes
12 cups shredded lettuce
6 corn or flour tortillas, crisped hard and flat just before
*   serving*
2 small cucumbers, peeled and cut into matchstick strips
1½ pounds cooked shrimp, peeled, tails removed, and
*   deveined*
2 batches of Fresh Tomato Salsa-Sour Cream Dressing
*   (recipe follows)*
2 tablespoons fresh tarragon leaves

1. Bring a medium saucepan of water to a boil. Add the sweet potato pieces and boil gently until tender but still firm, about 8 minutes. Drain in a colander; set aside to drip dry.

2. To assemble, spread about 2 cups shredded lettuce over each tortilla. Arrange about ½ cup each of sweet potatoes and cucumbers over the lettuce. Mound about ½ cup of the shrimp in the center. Top with a dollop of Fresh Tomato Salsa-Sour Cream Dressing. Sprinkle tarragon leaves over all. Serve the remaining dressing on the side. Eat right away while the tortilla is still crunchy.

▲▲▲▲▲▲▲▲▲▲▲▲▲▲▲▲▲

Our friend Mariano Rivera Velasquez, a denizen of Mexico City, describes how much Mexican cooking is European in tradition, refined, not all chili-powdered. His favorite haunts in Mexico City offer very light meals, roasted meats, fresh fish, simple salads. That's why we offer him this tostada topped with shrimp and sweet potatoes with its herbaceous French flair. He finds it "very Mexican" and devours everything except the underlying tortilla.

FRESH TOMATO SALSA-SOUR CREAM DRESSING

Makes about 1½ cups
Takes about 5 minutes

⅓ cup Fresh Tomato Salsa (page 37)
¾ cup sour cream
¼ teaspoon salt

Combine all of the ingredients in a mixing bowl and stir until well blended. Serve right away, or cover, refrigerate, and use within 3 days.

TOSTADA DEL PUEBLO

Tostada del Pueblo is a spicy, Mexican-style version of Greek village salad (*xoriatiki*) and American hometown spinach salad, with its accompanying bread served as an underlying crisp tortilla.

Serves 4 to 6
Takes 20 to 40 minutes

3 yellow wax chili peppers, stemmed and coarsely chopped
3 tablespoons grated onion (about 1 small onion)
¾ cup diced fresh tomatoes or ¼ cup canned crushed
  tomatoes
¼ cup red wine vinegar
¾ cup dry red wine
¾ cup olive oil
1½ pounds skirt steak
Salt and freshly ground black pepper, to taste
¼ cup pine nuts
Oil for frying
6 cups shredded spinach (about 1 pound)
6 corn or flour tortillas, crisped just before serving
¾ cup Calamata or other good black olives, pitted and
  halved
1 cup feta cheese, crumbled
2 tablespoons shredded fresh mint leaves

1. In a nonreactive dish large enough to hold the steak in one layer, mix together the chili peppers, onion, tomatoes, vinegar, wine, and olive oil. Add the steak, turn to coat both sides, and sprinkle liberally with salt and pepper. Marinate at least 15 minutes, and no longer than 1 hour, turning once or twice.

2. Place the pine nuts in a small frying pan, over medium-high heat and stir them until they are browned, about 3 minutes. Set aside.

3. In a large frying pan set, heat enough oil to coat the bottom. Remove the steak, reserving the marinade. Fry the steak, 2½ minutes per side. Transfer it to a platter.

4. Place the marinade in a small saucepan and bring it to a boil. Remove from the heat and set aside in a warm place.

5. Slice the steak crosswise into thin 1-inch-long strips.

6. To assemble, spread about 1 cup spinach over each tortilla. Top with about ½ cup steak strips. Arrange olives, feta cheese, and pine nuts over the steak. Drizzle on the warm marinade and sprinkle mint over all.

I n the Mexican village, or *pueblo*, as in villages throughout the world, food and drink are often a bit less complex than the city-slicker versions. Take for example the village *margarita*—Mexico's refreshing cocktail—that might accompany the village-style tostada. Brought to the table in plain pitchers and served in small glasses (not vessels large enough to swim in), the drink consists of simply tequila and lime, usually no ice.

■ To make village *margaritas:* The ratio is twice as much tequila as lime juice. For 2 to 3 drinks use 5 jiggers of tequila and 2½ jiggers of lime juice. Mix together and pour, over ice if you like them chilled.

■ The city version has an added twist. Take ½ cup ice, 5 jiggers of tequila, 2½ jiggers of lime juice, and for extra refinement, ½ jigger of Triple Sec. Put all the ingredients in a blender and blend them together while crushing ice. Salt the rim of the glass, as you like.

SIDE
SALADS

COOL DOWNS

A side dish of salad is a cooling antidote to the spiciness of well-filled tortillas.

Vegetables, cooked and raw, and fresh fruit slices have always played a role in embellishing rich tortilla fillings. They appear as chopped tomatoes on a ground beef taco, a scoop of guacamole on fish, a bit of banana on potatoes. Tortillas often need the crunch, the tang, the snap, the vinegar, the sweet, the wetness, the herbiness, the slickness of such salad elements. Sometimes, especially for a dinner party or festive occasion, an extra offering of *verduras* or *frutas* gives a counterpoint to a tortilla meal and rounds out the banquet.

AVOCADO AND GRAPEFRUIT SALAD WITH LIME-JALAPENO VINAIGRETTE

Hotels exist to soothe and comfort, and the fare in their dining rooms is often designed to do the same. A classic hotel offering is avocado and grapefruit salad—presented in a large leaf of iceberg lettuce! We admire the assuaging quality of creamy avocado juxtaposed with tart, refreshing grapefruit. But to travel with hot filled tortillas, the combo needs a bit more zip. Skip the iceberg lettuce, add a dash more citrus, along with a pinch of fresh chili.

Pale yellow to ruby, its carpels bursting with juice that tastes as dry as brüt Champagne, grapefruit—a native American species—is the most thirst-quenching, heat-soothing of the citrus fruits, and always good with well-filled tortillas.

Serves 6 as a side salad
Takes less than 20 minutes

2 grapefruits
2 ripe but firm avocados
¼ cup Lime-Jalapeño Vinaigrette (recipe follows)

1. Cutting deeply enough to reveal the pulp, slice the ends off the grapefruits. Set the grapefruit on one end and cut off the peel and white membrane all around, leaving only the pulp. Cut the pulp into ¼-inch-thick rounds or sections. Remove the seeds and arrange the slices attractively on a platter.

2. Cut the avocados in half and remove the pits. Cut each half in half again. Peel off the skins. Cut the avocado quarters, lengthwise or crosswise, into ¼-inch-thick slices. Arrange the slices attractively on the same platter as the grapefruit.

3. Pour the Lime-Jalapeño Vinaigrette over the avocado and grapefruit. Serve right away or chill up to several hours.

LIME-JALAPENO VINAIGRETTE

Makes ½ cup
Takes 5 minutes

¼ cup fresh lime juice
½ teaspoon minced jalapeño chili pepper
⅓ cup olive or peanut oil
¼ teaspoon salt

Combine all of the ingredients in a small bowl and mix together. Serve right away, or cover, refrigerate, and use within 3 days.

BEET SALAD WITH ORANGE VINAIGRETTE

Serves 6 as a side dish
Takes 20 to 40 minutes

1 cup plus 2 tablespoons cider vinegar
4 cups water
2½ to 3 pounds beets
½ teaspoon salt
½ teaspoon freshly ground black pepper
12 ounces daikon radish, peeled
¾ cup Orange Vinaigrette (recipe follows)
Finely chopped zest of ½ medium orange
¼ cup cilantro leaves

VARIATION

▼

■ If you can't find daikon, substitute that other humble, acerbic root, the turnip!

1. Combine 1 cup of the vinegar and the water in a non-reactive medium-size pot. Bring to a boil.

2. Cut the tops off the beets and reserve them. Quarter the beets and drop into the boiling liquid. Simmer until tender in the center but not mushy, about 15 minutes. Drain; set aside to drip dry.

3. Cut the beet greens from one of the bunches crosswise into thin shreds, stopping at the stems. (Reserve the remaining greens for another dish.) Wash the beet greens in plenty of water and dry in a salad spinner or on paper towels. Toss the dried greens with the remaining 2 tablespoons vinegar, ¼ teaspoon of the salt, and ¼ teaspoon of the pepper.

4. Peel the cooked beets; cut into thin slices. Grate the daikon through the large holes of a hand grater or with a food processor.

5. To assemble, spread the beet greens on a platter. Arrange the sliced beets over the greens; season with the remaining ¼ teaspoon salt and ¼ teaspoon pepper. Mound the shredded daikon in the center. Pour the Orange Vinaigrette over the salad. Sprinkle on the orange zest and cilantro. Serve right away, or refrigerate for up to several hours.

In Hungary they are pickled. In Romania they are shaved and simmered, sour-creamed, and made into borscht. In Greece they are so avidly awaited as February rolls around they haven't time to grow full bulbs. Their greens are boiled, oiled, and devoured. In Mexico slices of them sit on top of lettuce salads and tostadas. We as a country have strayed from beets, sadly, for their flavor is beyond compare. All alone, they are sweet and earthy, as befits a sugary root ripened in the soil. At the same time, they are ready for anything. Herbs, such as tarragon or cilantro, dress them in elegance. Vinegar makes their sweetness tart. Rarely do we unite them with fruit, yet they blend with fruit in flavor and color. Beet with pear—add a little cream cheese—makes a subtle union. Our beets with orange is a buoyant combination.

ORANGE VINAIGRETTE

Makes about ¾ cup
Takes about 5 minutes

¼ cup fresh orange juice
¼ cup cider vinegar
⅓ cup olive or peanut oil
1 teaspoon pure chili powder
⅛ teaspoon salt

Combine all of the ingredients in a small bowl and whisk together. Serve right away, or cover, refrigerate, and use within 3 days.

MEXICAN BEAN SALAD WITH RED CHILI VINAIGRETTE

Shiny, plump kidney beans, common in Mexican and Southwest cooking, hold their curvaceous shape when cold, absorb flavors of any dressing into their tender pulp, and best of all, add their glorious, ruddy cordovan color to any concoction. That's why they are the foundation of so many bean salads. Ours is a two-bean salad, the burnished kidney beans coupled with crisp green beans. A basic vinaigrette is reddened with chili powder to enliven the beans. The advantage to cooking your own kidney beans is you can keep them more *al dente,* less over-cooked. If using canned kidney beans, choose a brand, such as Progresso, that has no added sugar. For a more traditional, and more colorful, three-bean salad, add white beans as well.

Serves 6 as a side dish
**Takes less than 20 minutes plus 2½ hours if cooking
　　the kidney beans**

*1¼ cups dried kidney beans, or 1½ cans (15 ounces each)
　　cooked kidney beans*
½ pound green beans
2 large shallots, minced
½ cup chopped cilantro leaves
½ cup Red Chili Vinaigrette (see page 258)

　　1. If using dried kidney beans, place them in a medium-size pot, and cover with water by 1½ inches. Bring to a boil. Cook for 1 minute. Remove from the heat; set aside to soak for 1 hour.

2. Drain the beans. Return them to the pan with fresh water. Bring to a boil. Reduce the heat to a simmer, and cook until tender but still retaining their shape, about 1½ hours. Drain.

3. To cook the green beans, bring a medium-size pot of water to boil. Trim the stem ends off the green beans and cut the beans crosswise into 1-inch pieces. Drop the beans into the boiling water and cook until tender but still slightly crunchy, from 2 to 5 minutes. Drain; dry on paper towels.

4. To assemble, place the kidney beans, green beans, shallots, and cilantro in a bowl. Add the Red Chili Vinaigrette and toss. Serve right away, or cover and refrigerate overnight.

TIP

▶ Kidney beans can be cooked up to 3 days in advance. Refrigerate until ready to use. If storing, coat them with a little oil to keep them from drying out.

For those get-together occasions when you receive a note saying, "Everyone whose last name begins with the letters A to K, bring a salad" and you are an A to K—we offer you the classic answer: Mexican Bean Salad. Double, triple, and even quadruple the recipe and you have a pot luck or a school dinner dish that people swarm to. If you need to stretch the salad even further, we suggest adding a complementary grain, such as bulgur, or prosciutto or Parma ham strips.

▲▲▲▲▲▲▲▲▲▲▲▲▲▲▲

The Americas to the south of us are so rich in fruits we have never strayed into a market or past a fruit stand where we didn't find some pulpy berry or oddly shaped orb we had never seen before. There are corozos, tamarinds, sopodillas, canafistulas, cherimoyas, guanabanas, grenadillas, anons, feijoas, along with nisperos, mamoncillos, maracuyas, many kinds of bananas, guava, prickly pear, lima agria, mangos, papaya, and passion fruit. Allowed to mature on the vine and sent only to local markets, each piece we purchased—whatever flavor and texture, sweetness or sourness—was succulent, plucky, tart, syrupy. Each was indescribably its own fruit taste. When you find them, we suggest adding some exotic tropical and desert fruits to mixed fruit salads. Since these imported fruits have been picked underripe in order to ship some distance, allow them to ripen before serving. Find out from your greengrocer which like shade to ripen (as do pears) and which like sun (as do mangos), which like a hit of cold (as do persimmons) or some extra heat (as with passion fruit). The extra ripening time at home will open your fruit salad to full fruit ecstasy.

▼▼▼▼▼▼▼▼▼▼▼▼▼▼▼

RED CHILI VINAIGRETTE

Red Chili Vinaigrette dresses plenty more than beans. Use it on a salad of vigorous greens, strong vegetables such as broccoli or cauliflower, or on chicken, fish, roast beef, potato, or swordfish tostadas. To vary the vinaigrette, add a sprinkling of dried oregano, some minced garlic, or some finely grated onion.

Makes about ¾ cup
Takes about 5 minutes

1 tablespoon pure chili powder
⅛ teaspoon cayenne
¼ teaspoon salt
1 tablespoon fresh lemon juice
¼ cup red wine vinegar
½ cup olive or peanut oil

Combine all of the ingredients in a small bowl. Whisk until well blended but not homogenized. Serve right away, or cover, refrigerate, and use within 1 week.

MEXICAN FRUIT SALAD

Fruit of every sort is a major element of Latin cuisine from the beginning of the meal to the end. Fruit goes well with spicy cuisine and is a perfect complement to tacos. Here, we dress a selection of fresh fruit with a little lime juice and mild green chili pepper to give it a salady character. To use the same combination as a simple dessert, skip the chili pepper and top the fruit with toasted coconut.

Serves 6 as a side dish
Takes less than 20 minutes

6 cups mixed sliced or diced fresh fruit, such as banana, watermelon, cantaloupe (or other melon), pineapple, papaya, grapefruit, kiwi, mango, strawberry, orange, or grapefruit (see list for yield amounts for each fruit)
2 tablespoons (about ½ medium) minced Anaheim chili pepper
1 tablespoon fresh thyme leaves or ½ teaspoon dried
3 tablespoons fresh lime juice

Place the prepared fruit in a large bowl. Add the chili pepper, thyme, and lime juice. Gently toss, so as not to bruise the fruit. Serve right away, or cover and chill for up to 3 hours.

▲▲▲▲▲▲▲▲▲▲▲▲▲▲▲▲▲

CUP AMOUNTS FOR CUT FRUIT

■ 1 medium apple, cored, quartered, and cut into thin slices yields about 1½ cups.
■ 1 banana, about 6 ounces, cut into thin rounds yields ⅔ cup.
■ 1 medium cantaloupe, cut into ½-inch pieces yields 2 cups.
■ 1 medium grapefruit, peeled, sectioned, and cut into thin slices yields about 1 cup.
■ 1 regular-size kiwi, peeled and cut into thin quarter rounds yields about ½ cup.
■ 1 mango, 10 to 12 ounces, peeled and coarsely chopped yields about 1 cup.
■ 1 medium orange, peeled, sectioned, and coarsely chopped yields about ½ cup.
■ 1 papaya, about 1 pound, peeled, seeded, and cut into ½-inch pieces yields about 1⅔ cups.
■ 1 medium pineapple, peeled, cored, and cut into ½-inch chunks yields about 4 cups.
■ 1 basket strawberries, stemmed, cut into thin slices yields about 2 cups.
■ 1 quarter of a small watermelon, a 10- to 12-ounce piece, rind removed, seeded, and cut into ½-inch cubes yields about 1 cup.

▼▼▼▼▼▼▼▼▼▼▼▼▼▼▼▼▼

TOMATO, CACTUS, AND COTIJA SALAD

T o us, *nopales* is an anomaly of Mexican cuisine. In what is otherwise a hearty, forceful, and forthright style of cooking, cactus appears as a bland element. The paddles—that's what the petals or leaves are called—don't have a distinctive flavor, but they are fresh tasting and have a pleasing crunch to them. We include this esoteric and very Mexican salad, just in case you can get the ingredients, because it is refreshing and beautiful.

Serves 6 as a side dish
Takes less than 20 minutes

4 medium tomatoes, cut into ¼-inch dice
1 medium cactus (nopales) paddle (about ½ pound), cut into ¼-inch dice (see Tip)
½ small red onion, halved lengthwise and sliced very thin
¼ teaspoon salt
¼ teaspoon freshly ground black pepper
2 tablespoons red wine vinegar
1 tablespoon olive oil
½ cup cotija cheese, about 2 ounces, crumbled

In a bowl, gently toss together the tomatoes, cactus, onion, salt, pepper, vinegar, and oil. Sprinkle the cheese over the top. Serve right away or within 3 hours.

TIP

▶ Cactus paddles in most groceries already have their prickly nodules removed. In produce and country markets, they might still have their thorns. To remove them, protect your hands with gardening gloves or a folded dish towel and use tweezers to pull out the prickles.

▲▲▲▲▲▲▲▲▲▲▲▲▲▲

B ehind the house on the arid sand where Susanna lived in Los Angeles stood a high wall of prickly pear cactus. Perfect to keep stray dogs away, schemed the landscaper. Great to mix with eggs, Susanna thought. Gorgeous chopped and tossed into a salad to go with tacos mused the visiting Victoria. Both from dry climes in our childhood days, like two Br'er Rabbits in the briar patch, the thorns were no barrier to us. Using care, we raided the leaves year round, and waited avidly for fall when we could pick the fruit, pink and ripe, for cheek puckering and jam making. When using the paddles, don't let the prickles foil you. They are easy to remove (see the Tip).

▼▼▼▼▼▼▼▼▼▼▼▼▼▼

JICAMA-POMEGRANATE CHRISTMAS SALAD

Famed food writer Mimi Sheraton once devoted a whole article to how she would never buy a pomegranate again because the mess in her kitchen from seeding the fruit was not worth it. We think it is worth it. Our Christmas salad is a streamlined version of a classic Mexican dish served on Christmas Eve. If pomegranates are out of season, or you agree with Mimi Sheraton, substitute raspberries or watermelon in summer, strawberries in spring or fall, kiwis anytime.

Serves 6 as a side dish
Takes less than 20 minutes

1 pound jicama
1 large or 2 small pomegranates
2 tablespoons finely shredded fresh mint leaves
3 tablespoons fresh lime juice

1. Peel the jicama and grate through the large holes of a hand grater. Set aside.

2. Cut the pomegranate into quarters. With your fingers, gently remove the fleshy red seeds, separating them from the yellowish membrane as you go. Transfer the seeds to a bowl.

3. Add the jicama, mint, and lime juice. Gently toss together. Serve right away, or cover and chill for several hours.

Of all the holidays we and our families have enjoyed together, Christmas is the rare one we have never shared. Like others, we cluster with close kin. We have our ritual gathering of friends for gift exchange and sharing on the first night of Hanukkah so that it is still linked to a special observance. The highlights of the evening are two: small gifts under five dollars but precious in other ways (Guatamalan worry dolls, tiny picture frames just right for a child's school picture, miniatures of adobe houses to go in a potted plant), and Christmas salad. Each child has a pomegranate to peel—sparing our own hands, if not the premises, the bulk of the crimson stains. We shred the mint, usually running rampant through our gardens by this time of year, and the jicama. In the spirit of the occasion, Christmas salad is a joint gift to the table from all who partake in the joy of the occasion.

TORTILLA DESSERTS

DESSERT TACOS AND TOSTADA SUNDAES

We've turned tacos—and even tostadas, flautas, and chimichangas—into dessert. Heat or crisp a tortilla, this time with sugar. Fill it with fruit, ice cream, sweet vegetables, instead of the usual savories. Top it with a sweet, not spicy, sauce—Mexican Chocolate, Coffee Caramel, Pineapple Anisette—and sprinkle on sugared nuts or candied fruit.

Fruit, cheese, or cream-filled, tortillas move from the heart of the meal to the crowning touch. They can end the meal and end the day. Tortilla desserts are far faster to make than pies or cakes, and they are economical.

To make dessert tacos with a soft shell, we heat tortillas in a bit of butter and brown sugar. To make the tortilla shells slightly crisp, dappled with candy here and there, we use confectioners' sugar in the pan instead of brown sugar. To make crunchy dessert tostadas, perfect as an ice cream cup, we fry tortillas with butter and granulated sugar to candy them all over and quickly shape them in a bowl. One dessert taco per person is enough to satisfy almost any sweet tooth. One warning, when making dessert tacos, be careful to use tongs or some other instrument to turn the tortillas. Sugar gets very hot, and it's easy to burn your fingers.

SWEET BANANA TACOS WITH TOASTED ALMONDS

Turned in butter and laced with an extra touch of sugar, blanketed in cream, and dusted with toasted almonds, the pudding-like banana becomes a tempting sweet taco.

Serves 6
Takes less than 20 minutes

2 pounds red bananas, saba bananas, slightly green regular
    bananas, or sweet yellow plantains
6 tablespoons (¾ stick) butter
1½ tablespoons dark brown sugar
6 corn or flour tortillas
½ cup sliced almonds
1½ cups sour cream
1 tablespoon confectioners' sugar

1. Peel the bananas or plantains; cut into ¼-inch-thick rounds. In a large frying pan, melt 2 tablespoons of the butter over medium-high heat until foaming. Add the banana pieces and brown. Turn and brown on the other side, about 1 minute altogether. Remove from the heat; set aside.

2. Place 1 tablespoon of the butter and ½ tablespoon of the brown sugar in a frying pan large enough to hold a tortilla. Set over medium-high heat until the butter foams and the sugar melts. Stir, then place a tortilla in the pan and fry for 30 seconds. Turn and fry on the other side, until warmed through and sugar coated but still pliable, 30 seconds more. Remove and continue with the remaining tortillas, adding a little more butter and sugar to the pan as needed.

Tito Ramirez is one of the finest cooks on the Mississippi Delta, especially when it comes to bananas. Half Haitian, half Cajun, Tito uses bananas in a way most folks use apples. A cousin of a friend of ours, one day he came behind the counter of our cafe and wowed us with some of his banana art. Lately he's devised new banana extravaganzas—banana flambé all wrapped and sealed in a foil, ready to ignite to a big hurrah, and banana crêpes with almonds and cream. After his glorious visit, we had plenty of bananas and the aura of his creativity left. So we concocted this stellar banana taco.

3. Stir the almonds in an ungreased frying pan until toasted, 2 to 3 minutes.

4. Place the sour cream and confectioners' sugar in a small bowl and stir together until smooth. (This will keep covered and refrigerated for up to 1 week.)

5. To assemble, spread about ⅓ cup of the bananas in the middle of a sugar-coated tortilla. Top with sweetened sour cream and toasted almonds. Fold and serve.

M E N U
▼

PASCAL OR PASSOVER DINNER

Salsa-Poached Egg Tacos

Sole and Fried Potatoes with Ancho Chili Sauce in a Taco

Goat Steeped in Cider Vinegar and White Wine in a Taco

Good and Plenty Wine-Simmered Vegetable Tacos

Sweet Banana Tacos with Toasted Almonds

BAKED YAM FLAUTAS WITH PINE NUTS AND SESAME SEEDS

On Thanksgiving everyone awaits the arrival of the candied yams almost as much as the turkey itself. Roasted yams are so soft and buttery—almost caramel-like—you spoon them up to savor along with their dappled coating of nuts and marshmallows, and wish for them to come back for dessert. If you're lucky, yams will appear with pine nuts and sesame seeds in a dessert taco.

Serves 6
Takes 1½ hours

2 pounds yams or winter squash, such as acorn, banana, or
    Hubbard, halved and seeded
6 tablespoons (¾ stick) butter, softened
3 tablespoons dark brown sugar
6 corn or flour tortillas
½ cup pine nuts
2 tablespoons sesame seeds
1 tablespoon confectioners' sugar
1½ cups sour cream

1. Heat the oven to 375°F.

2. Place the whole yams or squash pieces on the oven rack and bake for 1 to 1¼ hours, depending on the size, until the pulp is soft through to the center. Scrape out the pulp into a bowl. Add 2 tablespoons of the butter and the sugar; stir with a fork to mix.

3. Place about ⅓ cup of the yam mixture in the center of a tortilla. Roll up the tortilla flauta style; secure with a toothpick.

▲▲▲▲▲▲▲▲▲▲▲▲▲▲▲▲

Throughout Wyoming, northern Colorado, and across the Great Basin of Utah and Nevada lived groups of Shoshone and Ute Native Americans whose main sustenance was pine nuts. Relying on pine nuts for a dietary staple is a hard way to live. Pine nuts arrive unpredictably, approximately every seven years, but sometimes sooner and sometimes later. To survive, the pine nut eaters had to know when a stand of piñon pines was about to produce and had to be there. The group split up in summer, searching until someone discovered pine cones bursting. The news was spread family by family, with the group rebanding to harvest. Fortunately for us, the product of the capricious conifer is easy to get now. All shelled and ready, we use pine nuts as a taste delight in pesto, a toasted crust on a soft cheese appetizer, or as buttery studs atop sweet yam tacos.

▼▼▼▼▼▼▼▼▼▼▼▼▼▼▼▼

4. Combine the pine nuts and sesame seeds in an ungreased frying pan. Toast, stirring, over medium heat until browned, 2 to 3 minutes.

5. When ready to serve, melt 2 tablespoons of the butter in a large frying pan set over medium heat until foaming. Add 3 or 4 flautas and fry for 1 minute. Turn and fry on the opposite side until browned and crisp, about 1 minute more. Remove to a platter. Add the remaining 2 tablespoons butter to the pan and continue with another round to fry all of the flautas.

6. Stir the confectioners' sugar into the sour cream.

7. Top each flauta with the sweetened sour cream. Sprinkle on the toasted pine nuts and sesame seeds. Eat while still warm and crunchy.

FRIED PINEAPPLE AND ORANGE TACOS WITH GRATED CHOCOLATE

Serves 6
Takes 20 to 40 minutes

½ medium pineapple, peeled, cored, and cut into ¼-inch dice
2 oranges, peeled, seeded, and sliced into ¼-inch-thick quarter rounds
2 tablespoons dark brown sugar
4 tablespoons (½ stick) butter
1½ tablespoons confectioners' sugar
6 corn or flour tortillas

As children we both loved pineapple upside-down cake, baked in a heavy pan with its irresistible layer of pineapple crystalized sweet in butter and brown sugar. We still lose all resolve around sweet fried pineapple, while tortes of chocolate and tarts with vanilla cream leave us cold. We have solved our craving by creating a dessert taco we can make in minutes, no batter and no baking.

TOPPINGS
1½ cups heavy (whipping) cream
½ cup shredded fresh mint leaves
2 ounces bittersweet chocolate, finely grated

1. Place the pineapple and orange pieces in a large, non-reactive frying pan. Sprinkle with the brown sugar. Cook over medium-high heat until they begin to brown, about 3 minutes. Turn and cook on the other side until the liquid evaporates and the pieces are browned, 2 to 3 minutes more. Remove and set aside.

2. Place 1 tablespoon of the butter and ½ tablespoon of the confectioners' sugar in a frying pan large enough to hold a tortilla. Set over medium-high heat until the butter and sugar melt. Stir. Add a tortilla and fry for 30 seconds. Turn and fry on the other side until browned and slightly crispy, 30 to 45 seconds more. Remove. Continue with the remaining tortillas, adding more butter and sugar to the pan as needed.

3. To assemble, beat the cream until soft peaks form. Spread about ⅓ cup of the pineapple-orange mixture in the center of a sugar-coated tortilla. Top with whipped cream, mint leaves, and a sprinkling of grated chocolate. Fold and serve.

TIP

▶ The pineapple and orange can be fried in advance, refrigerated overnight, and served cold.

▲▲▲▲▲▲▲▲▲▲▲▲▲▲▲▲▲▲

Once discovered in the New World, pineapples spread around the globe almost as fast as tobacco. They were called *pinas* by the first explorers because they were thought to resemble huge pine cones. Those first Europeans to taste pineapples were so enthralled that soon, reports say, their boats came back laden with the fruit. Not always successfully, though. Pineapples must be already ripening when picked, for they won't mature off the plant. Once ripe and harvested, they spoil rapidly. For that reason, they were a luxury and a rarity, save for the canned rings and pieces, until modern air freighting began. We find the lush sweetness enrapturing. We think of our Fried Pineapple and Orange Taco as an old and new West Indies taco because when the Spanish took pineapple from those islands, they brought back oranges and sugar cane in exchange.

▼▼▼▼▼▼▼▼▼▼▼▼▼▼▼▼▼▼

Mexican chocolate in our stores comes in thick 3-ounce disks packed in colorful octagon-shaped cardboard boxes, six to a box. It's dark and grainy from coarse crystalline Mexican sugar, mixed like a *mole* with crushed almonds, and heavily doused with fragrant, spicy cinnamon. To the Olmecs, Mayans, and Toltecs it was morning coffee, afternoon tea, the elixir for dinner. It still is to Mixtecs, Zapotecs, and other tribal peoples of Mexico.

When we were in college, Mexican chocolate was all the rage. We each had the native Mexican device, called a *molinillo*, used for spinning the chocolate disks into a frothy brew. A *molinillo* is shaped like a long stick with a cogged ball on the end and several free spinning rings spaced around the stick. You place the chocolate in a pan of heated water. With the *molinillo* ball in the pan, you hold the stick between your palms, pressed flat together as if you were praying, then rub your palms briskly back and forth. The stick spins, the rings dance and twirl, and the chocolate whips into the water.

LA BAMBA FLAUTAS

Mascarpone is a soft, spreadable Italian cream cheese, so rich and buttery it tastes like cream cheese ice cream. For a lavish ice cream sandwich, à la Mexicana, we roll it in a sugared tortilla, then smother it in chocolate sauce, brewed from heady, cinnamony Mexican chocolate. Finally we sprinkle on toasted and sugared nuts. Mascarpone, usually packaged in small tubs, is widely available in delis and cheese shops. If you can't find it, simulate its texture with a good-quality natural cream cheese and beat in two teaspoons heavy cream.

Serves 6
Takes 20 to 40 minutes

2 cups mascarpone cheese (about 1 pound),
*   at room temperature*
¼ cup heavy (whipping) cream
1 tablespoon confectioners' sugar
½ teaspoon vanilla extract
6 corn or flour tortillas
Sugared Nuts (recipe follows)
4 tablespoons (½ stick) unsalted butter or
*   walnut oil*
Mexican Chocolate Sauce (recipe follows)

1. In a bowl, mix together the cheese, cream, sugar, and vanilla until smooth. Spread about ⅓ cup of the mixture in the center of each tortilla. Arrange about ¼ cup of the Sugared Nuts over the cheese. Roll up each tortilla flauta style; secure with a toothpick.

2. When ready to serve, melt 2 tablespoons of the butter in a large frying pan set over medium heat. Add 3 or 4 flautas and fry for 1 minute. Turn and fry on the opposite side until browned and crisp, about 1 minute more. Remove to a platter. Add the remaining 2 tablespoons butter and continue with another round to cook all of the flautas.

3. Spoon Mexican Chocolate Sauce over each flauta and eat while still warm and crunchy.

flauta

SUGARED NUTS

S ugared nuts add texture and toasty flavor to many desserts. Sprinkle them over ice cream, serve a bowl of them alongside ripe pears, or embed them in a cheese filling and roll up for a dessert flauta as we do in the above recipe.

Makes 1½ cups
Takes about 10 minutes

3 tablespoons butter
3 tablespoons sugar
1½ cups shelled walnuts, pecans, macadamias, or peanuts
(about 6 ounces)

Place the butter and sugar in a frying pan set over medium heat. Heat until the butter foams and the sugar melts. Add the nuts and stir until the nuts are quite browned, 2 to 3 minutes. Transfer to a plate or waxed paper. Let cool before serving. Serve right away, or cover, refrigerate, and use within 2 weeks. These also freeze well, if you wish to store them for a longer period of time.

TIP

▶ You can spice up sugared nuts. After the nuts are browned, sprinkle on ½ teaspoon cinnamon or nutmeg and stir to mix in. Spiced sugared nuts are especially good on Gala Dessert Nachos (see Index).

▲▲▲▲▲▲▲▲▲▲▲▲▲▲▲

Hot chocolate . . . cocoa . . . the panacea of childhood, ski trips, and cold foggy mornings. To make hot chocolate Mexican-style, it's best to use disk-shaped Mexican chocolate. In a saucepan, place 2 wedges of a disk for each cup of milk and whisk over medium heat until the chocolate melts.

If you can't find Mexican chocolate, duplicate its special flavor by combining for each cup of milk: a ¾-ounce semi-sweet chocolate bar or ¾-ounce chocolate chips, 1 teaspoon sugar, a small pinch of cinnamon, and 1 tablespoon finely ground almonds. Or combine 2 heaping tablespoons unsweetened cocoa powder, 2 teaspoons sugar, 1 drop vanilla extract, a small pinch of cinnamon, and 1 tablespoon finely ground almonds. Whisk together over medium heat to make the beverage frothy.

▼▼▼▼▼▼▼▼▼▼▼▼▼▼▼

MEXICAN CHOCOLATE SAUCE

Makes about 1⅓ cups
Takes about 10 minutes

9 ounces Mexican chocolate
1 cup water
2 tablespoons Triple Sec or other orange liqueur (optional)

Place the chocolate, water, and Triple Sec in a small saucepan. Bring to a boil, stirring to dissolve the chocolate. Reduce the heat and cook at a bare simmer until slightly thickened, about 5 minutes. Serve right away, or cover, refrigerate, and use within several weeks. Reheat in a heavy saucepan over low heat.

SWEET HOMINY CHIMICHANGAS WITH FRUIT PUREES

There's Indian pudding, made from cornmeal, molasses, raisins, and sometimes pumpkin added. There's Louisiana Creole corn mush, sweet and soothing. But, the Zuni Indians of New Mexico make sweet corn into a still sweeter pudding by letting the corn kernels ferment, then crushing them into a sugary pulp. The texture of corn pudding—in this case made from big, white, easy to grind hominy—is much like tapioca or rice pudding, and it goes, as they do, with a fruit topping. Tuck the mush into a tortilla and top with a fresh fruit purée. It's as good as shortcake.

Serves 6
Takes 20 to 40 minutes

2 cups white hominy (about one 29-ounce can), drained
4 teaspoons confectioners' sugar
2 tablespoons heavy (whipping) cream
1 basket (1 pint) ripe strawberries, hulled
2 ripe mangos
4 tablespoons (½ stick) butter
2 tablespoons dark brown sugar
6 flour tortillas

1. In a food processor, blender, or food mill, purée the hominy. Stir in the confectioners' sugar and cream. Place about ⅓ cup of the hominy mixture in the center of a flour tortilla. Fold up envelope style.

2. Wash out the food processor or other machine and purée the strawberries. Clean the machine again.

VARIATIONS

▼

■ Fruit toppings are a perfect complement to hominy, but the fruit must be sharp and tart. Mellower fruits, such as pear, apple and papaya, don't have the flash or contrast. Beside mangos and strawberries you can use: Apricots; berries, such as boysenberry, blueberry, raspberry, and if you can find it, mullberry; cherries; guavas; mandarin oranges or other oranges and tangerines; pineapple; and peaches.
■ The fruit purées can be embellished with a dash of: brandy, cassis, grenadine, kirsch, and Triple Sec.

3. Peel the mangos; remove the pulp from the pits. Purée the pulp.

4. When ready to serve, melt 2 tablespoons of the butter with 1 tablespoon of the brown sugar in a large frying pan set over medium heat. Heat until the butter foams and the sugar melts, stirring to blend. Add 2 or 3 of the filled tortillas, depending on the size of the pan, and fry for 1 minute. Turn and fry on the other side until golden and slightly crisp, about 1 minute more. Remove to a platter. Heat the remaining 2 tablespoons butter and 1 tablespoon brown sugar. Continue cooking until all the chimichangas are done.

5. Spoon strawberry purée over one end of each chimichanga; spoon mango purée over the other. Eat while still warm and crunchy.

G uava, mango, and passion fruit pastes are intensely flavored. They are available in Mexicatessens. Candied orange and citron, or dried apricots, pineapple, figs, or dates are exotic and time-honored sweetmeats. They can be found in most supermarkets.

SWEET RICOTTA AND CANDIED FRUIT FLAUTAS

T he blintzes and sweet crêpes of Poland, Russia, Latvia, Estonia, Finland, and France are filled with cottage cheese or farmer's cheese and topped with fruit. They are a classic. In our version, to keep the tortilla more Copacabana than Danzig, we use the candied tropical dessert fruits typical of those cuisines.

Serves 6
Takes 20 to 40 minutes

2 cups ricotta cheese (about 1 pound)
¾ cup diced candied fruit, such as candied orange
*   or citron, or Mexican fruit paste, or dried*
*   apricots, figs, or dates*
6 corn or flour tortillas
4 tablespoons (½ stick) unsalted butter
1 tablespoon confectioners' sugar
1 teaspoon ground cinnamon

1. Mix the ricotta cheese and diced fruit in a bowl. Spread about ⅓ cup of the cheese and fruit mixture in the center of a tortilla. Roll up the tortilla flauta style; secure with a toothpick.

2. When ready to serve, melt 2 tablespoons of the butter in a large frying pan set over medium heat. Add 3 or 4 flautas and fry for 1 minute. Turn and fry on the opposite side until browned and crisp, about 1 minute more. Remove to a platter. Add the remaining 2 tablespoons butter to the pan. Continue with another round to cook all of the flautas.

3. Sprinkle the sugar and cinnamon over the flautas. Eat while still warm and crunchy.

TOSTADA SUNDAE WITH COFFEE-CARAMEL SAUCE

No glass sundae cup here. Instead fill a crunchy flaky caramelized edible cup made from a tortilla with ice cream. Vanilla is basic; it goes with any and every topping. Coat the ice cream with a rich coffee and caramel sauce, and you have a tostada sundae. Of course you can use any flavor of ice cream and choose a topping to suit any fancy.

Serves 6
Takes 20 to 40 minutes

1 to 1½ quarts vanilla ice cream
6 Dessert Tostada Cups (recipe follows)
Coffee-Caramel Sauce (recipe follows)

Place 2 or 3 scoops of ice cream in the center of each tostada cup. Top with Coffee-Caramel Sauce. Eat right away.

DESSERT TOSTADA CUPS

Makes 6 tostada cups

3 tablespoons butter
6 tablespoons sugar
6 corn or flour tortillas

Place ½ tablespoon of the butter and 1 tablespoon of the sugar in a frying pan large enough to hold a tortilla. Set over medium heat until the butter foams and the sugar melts. Stir. Add a tortilla to the pan and fry over medium to medium-high heat until the tortilla puffs up, about 1 minute. Turn and fry on the other side until well browned, about 1 minute more. Remove the tortilla to a small bowl, pressing down the center to fit the shape of the bowl. Let cool until set, then remove the tostada cup from the bowl. Add more butter and sugar to the pan and continue with another round until all the tortillas are fried and formed.

TIPS

▶ Tostada cups can be made several hours in advance. After cooling until set in a bowl, they hold their shape.

▶ Use 4-inch hors d'oeuvre-size corn tortillas for smaller desserts.

▲▲▲▲▲▲▲▲▲▲▲▲▲▲

T he form your tostada sundae cups take depends on the size you want to serve and whether your dessert crowd are the single scoop or banana split sort of sundae eaters. For a small single scoop sundae, shape your tortilla in a Chinese-rice or cup-of-soup size bowl. For hearty two-scoopers, use a cereal bowl. For those who can down a whole carton of ice cream plus nuts, fruit, and sauce, shape your tostada cup in a serving bowl using a burrito-size tortilla.

▼▼▼▼▼▼▼▼▼▼▼▼▼▼▼▼

COFFEE-CARAMEL SAUCE

Makes 1½ cups
Takes less than 20 minutes

2 cups packed dark brown sugar
¾ cup brewed very strong coffee
¾ cup heavy (whipping) cream

Place all of the ingredients in a small saucepan. Bring to a boil. Reduce the heat and simmer to just before the soft ball stage (about 230°F on a candy thermometer), about 15 minutes. Serve right away, or cover, refrigerate, and use within several months.

TIP

▶ Coffee-Caramel Sauce can be reheated over a double boiler or in a microwave oven.

COCONUT MILK ICE CREAM TOSTADA SUNDAE

N ever fear, you don't have to buy a whole coconut from the market, hammer it down, drain—or drink—the liquid, then grate the inner flesh to make coconut ice cream. That arduous task can be saved for special occasions. Coconut ice cream can be produced rapidly and readily from canned coconut milk. Imported from the Phil-

▲▲▲▲▲▲▲▲▲▲▲▲▲▲

O ne nestles in a protective pod. The other dangles berry-like in a cluster. Both are shiny and hard. Neither has any aroma until processed. Yet when processed, both vanilla and coffee, two seemingly unpalatable, unflavorful beans, release bouquets that have intrigued, enticed, and captivated the entire world.

Vanilla comes from the New World. The beans emerge from long flat pods that grow on orchid vines. Coffee comes from Arabia, where it was ground for flavoring long before it was brewed into a drink. Once imported to South America, coffee became a major crop of the Andes, where the highland chill provides the ideal growing conditions. Coffee beans take roasting to bring out their essence and incense. Vanilla beans need to sun dry to liberate their mellifluous flavor.

Here we combine both beans. One is in the world's most favorite ice cream flavor, where the vanilla shows in dark flecks throughout the cream. The other we caramelize with sugar almost to molasses consistency and use to top the tostada.

▼▼▼▼▼▼▼▼▼▼▼▼▼▼

ippines and Southeast Asia, it is now widely available in supermarkets. Once you've made the coconut ice cream, we have another hint for its use. Drop some into iced coffee or iced tea to reproduce the nectar-like Thai tea and coffee that lure so many of us to our local Thai restaurants.

Serves 6
Takes 20 to 40 minutes

1 cup coconut strips or unsweetened shredded coconut
1 or 2 batches of Coconut Milk Ice Cream (recipe follows)
6 Dessert Tostada Cups (page 276)
Pineapple-Anisette Sauce (recipe follows)

1. Place the coconut in an ungreased skillet and stir over medium heat until dotted with golden brown spots, about 2 minutes.

2. To assemble, place 2 or 3 scoops Coconut Milk Ice Cream in the center of each tostada cup. Top with Pineapple-Anisette Sauce and the toasted coconut strips. Eat right away.

COCONUT MILK ICE CREAM

Makes 1 quart
Takes 20 to 40 minutes

1 cup sugar
2 large eggs
4 cups canned coconut milk

1. In a bowl beat together the sugar and eggs until pale in color, about 5 minutes. Beat in the coconut milk.

2. Freeze in an ice cream maker according to the manufacturer's instructions. Serve right away or store in the freezer.

TIPS

▶ If your ice cream maker turns out somewhat soft ice cream, you may need to allow extra time for hardening in the freezer.

▶ If you lack the time or equipment to make coconut ice cream or the coffee ice cream in the following recipe, you can always purchase any good-quality ice cream to make dessert tostadas.

PINEAPPLE-ANISETTE SAUCE

Makes 1½ cups
Takes less than 20 minutes

2 cups fresh pineapple chunks (about ½ medium pineapple)
2 tablespoons Anisette liqueur

1. In a food processor or blender, or with a chef's knife, mince the pineapple pulp until it is well crushed but not yet a fine purée.

2. Place the crushed pineapple and Anisette in a small non-reactive saucepan. Bring to a boil. Reduce the heat, and simmer until the pineapple is well wilted, about 5 minutes. Chill before serving, or cover, refrigerate, and use within 3 days.

There's nothing quite like an after-dinner-dessert party where you enter a room to find displayed before you a banquet of luscious sweets of every flavor. To throw a party well-filled style we suggest you set out a variety of sweet tortillas. For a successful array try: Fried Pineapple and Orange Tacos with Grated Chocolate, La Bamba Flautas, Sweet Hominy Chimichangas with Fruit Purées, Coconut Milk Ice Cream with Pineapple-Anisette Sauce and Coffee-Caramel Sauce in a Tostada Sundae

COFFEE ICE CREAM WITH ORANGE-GINGER SAUCE

You can turn coffee into a classic granita dessert ice simply by freezing sugared strong coffee, then crushing the ice into a luscious brown snow. You can also make classic coffee sorbet using egg whites. For a dessert tostada we prefer a sumptuous coffee ice cream, which you can accomplish only by adding thick whipping cream. We top our coffee ice cream tostada with a spicy, tropical Orange-Ginger Sauce to give the coffee ice cream a flowery, exotic veneer.

Serves 6
Takes 20 to 40 minutes

Coffee Ice Cream (recipe follows)
6 Dessert Tostada Cups (page 276)
Orange-Ginger Sauce (recipe follows)

Place 2 or 3 scoops of Coffee Ice Cream in the center of a tostada cup. Top with Orange-Ginger Sauce. Eat right away.

COFFEE ICE CREAM

Makes 1 quart
Takes 20 to 40 minutes

1 cup water
1 cup sugar
4 egg whites
2 cups brewed very strong coffee, at room temperature
1 cup heavy (whipping) cream

1. In a small saucepan, simmer the water and sugar together until thickened, about 6 minutes. Cool.

2. Beat the egg whites until stiff peaks form.

3. In a bowl, mix together the sugar syrup, coffee, and cream. Beat in the egg whites until blended and smooth.

4. Freeze in an ice cream maker according to the manufacturer's instructions. Use right away, or store in the freezer.

ORANGE-GINGER SAUCE

In an out-of-the-ordinary ice cream sauce, floating matchsticks of fresh ginger add an unexpected nip and a glorious golden tone.

Makes 1¼ cups
Takes 20 to 40 minutes

1½ cups fresh orange juice (4 to 5 medium oranges)
½ cup Triple Sec or other orange liqueur
1 cup sugar
1½ ounces fresh ginger, peeled and cut into very thin 1-inch-long matchsticks, about ¼ cup

Combine all of the ingredients in a small nonreactive saucepan. Bring to a boil, stirring to melt the sugar. Cook at a low boil until the mixture lightly coats a wooden spoon and drips rather than runs off the spoon, about 30 minutes. Chill before serving, or cover and refrigerate for up to several weeks.

▲▲▲▲▲▲▲▲▲▲▲▲▲▲▲

We call Orange-Ginger Sauce our "peculiar" sauce because it never freezes. Stored in the freezer virtually for months, it keeps perfectly, but never becomes solid. It's a blessing for an unexpected party. Since it stays semi-liquid, it's always ready to pour over tostada sundaes. Indeed, it gives them an extra frosting.

▼▼▼▼▼▼▼▼▼▼▼▼▼▼▼

GALA NACHOS WITH MANGO-TEQUILA SAUCE

▲▲▲▲▲▲▲▲▲▲▲▲▲▲

A lice Medrich, creator and owner of the famous Cocolat stores, first started selling her renowned chocolate truffles—the basic one rolled in cocoa powder— at the Pig-By-The-Tail. Within a few months she added her first molded truffle, much larger, which we dubbed "son of truffle." The success of the truffles was enormous, and Victoria sold scores of them daily. It was with that success that Alice went on to open the first Cocolat shop near Victoria's deli. It's to Alice and the many flavors that she soon encased in her dulcet truffles that we dedicate the chocolate drop addition on our gala dessert nachos.

▼▼▼▼▼▼▼▼▼▼▼▼▼▼

W hether you are 2 or 10 or 20, it's always joyous when a big tray of nacho chips, oozing with melted cheese, comes to the table. More gala, more festive, and evoking still more shouts of praise is a tray of sweetened nacho chips oozing with ice cream, bedecked with fruit, befrilled with chocolate, and drizzled in Mango-Tequila Sauce. Gala Dessert Nachos can be made for any number. We have written the recipe for six, but you can simply add more tortillas, more ice cream, and more trimmings. The ice cream flavors are up to you. For extra cachet add a second sauce, such as Mexican Chocolate Sauce (page 272) or any of the others listed at the end of this recipe.

Serves 6
Takes 20 to 40 minutes

6 corn or 4 flour tortillas
3 tablespoons butter
6 tablespoons sugar
1 to 1½ quarts ice cream or sherbet, or a mixture
3 cups cut fresh fruit (see list on page 259)
Mango-Tequila Sauce (recipe follows)
Sugared Nuts (page 271)
¾ cup chocolate chips

1. Stack the tortillas in one pile and cut into triangles, 6 each for corn, or 8 each for flour.

2. Place ½ tablespoon of the butter and 1 tablespoon of the sugar in a large frying pan. Set over medium heat until the butter foams and the sugar melts. Add as many tortilla triangles as will fit without overlapping and fry until they puff up, about 1 minute. Turn and fry on the other side until golden, about 1 minute more. Remove to a plate without overlapping. Add more butter and sugar to the pan and continue more rounds until all of the triangles are crisped.

3. To assemble, arrange scoops of ice cream or sherbet in the center of a large platter. Strew fruit pieces around the ice cream and tuck tortilla triangles in here and there. Spoon Mango-Tequila Sauce over all. Dot with Sugared Nuts and chocolate chips. Serve right away.

MANGO-TEQUILA SAUCE

Makes 1 cup
Takes less than 20 minutes

3 ripe mangos
3 tablespoons tequila, preferably gold
½ teaspoon ground nutmeg

1. Peel the mangos; cut the pulp off the pits. In a food processor, blender, or food mill, purée the mango pulp.

2. Place the mango pulp and tequila in a small nonreactive saucepan. Bring to a boil. Stir and remove from the heat. Stir in the nutmeg. Chill several hours before serving.

M E N U
▼

SUMMER HARVEST SPREAD

———

Pork and Corn Meatball Tacos

Breaded Eggplant Tacos

———

Tomato, Cactus, and Cotija Cheese Salad

———

Gala Nachos with Mango-Tequila Sauce

PARTY MENUS

There are times when you want to trumpet a fiery salute, paint the day a chili red, or give someone a hot and happy banquet. For the occasions when you want to make merry, laud someone, or commemorate something in a jubilant and distinctive way, we suggest a tortilla table. Throughout the book we outline party menus to aid your planning. Serve an intimate dinner or an elegant gala, sit-down style. Or, for larger, looser, livelier jamborees, arrange a buffet.

chimichanga   tostada   quesadilla   flauta

INDEX

A

B

O

P

Lizard and Snake needed coin.
They shared a taco and set to work.